INDUSTRIAL MANAGER'S DESK HANDBOOK

INDUSTRIAL MANAGER'S DESK HANDBOOK

Thomas T. Samaras

PRENTICE-HALL, INC.

ENGLEWOOD CLIFFS, NEW JERSEY

Prentice-Hall International, Inc., *London*
Prentice-Hall of Australia, Pty. Ltd., *Sydney*
Prentice-Hall of Canada, Ltd., *Toronto*
Prentice-Hall of India Private Ltd., *New Delhi*
Prentice-Hall of Japan, Inc., *Tokyo*
Prentice-Hall of Southeast Asia Pte. Ltd., *Singapore*
Whitehall Books, Ltd., *Wellington, New Zealand*

Library of Congress Cataloging in Publication Data

Samaras, Thomas T
Industrial manager's desk handbook.

Includes bibliographical references and index.
1. Industrial management. I. Title.
HD31.S312 658.4 79-21418
ISBN 0-13-461491-7

Printed in the United States of America

Dedication

To:
Mary June
My mother and Laura Stenning

ACKNOWLEDGMENT

Special thanks are given to Del Carlson, Kenneth Garcia, Larry Hambright, Robert Stokeley, and Kim Yensuang for their help during the preparation of this book.

What This Desk Handbook Will Do for You

Many managers feel that a heavy emphasis on sophisticated management techniques is needed for today's industry. This is not true. Very often *simple management tools are most successful in dealing with the contemporary industrial problems of change and complexity.*

This book will help managers refocus on fundamental and practical management techniques. Instead of concentrating on managers' efforts in complex paperwork systems or new management philosophies, it will guide managers in working on basic things such as predicting and controlling future events, increasing their staff's productivity and creativity, identifying their company's key needs, being responsive to customer requirements, and reducing disorder.

The consistent use of basic management techniques and systems will give the manager more successful results than the "jumping bean approach"—bouncing from one new management technique or system to another every time a problem occurs or someone gets a new idea. As the book shows, frequent changes in management procedures and systems drain resources, confuse people, and burn out conscientious workers. One management expert reports that the economy loses billions of dollars a year due to lost productivity, job turnover, absenteeism, and illness—all caused by on-the-job frustration, distress, and burn-out.

The need for a return to simplicity and basics in managing the industrial enterprise is wide-spread. (This is illustrated by the popular acronym KISS—Keep It Simple Stupid.) Thus, small, medium, and large companies need to reassess their practices to counteract the trend of ever-increasing complexity, red-tape, and instability that greedily siphon off human and other resources into the wastebin of business failure.

While this desk handbook emphasizes a return to basic management practices, it also recognizes that some problems need new, advanced or complex techniques. Thus, the intelligent use of computers, zero-base budgeting, configuration management, and performance measurement systems is also presented.

Stability is also emphasized as a desirable quality. However, it is not the purpose of this book to urge stagnation. Change, when it leads to simpler and improved operations, is encouraged and detailed methods for managing constructive changes are provided.

To enhance the practical value of this desk handbook, numerous examples are given of techniques that have resulted in saving millions of dollars a year. These include:

- How one electric utility company saved $300,000 a year by replacing an outside vehicle maintenance agency with a modest increase in its own maintenance staff.
- How a small electronics company obtained an additional $50,000 from the customer by a simple change in the operating procedures of its project managers.
- How a high-technology company saved $150,000 a year through simpler processing of supplier documents.
- How a chemical company saved $140,000 a year in bulk materials by using computer simulation techniques.
- How a manufacturing and R&D company saved over $70,000 a year by stopping unneeded scrapping of existing manuals and procedures.
- How a medium-size manufacturing company earned hundreds of thousands of dollars a year by salvaging and selling its production wastes and obsolete stock.

Working exhibits and tools are also an integral part of the entire handbook. These exhibits are designed to provide valuable, simple-to-use aids for the busy manager. Their effective use can help solve stubborn problems, untap the hidden potential of your people, and improve profit margins. A small sample of these working tools includes:

- A decision-making matrix that helps you pick the right technique for making a decision
- A 41-question self-test for evaluating and improving your current administrative practices
- A communication guidelines checklist for improving the exchange of ideas with your staff

- A set of troubleshooting charts that identify various problems, their causes, and their solutions
- A package of rules for improving interfaces with other groups in your company
- A set of rules for keeping disorder from growing in your company
- A checklist for what makes an organization run well
- A sample work plan for improving project performance
- A single sheet integrated cost-schedule-performance management report for providing managers with greater visibility
- A checklist of 39-cost reduction ideas for improving your company's performance

Although primarily oriented toward the middle manager, this handbook can be used to help a variety of people including recent business graduates, industrial engineers, and seasoned executives. It can be used in these ways:

1. To look up a variety of management practices and facts used in industry.
2. To learn about new management techniques or tools that are being used by other companies successfully.
3. To avoid the mistakes of other companies.
4. To review traditional practices or techniques that have been pushed aside, but deserve much more attention because of their proven value for effective management.
5. To help crystalize and develop ideas in managers' minds that have been latent or unused.
6. To accelerate the development of recent business graduates and junior managers by exposing them to the realities of the industrial world.
7. To help seasoned managers re-evaluate their present attitudes and practices in terms of their effectiveness in attaining needed and desired results.

All 17 chapters are packed with many benefits to the manager open to improvement and growth. These benefits are aimed for use in the real industrial world and by the manager who realizes that his primary function is to help people produce goods and services when needed and at minimum cost and confusion. The next section highlights 40 ways this handbook will help you achieve your objectives of increased productivity, lower cost, greater influence and recognition, improved staff morale, and added work satisfaction.

Ways This Book Will Help You

This book gives 40 innovative ways to help you increase efficiency, performance, and profits. It will help you take a systems approach to management which can reduce problems that wipe out budgets, create disorder, deplete human energy from application to profit-making activities, and delay completion of work.

For any manager interested in improving personal or staff performance this book—

1. Shows you why a practical approach to management is the best way to achieve organizational objectives. (Chapter 1)
2. Alerts you to the dangers of uncontrolled innovation and change. (Chapter 1)
3. Provides you with an inventory of management responsibilities. (Chapter 1)
4. Helps you understand how management skills are acquired. (Chapter 1)
5. Gives you a profile of a successful manager (Chapter 1)
6. Presents a test for appraising your management skills. (Chapter 1)
7. Shows you how to avoid being stung by using new and costly management theories that may not apply to your organization. (Chapter 1)
8. Gives you a checklist for evaluating a well-run organization. (Chapter 2)
9. Presents an overview of what makes a good leader. (Chapter 2)
10. Offers you a checklist for improving your communication abilities. (Chapter 2)
11. Introduces you to a practical application of the entropy theory and describes how it can help you without requiring any direct organizational changes or special management systems. (Chapter 2)
12. Gives a summary of how to organize and staff for effective management. (Chapter 3)
13. Pinpoints criteria for evaluating or designing an effective organization. (Chapter 3)
14. Provides a checklist for selecting managers for your organization. (Chapter 3)
15. Presents sample position and job descriptions. (Chapter 3)
16. Spells out guidelines for external and internal communications of project and functional staff. (Chapter 3)
17. Identifies organizational pitfalls to avoid. (Chapter 3)
18. Sets forth practical guidelines for planning, scheduling, and budgeting work. (Chapter 4)
19. Presents you with a simple work plan for use on small and large projects. (Chapter 4)

20. Introduces you to the concept of zero base budgeting. (Chapter 4)
21. Gives you an overview of various methods for controlling activities and operations. (Chapter 5)
22. Features performance measurement techniques that can provide you with better control and visibility. (Chapter 6)
23. Gives a number of tools for improving your decision-making ability. (Chapter 7)
24. Includes a decision-making matrix outlining the advantages and disadvantages of each tool. (Chapter 7)
25. Tells you how to avoid traps in the decision-making process. (Chapter 7)
26. Gives you a variety of techniques for increasing productivity and efficiency. (Chapter 8)
27. Offers a checklist of 39 cost reduction ideas. (Chapter 8)
28. Introduces the relatively new discipline of configuration or product management and shows how it can help you ensure quality control and customer satisfaction. (Chapter 9)
29. Presents a chart of the areas that need to be evaluated for good configuration management of products. (Chapter 9)
30. Outlines the baseline management technique for helping you control new product design and development. (Chapter 9)
31. Gives you a review of how small computers can help improve business performance and what pitfalls to avoid in their use. (Chapter 10)
32. Sets forth clear guidelines for improving interfaces with other groups. (Chapter 11)
33. Gives you guidelines on how to manage industrial documentation effectively and save money. (Chapter 12)
34. Tells you how to critique and improve existing systems, operations, and products. (Chapter 13)
35. Tells you how to evaluate the need for and to design new systems and operations. (Chapter 14.)
36. Shows you how to implement new systems effectively. (Chapter 15)
37. Gives you managers' troubleshooting charts. (Chapter 16)
38. Provides 36 ways to promote your personal performance. (Chapter 17)
39. Sets forth numerous practical examples or case studies of how companies have improved performance or saved money by using certain practical management techniques. (Most chapters)
40. Includes practical examples of how companies got into trouble because of certain poor management practices, and points up what they should have done. (Many chapters)

You are invited to apply the answers in this handbook to your individual situation. The step-by-step program will act as a powerful catalyst for triggering your own creative powers—powers that will improve management skills for leading your people to excellence in performance.

Thomas T. Samaras

CONTENTS

LIST OF ILLUSTRATIONS

1

A Practical Industrial Management Approach

Effective management generally involves 95% practical, down-to-earth techniques and only 5% theory and science. While this book offers answers in both areas, *its primary focus is the pragmatic, real world of industrial management*.

Practical management, in terms of this book, is a discipline devoted to getting the job done right in the shortest possible time and with minimum resources. Its focus is not on making people happy, but in getting them organized, motivated, and productive. While the happiness of people is important, the main aims of industry are to serve society and make money. Too often, we forget that there are people in need of the products our companies make. This need is not just for pleasure or comfort, but for life itself. Companies that produce medical instruments, energy, food, production equipment, medicine, automobiles, bicycles, homes, hospitals, bridges, and sea vessels are only a few members of industry that have either direct or indirect influence on the health, safety, and welfare of millions of Americans. That is why this book approaches the management process as primarily oriented toward getting the job done effectively rather than one of keeping people who make the products happy. However, most people in industry will be happy by virtue of doing a good job, serving others, and sharing in the rewards of improved performance. The communication of this service concept is an important challenge for the industrial manager.

1.1 Benefits of Practical Management

A practical management focus can provide many benefits. One of them is the avoidance of being distracted by theories, techniques, and new systems that burn up incredible amounts of energy without worthwhile increases in production or product quality. The English economist, E. F. Schumacher, observed that modern industry produces an incredibly small amount in proportion to the manpower and energy it consumes. While this is certainly not true for many companies, there is no doubt that a large number of companies are only 30% to 60% efficient. Some of the reasons for this low efficiency are overconcentration on human relations, lack of motivation, misapplication of participative management concepts, and unrealistic policies. These conditions lead to dissipation of productive energies that could have been focused on the end product of the organization.

Another benefit of practical management is that the manager can avoid the energy traps of those who want to scrap existing operating or production systems because they didn't invent them or because they found a few flaws or problems. A practical manager realizes that no system is perfect, except perhaps on paper, and he will not be led into premature dumping of basically good and proven systems that merely need some new elements or minor modifications. The extent of this dumping of existing systems is illustrated by the following plea made by a director of a company in a western state.

> ". . . I would once again request that we minimize the complexity of our management systems and avoid frequent changes. It takes time for people to get used to a given system and for it to work effectively. Constant changes in systems, as we have had at T.D. Growth Corp. for the last several years, create confusion and adversely impact employee morale. It is better to keep or modify slightly an existing system that is 75% effective than to introduce a new system which may be 80%-85% effective. So my over-riding recommendation is let's settle on a simple system that is as much like existing systems as possible and then plan on using the same system for many years."

The experience of finding that a new management technique or equipment is less productive than older systems is not uncommon; however, most companies live with changes once implemented to create the illusion of progress or because of the political repercussions that would result from admission of an error in analysis or judgment. One company, however, found it profitable to undo its mistake and rid itself of a new system that wasn't working out.

> **Case in Point:** About two years before, the company had installed a new automated system for producing reports and other documents. A manager had convinced the company that its older methods weren't efficient. Unfortunately, the staff wasn't convinced and the system failed to be fully utilized. A re-evaluation resulted in the

removal of the system. The company saved $14,400 a year by eliminating unnecessary computer costs.

While the preceding may appear to be an attack on new systems, techniques, and equipment, it is not. It is intended as a caution to blindly accepting things because they are new or recommended by an expert or influential person. Innovation plays a key role in industry. However, it has become a way of life for some managers. One fairly young manager, with a master's degree in business administration, stated:

"I consider my primary mission at Baxter-Z Corp. to be a change-provoker. Innovation is the name of the game and I intend to be in the forefront."

His first step was to discard an existing scheduling and control system in favor of another one that he had used when he worked in the production department of another company. While the process of conversion burned up over 100 hours of his staff's energy and time, the end result was something more complicated, but not better. A few months later, his boss told him to scrap the system because it was impractical and to go back to the old one.

The preceding example leads into another benefit of practical management. This benefit deals with working on things that are really important and that can be successfully implemented. Too often, managers spend their time on unimportant or marginally attainable areas and thus deprive areas of real need of their experiences and energies.

Case in Point: A growing company in the midwest was constructing a new corporate facility. The president, enthusiastic over the new building, allowed himself to get involved in the office layout plans to the extent that he spent many hours trying to decide how the offices should be arranged and furnished. While this was fun for him, it didn't indicate a recognition that the company had more important problems that needed his help for solutions.

Although this is an obvious example of not working on the right things, other less obvious examples occur every day. These include managers who delve into minor details of work, who think that they are editors, or who get embroiled in the production of a company newsletter.

Another benefit of practical management is in promoting simplicity of operations and products. In today's society, people tend to associate complexity with superior ability. Actually, the company that gets its work done with simple techniques and procedures is inherently more efficient, effective, flexible, and capable of survival.

Case in Point: One major industry in the U.S. has become so complex and entwined with rules and regulations that it takes over five years to get a product to the user. The remoteness of visible benefits and extremely high costs threaten the survival of this industry.

Simple operating systems and products have the advantages of being cheaper to design, install, and maintain; are more reliable, and more readily changed when problems or new conditions occur. Some of the problems avoided by simple systems include:

- Staff spends too much time learning about and maintaining the system than doing work.
- Staff makes more errors because it is more difficult to work with the system.
- Managers find more things wrong with the system and therefore keep modifying it.
- Simple changes have ramifications that no one could foresee because of all the interactions among subsystems that are possible.
- The system is used as an excuse for not getting the job done. (Complex systems tend to overshadow individual performance and people naturally blame the system for their failures or inadequacies.)
- The system is used as a substitute for personal communications and contacts.

Actually, effective simple management systems and company products generally require more creativity, experience, and ability to produce than more complex ones. Experience and confidence eliminate the need to develop complex systems that demonstrate one's sophisticated design talents. For example, the designer may make a product complicated or sophisticated because it is professionally more challenging and satisfying than using a previously proven or simple design.

Case in Point: One young engineer with two to three years experience remarked to his associate that he preferred to design complex products because it forced him to use advanced techniques and new components that increased his design capabilities. Besides, it wasn't very interesting to use a simple, proven design that someone else had created years before.

While complex systems and products are here to stay, the manager need not contribute to their unnecessary growth. He is in an excellent position to guide his staff toward simple designs in hardware or paper systems whenever they can do the job as well as complex ones. He can help motivate his staff by rewarding or promoting those engineers who show outstanding ability in designing simple, reliable products.

1.2 Who Needs Practical Management?

Virtually everyone can benefit from a practical management orientation. The need for practical management is greatest in industry—where the hard goods needed by the public are produced. Of course, the degree of need for this management orientation varies, depending on the experience and training of the managers involved. But even an experienced and successful manager can have voids in his background, may have forgotten old rules that he learned the hard way, has failed to put good rules or techniques into practice, or is not aware of some of the newer systems that have been found effective management tools.

A summary of who can benefit from a sharper focus on practical management techniques follows:

- *Recent business graduate:* Most of your training has focused on ideal and often sophisticated systems and techniques, but you have not been exposed to the problems involved in working with others with different ideas, experience, and backgrounds. You have also not lived in an environment where lack of production and money will destroy your company. In addition, the opportunities to apply things you have learned will be very small compared to the demands to learn new, less theoretical techniques to survive.
  Caution: Past academic excellence is no guarantee that you will succeed in the actual business world.

- *Junior or moderately experienced manager* You have probably been with one or two companies during your career and your background is therefore somewhat narrow and reflects the experiences of your company's key executives. This is as it should be, but your growth and contributions can be enhanced by a more structured approach to management that reflects a greater variety and broader base of experience.

- *Experienced manager or executive* While your success attests to your management skills, there is always danger of obsolescence and deterioration that comes with time, when growth stops or when someone has had a job for a long time. Therefore, practical management can rekindle ideas or techniques you learned a long time ago, introduce some ideas or tools that you may not be aware of, or trigger new ideas of your own that have been in your subconscious and need more aggressive development on your part.

The need for practical management in industry is illustrated by the following example:

> **Case in Point:** After 26 years existence, one company on the East Coast was still having its managers trained by management experts from an eminent university. This training went on while middle managers wondered when top management would spend some time solving internal problems, such as lack of unified and central control, weak direction from the top, and periodic reorganizations that didn't solve anything

Another example is illustrated by a promising executive of a small company in Los Angeles who found himself booted out of a top management spot in the prime of his professional life. While he wondered why and how his career had abruptly come to an end, he failed to associate his personal tragedy with the fact that he simply could not do an effective job when he spent half his working day away on personal business having nothing to do with his company's needs.

Even people who teach others about management need help. The confusion and disorder in some universities in conducting their daily operations has been reported by many people. One graduate business school had these basic problems while it was teaching students how to run industry:

1. Its accounting system was out of control—about 20% of the students either didn't get billed or got multiple billings. It took three years to straighten out the mess.
2. Students did not receive responses from the Graduate Office to their requests for help in understanding or following the school's graduation practices until they complained to the Dean. And only the person complaining was helped.
3. Students with over 50% of their research work done were being told that they didn't meet minimum requirements even though a previous professor had approved their initial plans. As a result, in some classes, 50% of the students failed to graduate because they never finished their research projects.

A manager in a large company in Southern California was surprised when one of his key staff members quit. He couldn't understand why, with all the in-house training and invitations to meetings, he wasn't happy. However, the person leaving confided to an associate that he couldn't stand spending hours a week listening to abstract lectures on leadership and attending meetings that produced no output.

One executive recently observed that many managers are amateurs. Perhaps the pace of the modern world has been too great for any but the most talented to become good managers. However, regardless of whether a manager is an amateur or professional, the need for continual professional growth and the application of practical management techniques is essential in today's complex and dynamic industrial environment.

1.3 Practical Manager's Inventory of Key Responsibilities

Practical management involves focusing the manager's attention on a relatively small number of critical functions that can be effectively applied to achieve successful achievement of work needs. The following checklist pertains:

- Keep in touch with overall company objectives, plans, and needs and communicate them to your people.
- Focus manager and staff's attention on tasks, ideas, and products that will provide the company and customer with the greatest payoff.
- Help your people get work done efficiently by providing needed facilities, tools and people and removing roadblocks when they occur.
- Provide leadership by choosing or helping your people choose the right things to work on and the best methods to accomplish this work.
- Provide discipline; even highly motivated people need to have some framework, rules, or system to work within (although they may not want to admit it).
- Be a catalyst for fruitful innovations in operations and production.
- Solve people and unfair reward problems effectively and quickly.

Case in Point: Delays in promoting an underpaid staff member, goaded him into looking for another job. Several months later he resigned. His supervisor stated that the approximate $1,000-a-year raise was a fraction of the cost to retrain a new person, who would also have to be paid more money to leave his present company. Retraining would cost about $10,000.

- Prevent your people from accepting unrealistic budgets and schedules that are bound to lead to failure and demoralization.
- Protect your people from unnecessary or marginal value tasks requested by other functions in the company.

This list of responsibilities can be expanded to many more items. However, a longer list would tend to obscure the manager's focus and eventually make him ineffectual. Of course, a list like this is somewhat subjective. Therefore, each manager should delete some items and add responsibilities that his environment and experience tell him are most important for him and his company.

1.4 How Are Effective Management Skills Acquired?

Management is an overwhelmingly practical discipline—theory and academic knowledge are certainly important, but the people who ran the ancient Egyptian, Greek, and Roman societies weren't educated in the sense of the modern manager. Yet those societies flourished and lasted from 400 to thousands of years. Since then, of course, other societies, such as the English, Dutch, German and French came into being and have existed for a long time. While the leaders of these older societies were probably literate and intelligent, their range of knowledge in no way compared with that of today's master's graduate in business or management. Therefore, it appears that effective management skills were acquired from others or through personal experience.

Today, the process is essentially the same except that a much larger base of knowledge is needed before the aspiring manager can even begin to learn management skills. Unfortunately, in acquiring this large reservoir of general information and specialized knowledge, the manager loses sight of basic and simple techniques for developing skills. He tends to get lost or enmeshed in the complex and ever-changing patterns of social, environmental, business, and personal life. As a result, little time or attention is given to the acquisition of the ability to manage people and organizations. Part of the problem is that in the face of growing technology and related sciences, management appears to be a relatively simple process. The fact that the practice of management is a rigorous and demanding discipline is not realized and most managers feel that understanding the paperwork system, company operations, and internal politics is all they really need to be effective. Of course, this belief leads to mediocrity in managers and prevents them from acquiring real management skills.

For the manager who realizes that management is a practical but demanding discipline, the process of acquiring effective management skills requires first that he obtain a basic level of knowledge about his company, industry, and product and second that he take the following steps. (While most of these steps seem obvious, social conditioning makes many people think that schooling, seminars, and books are the primary path toward development of management skills and that the steps presented next are not needed or of little importance. In contrast, these steps are all-important.)

1. Follow examples of good managers—if one isn't available with overall superior skills, follow different people who excel in specific areas, such as organization, planning, leadership, or decision making.
2. Practice the management skills. (The scope of knowledge and skills required these days is so great that little time exists to master them as our forefathers mastered the work skills of the past.)
3. Acquire skills gradually through step-by-step growth process and evolution into more difficult management jobs.
4. Maintain a desire and openness toward growth in management skills even if you are already performing well.
5. Be consistent in application of these skills and work hard at their development.
6. Learn from the mistakes and successes of others and consciously avoid or follow them. This may require keeping a notebook where mistakes and successes are recorded, analyzed and reviewed at a later date so that they are not forgotten.
7. Follow the Golden Rule. Today, anyone who steps on and abuses others is bound for failure. Experience has shown that the others will eventually destroy him unless he already has great power: whereas managers who are fair usually get equal treatment from other managers and people so that their promotions are based on performance.

Case in Point: One manager was well-known in a West Coast company for his lying and abuse of others. When a reorganization occurred, he found his job abolished and there was no other position for him.

8. Learn from your own mistakes and experience. See 6.
9. Develop a realistic understanding of human foibles, strengths and weaknesses through a genuine interest in, and openness to, people; listen to their complaints and their injuries by others so that you can avoid them with your own people.
10. Prepare and follow a management plan.
11. Keep up with new developments in your business, your competitors, management theories, and changes in laws, society's standards, directions, and expectations.

While the preceding list seems to ignore formal education, items, 9, 10, and 11 really deal with formal and informal educational growth. In today's complex world—which may have exceeded our capacity to deal with its constantly changing features—formal learning is essential for most people who want to become effective managers because some areas of business are often not learned unless a formal program of study is followed. Thus, subjects like operations research (OR), management science, PERT, statistics, computer information systems, and economics may never be properly understood by many managers without formal courses or seminars. However, the problem today is not just technical or academic ignorance, but the ability to get the job done efficiently. Too many people focus on exhibiting knowledge of various theories or mathematical techniques and play down the functions of meeting goals or producing good work. Perhaps the steps for being a good manager are too simple and obvious to be given much attention. Yet, experience with managers who spend too much time reading and trying to follow all the new methods and systems of behavioral management theorists indicates that they are not very effective.

Experience also indicates that people who have grown on down-to-earth practices, attitudes and beliefs, take a systems approach,[1] and are open to new ideas and personal growth become the best managers.

1.5 Profile of a Successful Manager

The successful manager has one common characteristic with other successful managers—he gets his project or work done to specifications and within budget and time allocations. Other than that, he cannot be pinpointed by physical and personal qualities although behavioral scientists can obtain some indications from psychological tests that tell whether he is a follower, compromiser, doer, or executive type. However, good managers come in all sizes, shapes, and backgrounds, except when the top executive exercises a culling practice that eliminates potential managers who do not fit the "correct image," which usually means meeting the physical, cultural, religious, and educational preferences of the owner or president of the company.

Recognizing that there can be personality extremes that may prevent a potentially effective manager from being successful, the successful manager possesses the following qualities:

- *Leadership ability:* sets goals and motivates people to achieve them. Knows what is needed and how goals will be met.
- *Integrator:* brings various factions or groups together harmoniously to get the job done.

---

[1]See Section 2.2 for definition of systems approach.

- *Strong Drive to Meet Objectives:* exhibits a real drive to achieve his group's objectives.
- *Good Decision Maker:* makes decisions when adequate information is available and is right most of the time on routine items and almost all the time on critical decisions.
- *Charisma:* has an undefined personal quality that induces confidence, respect and awe in others.
- *Rapport with Higher Management:* relates well to upper management; has their trust and can negotiate effectively with them.
- *Rapport with Peers:* has open, cooperative relationship with other managers.

Case in Point: One manager who had charisma and good leadership qualities with his own staff failed to relate with other managers. Instead he stayed in his own area and rarely took the initiative to develop bonds with other managers. As a result, he wasn't in a strong position when it came to persuading others to alter operations and interfaces with his own group.

When the fortunes of the company turned down and staff reduction was necessary, he had no supporters and was easy prey for the layoff list.

- *Rapport with Staff:* the ability to relate to and understand the needs, problems, and anxieties of his staff and to communicate this understanding to them. Also includes mutual trust.
- *Knowledgeable:* knows the business, but not necessarily all its details.
- *Good Planner:* understands the principles of planning, budgeting, and scheduling a project and makes sure these activities occur.
- *Knows What's Important:* works on those things which are most important to the company or his department and makes sure his people do too. Doesn't get diverted into wasting time on low-payoff activities.
- *Arouses Loyalty:* creates loyalty in people so that they will do what's best for their boss and the company—even when the boss isn't around.
- *Helps Others Grow:* provides job assignments that are slightly more difficult than the person thinks he/she can do so that he will make an extra effort to succeed.
- *Isn't a Glory Hog:* shares credit for successes with his staff, but takes a lion's share of the blame when things go wrong.
- *Is a Fighter:* fights for his ideas or people when they are right, but knows when to back off and does not become personally offensive.

CAUTION: in some companies, anyone who fights too hard—even for a good reason—may find himself out of a job. Thus, good sense is needed to know when to back off.

- *Confident:* really confident managers are rare; perhaps this comes about because the complexities and demands of modern industry keep people close to their levels of competence, or below it. But confidence can be a powerful quality in getting things done and in obtaining the support of higher management as well as his staff. (However, there needs to be a discrimination between confidence based on ability and that based on a false view of one's abilities.)
- *Determined:* won't let circumstances, criticism, or other people's opinions deter him from his course or plan.
- *Good Staffer:* able to select or identify doers vs. talkers.
- *Sense of Humor:* too much tension or pressure can act as blocks to thought, creativity, and production. A sense of humor can relieve the staff's tension and promote a good group spirit. Also a depressed or worried manager projects an unsettling image to his people which in turn lowers their morale and productivity.

Table I is a management self test. It can be used to see how you rate in terms of characteristic traits or practices of a successful manager. A score of over 30 is very good. However, the primary purpose of the test is to stimulate your reactions and thoughts to the questions and not to rate you against some arbitrary standard.

TABLE I

INDUSTRIAL MANAGER'S SELF TEST

1. Do I have my objectives written down and issued to my staff? Y__ N__
2. Am I in touch with all key aspects of my operation? Y__ N__
3. Do I see most of my people at least once a week? Y__ N__
4. Do I have a management plan? Y__ N__
5. Do I make sure that my staff is planning and scheduling all work before it is started? Y__ N__
6. Has my organization's efficiency, productivity, work quality, or performance improved each year under my leadership? Y__ N__
7. Are my working relations with other managers reasonably smooth, cooperative and open? Y__ N__
8. Do I have a turnover of less than 5% a year? Y__ N__

9. Do I provide rapid response to requests for decisions or help for my staff? Y__ N__
10. Do I meet my promises? Y__ N__
11. Do I really delegate responsibility to my people? Y__ N__
12. Do I help people develop professionally? Y__ N__
13. Do I not take it for granted that the job will always be done on time and within budget? Y__ N__
14. Do I spend more time with my people than with people of power? Y__ N__
15. Do I avoid blaming problems or errors on my boss or staff when someone brings them to my attention? Y__ N__
16. Do I have 8 hours a week of free time to think about potential opportunities, improvements, and problems? Y__ N__
17. Do I avoid getting mad when my actions or mistakes are criticized? Y__ N__
18. Do I put getting the job done right before being liked by my people? Y__ N__
19. Do I have a sense of humor? Y__ N__
20. Do I show recognition when I pass someone in the hall who works in my group? Y__ N__
21. Do people feel free to speak up and disagree with me? Y__ N__
22. Do I thank or praise people for their help? Y__ N__
23. Do I avoid favoritism based on personalities or other qualities not related to performance? Y__ N__
24. Do I follow the rules I expect my staff to follow? Y__ N__
25. Do I take the lead in improving operations and performance of my group? Y__ N__
26. Do I generally make the right decision on key issues? Do I keep a record of my failures? Y__ N__
27. Do I normally obtain the cooperation of higher management on my requests for help or more resources? Y__ N__
28. Do I work well with other managers on my level? Y__ N__
29. Do I fight for my people when necessary, e.g., to get a promotion or interim raise? Y__ N__
30. Do my people support me when things are not going well? Y__ N__
31. Do I criticize people in private? Y__ N__
32. Do I keep my people informed of what is happening in the company? Y__ N__
33. Do I give my people feedback on their progress on a regular basis? Y__ N__

TABLE 1 (CONTINUED)

34. Do I get new ideas and suggestions for better operations from my people? Y__ N__
35. Do I give the staff clear and complete instructions? Y__ N__
36. Do I usually counsel problem people effectively? Y__ N__
37. Do I really listen to what others say? Y__ N__
38. Do I coach my staff effectively so that they will improve their efficiency and performance? Y__ N__
39. Do I present my ideas and needs clearly and effectively to others? Y__ N__
40. Do I take concrete actions to continually improve my managerial ability or performance? Y__ N__
41. Do I say no to requests for more work or special assignments when my staff is already overworked? Y__ N__

Note: All answers are yes.

1.6 Facing Criticism

We live in a society that is always fault-finding. Industry is not exempt from this condition. Managers frequently run down their peers, higher management, and people who work for them. People who are not in managerial jobs are often even more critical of administrators than the other way around. Many years ago when people were in power because of birth, leaders had a much simpler environment and standards to work with; the potential areas of criticism were much fewer. However, today standards and reference points are so diverse, that a manager is often attacked by his peers or his staff. In most cases, these attacks are behind one's back and many people are completely unaware of what others think of them. Sometimes, however, a specific issue may bring opposition or hostility into the open, as one executive of a fairly large organization found.

Case in Point: A competent executive in one organization in Chula Vista had held his position for 16 years and generally had the full support of the board of directors. He had a number of fine administrative qualities, such as organizational and decision-making abilities, fiscal responsibility, and keeping friendly and informal relations with his staff. He often sat with the working staff and entered into casual conversation. He also took strong and effective actions to keep from laying any full-time staff members off when funds were low. He was generally fair, although his decisions were not always popular. One year, when funds were short, he opposed popular

> pressure to raise staff wages and to take cost-foolish actions. The frustrated staff held a confidential vote of confidence on his leadership ability. The results were not good and a considerable fuss was made. Much of the good will developed over the years seemed to have evaporated and he wondered what had gone wrong.

A situation like this is very trying on even the strongest executive. A natural feeling is to resign or start looking for another job. But before this is done, the executive would do well to evaluate his performance and goals on an objective basis. If his goal is to achieve popularity, then this kind of a vote would certainly be devastating. However, as mentioned in a previous section, popularity, while desirable, is not the primary goal of a true executive. His aim is to get the job done right with minimum cost and time. If a review of one's performance on these grounds reveals no failure, then the executive should stand firm and let time smooth things out. If specific complaints are made, these should be evaluated and corrected if valid.

While specific actions and support from other executives can lessen some of the pain, there is still a psychological factor that must be dealt with. Any sensitive person is going to have some self-doubts when he is attacked by others. In dealing with these attacks on an internal level, the executive or manager must consider these questions:

- Is there a specific thing that I denied the staff or someone that would make them turn against me?
- Are there other events that made people unhappy and got them near the edge of anger with my minor action serving as the fuse to their explosive opposition?
- Are there a few strong leaders who oppose me or my policies who have stirred up other managers or my staff? Are they manipulating the weaker people on my staff?
- Have other managers or executives been subject to open or covert criticism during the last year or two?
- Are people jealous of my accomplishments and power? (There are always some people who resent successful people.)
- Do the critics have all the information that I have about the situation?

Very often people in industry criticize others on a superficial understanding of the situation. They rarely know the background, corporate objectives, specific instructions or goals given to the manager by someone above him. They also don't know what problems or trends in company operations have created a need for unpleasant decisions that the executive must make.

Case in Point: The staff that rebelled in the previous example, did not know that if the expensive demands were met, many people would have to be laid off the following year and that other undesirable repercussions would follow if costs were not held in line.

Another consideration for the embattled manager is whether he really wants to be his own man and really lead his organization. If he or she is committed to being a leader, then he or she must recognize that the majority is not always right and that very often the actions and beliefs of the minority turn out to be right. History attests to this because virtually every popular belief about business, politics, religion, science and the future was at one time a minority opinion.

In summary, as people's literacy and expectations continue to increase, their disappointments are bound to be greater. Mixing these higher expectations with our increasingly complex and dynamic society and industry, will result in even greater criticism of executives in the future. Perhaps desensitivity training may become a necessity for many leaders who hold their jobs because of performance and not popularity.

1.7 Role of Management Theory in Practical Management

While management theory is played down in this book, it still has considerable value because changing business requirements often require new ideas, approaches, and techniques. Also, a theory of management can help a manager make decisions when experience is not available to point the way. The key management theories include the behavioral approach, scientific management, systems management, administrative management, and bureaucratic administration. This book does not specifically reflect any one theory, except by accident, because it is based on experience with a variety of companies, small and large, in commercial, military, and aerospace fields. However, the experience of any one person is limited and, therefore, material from management experts and other managers is inevitably blended with direct experience.

1.8 Confusion Over Success in Business and Success in Management

There are two basic types of leaders in the industrial world. The ones who have an idea for a new product or company and have the drive and risk-taking abilities to create an organization almost single-handed. They are usually called entrepreneurs. The other types of leaders are the ones who step into an existing organization and create order and efficiency out of chaos and waste. They are referred to as managers or executives.

The world needs both kinds of leaders because they are usually not interchangeable. The reason for this is that the qualities for success are somewhat different. Entrepreneurs thrive on risk, obsessive drive, luck, new ideas, intuitive decision making, aggressiveness, and salesmanship. In contrast, managers thrive on order, stability, planning, informed and reasoned decision making, controlled innovation, and expertise in some area, such as finance, marketing, engineering, or production. The founder of a successful medium-size company illustrates the qualities of an entrepreneur:

> **Case in Point:** H. Z. Stokes was an engineering genius who developed a unique instrument for industrial testing that soon grew in demand and resulted in the creation of a thriving manufacturing and engineering company in San Diego, California. His drive and quick mind were highly respected by his staff, but now that the company was becoming established, new and different problems had to be dealt with, such as better planning and business forecasting, people matters, and the needs and frustrations of the managers of various departments. However, Mr. Stokes continued to poke into most areas of the company and was often a disrupting and irritating element. The managers and staff found his presence and meddling offensive because he often berated people for being slow or unimaginative. He also tended to take other's ideas and run with them, leaving the originator angry, frustrated and resolved to keep his next idea to himself.
>
> His ownership of the company and short fuse made it difficult for the other managers to deal with him. However, after a consultant explained what he was doing to his company, he gradually relinquished his control over day-to-day affairs and began concentrating on new product ideas and the larger picture, allowing his professional managers to operate the company.

People often confuse the above-type leader with the subject of effective management. This book does not deal with this type of manager. But it is important for the industrial manager to be able to identify the entrepreneur type so as to develop a strategy for working effectively with him. This knowledge can also prevent an effective manager from assuming that he can set up his own business based on his performance in an already established organization.

1.9 Beware of Distorted Perspectives

Specialists in management and business tend to develop their own brand of management style, approach and philosophy to problems. Each approach usually has merit, but its application can create disaster if followed blindly by others; e.g.,

> **Case in Point:** The President of a highly successful manufacturing company became enamored with academicians' ideas on human relations and participative management. He invited a number of these experts to help set up an open company that would be directed by the staff in a decentralized mode. The executives were assigned to a management committee whose mission was to advise the various working groups when asked for help; but they had no direct authority over activities and direction of the company. Performance and other accounting records were abolished and disciplinary action authority was given to the various decentralized groups of 3 to 12 people. In theory, this organization was intended to make people feel that they had a say in how the company was run and this in turn would release a wellspring of creative and productive energy that would make the company even more profitable and successful.
>
> Workers were happy with the new system, but the leaders/managers withered and became bored. Also the benefits of their experience were lost because they had no authority over the staff if it chose to ignore their advice. Within a few years, this leader in a specialized area of the industrial market found that it was heading for disaster.
>
> After five years, a reassessment of the situation resulted in going back to the more traditional organization.[2]

This example is not intended to discourage new approaches to business organization and philosophy, but the use of a psychologist's ideas to reorganize an industrial firm must be very carefully examined because the two areas are not that closely related. There's a big step from the chair of a brilliant academician to the world of making a profit. Therefore, it is recommended that the following checklist be reviewed before embarking on the use of someone's theory, whether he be an academician, successful executive, or practicing expert in industrial management.

TABLE II

CHECKLIST FOR USING A NEW THEORY OR SYSTEM IN YOUR COMPANY

- Was it successfully used in other companies similar to your own?
- Has the system been in effect long enough to demonstrate its long-term effectiveness? (Sometimes a new system increases productivity for a short time and then it returns to normal.)

---

[2]Erwin L. Malone, "The Non-Linear Systems Experiment in Participative Management," *Journal of Business*, Vol. 48, no. 1, Jan. 1975.

- Were there differences or special factors working in the organization that made the application successful, e.g., was the staff ready or eager for a change or did the staff share in the added profits obtained?
- Is the cost of implementation worth the benefits?
- How were the reported benefits measured? Were these methods objective?
- Will your people be able to work with this system or are they already cynical and uncooperative because of past failures?
- Is the system based on assumptions that do not apply to you or your organization, e.g., a certain level of maturity, large resources available, or availability of systems specialists?
- How many companies have successfully applied the concept? How many have failed?
- How is your organization similar or different to the ones that failed?
- Will you get aggressive top management support to implement it?
- Does the creator or architect of the system have practical experience?

2

Checklist for a Well-Run Organization

What constitutes a well-run organization? Many managers would answer that a well-run organization is one that meets its goals within the boundaries specified by higher management and the customer. However, this is more an after-the-fact description of an organization and is not useful in designing an organization that will achieve its goals or in correcting an organization that is having performance problems. A specific set of standards or qualities needs to be defined and evaluated to satisfy these needs.

This chapter is a checklist for evaluating an organization, whether it be a company, division, or department. Each item is presented in the form of a question followed by a commentary.

2.1 Is Good Leadership Provided?

Leadership is a rather difficult quality to define. Many people assume that a person who has an authoritative manner and is openly aggressive in achieving his goals is a leader. Certainly these qualities are important, but in today's complex world they are hardly sufficient to qualify a person as a leader. In fact, these qualities are inadequate by themselves and may even be replaced by other characteristics. In today's industrial world, these qualities may backfire on the manager or leader because people may rebel or shift to low gear when confronted by someone who is too authoritative and too aggressive.

Therefore, the picture of an effective leader is not easily portrayed. However, there are a number of qualities that experience indicates are valuable elements in the leader's ability to get the job done well. These are given next:

- Clear understanding of what has to be done and the best way to do it
- Strong drive to meet objectives
- Genuine interest in one's people
- Openness to ideas and criticisms from his staff

Case in Point: One manager reacted emotionally to the suggestion of another manager who recommended that he ask his key staff members to criticize his actions at weekly meetings. The manager felt this would undermine his authority and cause the loss of respect of his people. While the other manager agreed that a staff of immature people might not be able to handle this situation, he found the technique very productive in creating freer communication and as a method for further development of his leadership abilities.

Caution: The request for criticism from staff members is not recommended if the manager (1) is not already well established and (2) does not feel comfortable and natural in the responses that follow.

- *Visibility:* people like to see that their managers are interested in what they are doing. Managers who lock themselves in their offices doing paperwork or associating only with higher level managers tend to lose respect, influence, and authority among their people. They also lose a valuable technique for making people feel worthwhile and in motivating them.
- *Ability to pitch in:* when a tight schedule needs to be met or a crisis must be resolved, active participation of the manager is a tangible sign of the importance of the situation and the staff will provide greater effort in finishing the work.
- *Follows up on work and goals:* a good leader does not assume that things will get done simply because he issued an order. He periodically checks up on work in progress.
- *Communicates well:* is capable of giving and receiving information efficiently. This includes oral, written and body[1] communication.
- *Applies consistent discipline:* people expect a certain amount of disciplinary action (if applied fairly) from their leaders. Although rarely needed, the staff should be sure that the leader will take corrective action when a situation calls for it, including firing someone.
- *Not overly concerned with being liked:* a good leader should want to be liked, but he or she should never make it a requirement of his leadership quality inventory. A leader who is in quest of popularity

[1]Facial expressions, hand movements, and pats on the back.

and rarely disciplines, irritates, or disappoints his people is very likely running an inefficient operation.

- *Avoids demotivating people:* very few managers can motivate people because motivation is primarily a personal quality. However, a good leader is careful not to create an environment that demotivates his staff. A demotivating environment includes one that is highly political—special friends or relatives get the best jobs and pay, involves a lot of waste, or sets up roadblocks to getting work done efficiently. (see Section 17.12).

Case in Point: Leonard R. Sayles, business consultant, reported that "many more workers are turned off by obvious managerial wastage, the ignoring of equipment or procedure malfunctions and the tolerance of inefficient methods than by boring jobs."[2]

- Able to admit that he doesn't have all the answers:

Case in Point: One manager tended to take on a paternalistic manner with his staff and felt compelled to always have an answer to every question. However, his staff often complained that he would give them wrong answers or talk around them when he wasn't sure. They much preferred to be told: "I don't know but I'll check it out and get back to you later."

- *Able to make good decisions:* some management experts say that a manager who's right 50% of the time is doing well. However, this figure is highly variable, depending on the organization and environment. Chapter 7 will provide guidance for effective decision making.
- *Capable of delegating authority:* this is a classic textbook quality, but also applies to practical management. Many managers have great difficulty delegating authority because they don't think others can do the job as well as they, are insecure, or haven't found more important things to do. The effective manager, however, delegates as much authority and responsibility as he can and then holds his people accountable for their decisions or actions. However, he is still responsible for the successful accomplishment of the work.
- *Has a sense of humor:* see Chapter 1.
- *Schedules only 80% of his time:* a good leader should have at least 20% of his day free to deal with unforeseen emergencies, patch up deteriorating relationships, plan for the long term, or consider organizational changes or operational innovations that can improve productivity and efficiency.

---

[2]"Whatever Happened to Job Enrichment?" *Iron Age*, Nov. 8, 1973, p. 36.

- *Keeps his personal life in order:* a manager who has serious family, financial, or health problems can't help but have his performance at work degraded. Therefore, the manager who successfully controls his personal life can apply more energy and thought to managing his own organization.

2.2 Is a Systems Approach Taken?

A systems approach is one which is based on taking a look at the entire product or organization's life cycle and designing the product or organization to achieve the desired end results. This contrasts with the common technique of working solutions in pieces. For example, in designing an engineering document system, the entire process is identified, starting with the concept and proceeding through the various stages of the production drawing's preparation and use until the document is stored and eventually destroyed. Thus, an overall picture is created so that all the requirements and interfaces are defined and resolved at one time so that the system elements are not fragmented and poorly designed.

Another aspect of the systems approach, which is as important as the life cycle design approach, is commitment to the welfare of the total organization or product rather than to specific sub-elements. Thus, project and other managers make decisions that will increase the profitability and success of the company as a whole even if their areas may suffer somewhat.

> **Case in Point:** The president of a medium-size company issued an edict to his managers to cut overhead costs by 20% by the end of the upcoming new year. The manager of industrial relations found that by delivering internal mail to the secretaries of each department rather than to the individuals, he could reduce his mail clerks from three to two and save the department $12,000 a year. However, when another manager heard about the proposal, he noted that at another company, this action was found to be more costly. The saved mail clerk's costs were multiplied several times because (1) higher paid secretaries spent time running around delivering mail and (2) the secretary's other work sometimes interfered with getting the mail to the staff until a day or more later. Sometimes actions or meetings were missed because of these delays in mail receipt. The cost to the company was found to be well over $20,000 a year. After further thought, the industrial relations manager rejected the idea and searched for another method that would not increase total company costs while reducing his department's expenses.

2.3 Is Authority Undiffused?

When power within the organization is dispersed too widely, it becomes very difficult to get things done, especially when the task requires participation of relatively autonomous groups or divisions with somewhat different objectives and needs.

To avoid this, an operations manager, vice president, or the president must assume an overall leadership role at the operations level to minimize unintegrated activities that create internal conflicts and inefficiency. Otherwise, redundant supporting operations will occur within each group that will increase total company expenses and promote separatism.

2.4 Is the Organization Flexible and Versatile?

A flexible organization is one that can adjust its operations to account for an unexpected project, to a temporary increase in production, or to deal with a loss of a big order. The flexible organization can also efficiently handle changes in systems, procedures, product specifications, policies, public tastes, and governmental regulations without going out of business or becoming unprofitable. Flexibility can be enhanced by establishing procedures for using job shoppers, multiple shifts, overtime, rental of additional facilities or equipment or use of subcontractors.

The versatile organization can switch from one product line to another without too much of an upheaval. Or it can provide different types of skills and abilities to meet new task requirements. The job rotation technique described in Chapter 8 (Section 8.18) is a technique for increasing both the flexibility of the organization and the versatility of the staff.

2.5 Is Effective Planning Done?

Lack of planning is generally the major reason for the failure of a project. Without good planning, the project work is not identified, broken out into manageable tasks, and assigned to the best people qualified to do the work. Nor is a reliable strategy in getting the work done developed. Therefore, the organization that takes on a new job without doing all the necessary planning up front where it really counts has a high probability of fighting a number of brush fires along the way with consequent loss in efficiency, time, and energy. Poor planning also compounds problems by lowering staff morale and by lowering the confidence of customers in the company, which can lead to loss of future business.

2.6 Does a Non-Political Atmosphere Exist?

Politics in a company leads to internal strife, non-productive competition, loss of good people, and retention of people with a gift for survival and advancement. However, these survivors contribute a small output in terms of what they take from the company. With humans what we are, politics can't be eliminated, but it can be kept at a low level through conscious and explicit opposition to it by higher management.

2.7 Is Internal Competition Minimized?

Internal competition is desirable if it is conducted in the right spirit and under the right conditions. However, internal competition often leads to internal strife in both subtle and open form. When it is open, management can deal with it, but when subtle, it can eat away at the company's productivity and efficiency in these ways:

- People will not work smoothly with each other.
- People will not share information, tools, or techniques for improving operations.
- People may sabotage others so that they will look better.
- People will oppose good ideas because they didn't think of them.

Case in Point: Two administrators had developed a competitive spirit between them which was nurtured by management. As a result, bad feelings pervaded the two during meetings and each was often diverted from productive work fuming over the other's victories. The situation finally became obvious to all when a report that one of the administrators had submitted for typing disappeared from the secretary's desk during lunch hour. A thorough search did not find the report. It had to be rewritten. About two months later, the original report was anonymously returned in the mail to its author.

2.8 Is the Staff Competent, Conscientious, and Motivated?

Regardless of the leader's qualities, company facilities, and quality of tools and equipment, a company needs competent people to get the work done. Of course, if they are not conscientious and motivated, the work will still not get done well or efficiently. Thus, the effective organization must be staffed with experienced and capable people who want to get the job done well. However, a mediocre staff that is motivated and well-led can outperform a staff of exceptionally competent people who suffer morale, organizational or leadership problems.

Considerable talk goes on about how managers can move people to improve their performance. Experience shows that very few managers are capable of motivating people on a sustained and large scale. The reasons for this are twofold. First, to motivate someone the manager must discover a need or desire in that person which is so strong that when triggered, it will result in a greater effort by the person. Years ago, money was considered a general motivator, but now it has been downgraded to a minor position, with work satisfaction, growth, recognition, responsibility, respect, and challenge taking more important roles. Thus the process of discovering a person's real need or desire is much more difficult. Second, once the manager has discovered the need, he must be in a position to use a triggering device that will activate the person into the desired efforts. This triggering device must represent a tangible or intangible idea of exchange. That is, the person to be motivated must be convinced that if he or she works hard, the manager or company will respond by helping the person satisfy his/her needs or desires.

While the steps in the motivation process are simple, their successful implementation is difficult because people don't normally reveal their basic needs or desires to their managers and managers have constraints and limited capability to satisfy their people's real needs.[3] Thus, external motivation is indeed difficult to attain on a wide scale and for a long time. The practical solution is to find and keep people who are self-motivated. Then all the manager needs to do is to identify their de-motivators and make sure they are kept out of the work environment. This is a simple process because it takes considerable ineptness to turn off a self-motivated person.

2.9 Is Good Communication a Reality?

The need for good communication has been a recurring theme in management books, seminars, and articles, but industry still has a problem with this management quality. Companies still give their people short shrift when it comes to keeping them informed of new developments. A number of reasons exist for this deficiency: lack of time, de-motivated managers, a desire not to interfere with the staff's work, or the belief that people aren't really interested or don't need to know.

People, no matter what their level in the management tree, like to know about their company. It makes them feel included in the company's plans and makes them feel accepted. When left out of the communication network, they feel unwanted, hurt, or angry.

Once management has decided to reveal new information to the staff, it should be provided right away. Otherwise, the informal communication system may spread the word before management does. When this happens, confidence in the official communication system will decline and managers will look foolish presenting information that everyone already knows. Townsend already noted that very little information is really secret in an organization once it has been exchanged between two people, espe-

[3]Also, once satisfied, a new desire has to be identified and future satisfaction offered based on improved performance.

cially if written down. Therefore, very tight security is needed to keep confidential information from being picked up by the grapevine.

What kinds of information do people want to hear about? This depends on the type of people employed, the nature of the company, and the environment. The National Industrial Council reported that people want to know the following:[4]

1. History and organizational structure of the company.
2. The products and services provided, including how they are provided, why the are needed, and who uses them.
3. What new products, services, and operating systems are in work.
4. What the company expects from them and how they measure up to these expectations.
5. How they fit into the organization and their advancement opportunities.
6. Company income and profitability.
7. Advance warning of layoffs. Why they are needed and who will be affected.

A checklist for improving communication ability is given in Table III.

TABLE III

COMMUNICATION PROCESS CHECKLIST

1. Do you plan what you want to say and the best way to say it?
2. Do you explain what you mean, using short, familiar words and sentences?
3. Do you individualize your message by focusing it at as many individuals as practical?
4. Do you appeal to as many senses as feasible—hearing and seeing.
5. Do you listen to what your people are saying so that you can understand what they are thinking or feeling?
6. Do you repeat your key points? People often don't get the message right and silence does not necessarily mean understanding.

Case in Point: A manufacturer discovered that verbal orders passed along through various levels of management met these results: The second level under the top understood from 75% to 95% of what they were told. The shop supervisors understood from 50% to 75% of what higher management said, foremen understood about 35% and the staff understood about 25%[5]

[4]*The Small Business Report*, Oct. 1978, p. 8.
[5]MANAGING YOUR MANPOWER, Dun & Bradstreet, Thomas Crowell, 1967, p. 160.

TABLE III (CONTINUED)

7. Do you act on what you say? Failure to follow through on things agreed to or stated, reduces your credibility and communication effectiveness at subsequent meetings.
8. Do you evaluate the effectiveness of your communication by checking to see that the actions requested are being done or that a sampling of the listeners indicates an understanding of the message?

2.10 Are People Cost Conscious and Do They Control Costs?

An aura of cost consciousness is a needed quality for the effective organization, even when the money supply seems infinite. There will always come a time when the source of funds dries up because the customer can't afford to buy the product, goes out of business, or a competitor grabs a large share of your market with a product breakthrough. This could mean the death knell for the organization if its staff can't quickly adapt to effective cost reductions. Therefore, a respect for money should always pervade the organization so that frills, unneeded purchases, poor maintenance of expensive and inexpensive equipment, or waste of labor and material is considered a serious breach of company policy.

> *Caution:* If higher management is not aware of a department's self-initiated cost-cutting activities, the department manager may get into trouble when a directive is issued to cut costs to the bone; he'll be caught with little to eliminate and will look bad compared to managers who have a lot of fat in their budgets. (Hopefully, higher management will not penalize the cost-conscious manager under these conditions.)

2.11 Is Innovation Controlled?

Innovation is good. Innovation is needed. However, it cannot be handled in a loose or uncontrolled manner because it can wind up costing the organization more than its worth. Innovation can be dangerous when uncontrolled because:

- It is not objectively evaluated before implementation to be sure it will work and that it will save more money than it costs.
- It is not objectively studied to be sure it will really solve the problem that gave rise to the need for a change.

- People will push changes that they find interesting or professionally stimulating, regardless of the benefits or lack of benefits the company will realize.
- It can alienate people and reduce their productivity and quality of work. It may also cause them to leave the company.
- Implementation of a change or innovation can increase disorder elsewhere while reducing it at the source of implementation.

2.12 Is Information on the Company, Its Products, and Its Industry Readily Available?

Studies have shown that 25% to 50% of the work on new product development and design is wasted because it was done by the company on previous projects. The reason for this is that the retrievability of design or product information is not systematized so that designers, engineers, and scientists can quickly find out what is in process or was done in the past on similar projects. Other types of information not readily available include company business statistics and records on past costs and time needs to build a product.

A few sources of information that can help the staff and managers include:

- A design retrievability system that allows the engineer to find out what documents have been prepared in the past that are similar to what he plans to design.
- A management information system that provides information on various projects. This information includes work status, costs spent vs. budgets, milestones achieved vs. those behind schedule, rates of various labor categories, material costs, overhead rates, vendor delivery records, factory equipment utilization rates and current usage status.
- Seminars/conferences can provide ideas and information on new management systems, techniques, and practices.
- An information center which reviews abstracts and other industry publications and sends notices of useful information to appropriate managers, engineers, and others.
- Books on such subjects as management, manufacturing, computers and quality assurance can be ordered for the staff. *Books In Print* is a reference book at the library that can supply titles on subjects of interest to the company. Also book publishers issue bulletins, abstracts or flyers on new books to those that have requested to be on their mailing lists.

Case in Point: A flyer from Prentice-Hall described the availability of the CORPORATION GUIDE that would be automatically updated with new developments in corporate organization, financing, taxes, practices, procedures and offers of what to do suggestions.

Other information sources include:

- Industrial Arts Index
- Business Index
- Selected Categories in Research in Microfiche (U.S. Department of Commerce)
- Professional and Technical Journals
- Business and Professional book clubs
- Other companies
- Personal contacts or friends with experience in an area of interest or need
- Trade and Professional Associations (Library has reference books on various associations)

2.13 Is Entropy Kept Low So That Disorder Is Minimized and Energy Fully Utilized?

Science tells us that it is natural for any system involving a spontaneous process to become increasingly disordered unless work is done to maintain its configuration. This natural tendency for systems to deteriorate is defined by the term "entropy," which is a measure of the internal disorder within an organization and the degree in which energy is diverted from real production.

The concept of entropy is taken from the fields of thermodynamics and statistical mechanics, where it is considered one of the most basic laws of nature. Although each field has its own mathematical formulations for entropy, its conclusions are the same: a physical system left to itself will always distribute its components and energy so that its state of disorder increases.

Table IV lists the key features of the entropy theory. It should be noted that management experts have observed the entropy law in action although they may not have related it to a physical law of science. For example, Peter Drucker reported in his book "The Effective Executive":

> "The fewer people, the smaller, the less activity inside, the more nearly perfect is the organization in terms of its only reason for existence: the service to the environment."

Drucker's ideas relate closely to items 4 and 7 in Table IV.

TABLE IV

ENTROPY CHARACTERISTICS IN RELATION TO ORGANIZATIONS

Rule 1—In an on-going process, such as the human organization, entropy (disorder) always increases with time unless work is expended to reduce it.

Rule 2—Entropy is never negative and is always greater than zero.

Rule 3—Entropy can be reduced by reventropy[6]—work done on the organization itself, rather than on the products it makes.

Rule 4—Entropy increases as the number of people and the budget/funds increase.

Rule 5—The greater entropy is, the greater is our ignorance about the state of the organization.

Rule 6—Entropy is additive. The entropy of an organization is equal to the sum of the entropies of its parts (departments, divisions, etc.).

Rule 7—Complex and large organizations usually have higher entropies than simpler, smaller ones.

Rule 8—Entropy is a function of the number of accessible or possible states that an organization can be in. (The more options or choices a manager or worker has, the more entropy there is likely to be.)

Rule 9—Entropy indicates the degree that energy or ability to get work done has ceased to be available for productive uses.

Rule 10—Entropy expresses the rule that something (e.g., order or organized actions) cannot be had for nothing. Therefore, work must be expended to maintain an organization in a healthy state.

The famous MURPHY'S LAW is also closely akin to the entropy law. His law says:

"When left to themselves, things always go from bad to worse."

This is another way of stating the entropy theory, which was originally formulated by the scientists Rudolph Clausius and Sadi Carnot in the 19th Century.

John Gardner and Chris Argyris have also concurred that the dry rot in organizations will become so bad that they will eventually collapse.

Economist Georgescu-Roegen also reported that there is a continuous and irrevocable degradation of energy into an unusable form.

While the entropy theory provides a negative view of the world, it can

[6]Reventropy is made of two words "reverse entropy."

still be a very effective tool in dealing with management problems and in providing signposts for avoiding disaster. A few of these include:

- It warns the growing company or organization that a doubling of the staff is not likely to double the output and that efficiency is likely to drop.

Case in Point: One medium-size manufacturing company in Del Mar, California, found that an increase in staff from 240 people to 340 people (a 42% increase) only resulted in an increased factory output of 30%.

- An increase in a company's size inevitably requires a major change in the organizational structure and operational techniques.
- Providing more money will not necessarily guarantee that a difficult job will be done in less time or better.
- Discipline is a necessary component for a successful organization and random operations inevitably lead to disorder, lost energy, and reduced productivity.
- An organization, even when well-designed, will start to decay as soon as its construction has been completed.
- An additional, unneeded member at a meeting or on a committee will increase disorder and deplete the energy of the group by some measurable amount. He may even reduce the group's output to zero.
- The assemblage of equal-power people for some purpose will increase the number of interchanges by a large amount if one member is not more powerful than the rest. This will occur at a faster rate than the number of people added.

In the worst case, the number of communication links (C.L.) within the group can be calculated by this equation:

$$\text{C.L.} = \frac{N(N-1)}{2}$$

Thus, it is evident that if anything is to get done under these conditions, the group must be kept small. For example, the communication links for a 4-person and an 8-person meeting are:

$$\left.\begin{aligned}\text{C.L.} &= \frac{4(4-1)}{2} = 6\\ \text{C.L.} &= \frac{8(8-1)}{2} = 28\end{aligned}\right\}\ \text{Twice as many people but } 4\tfrac{2}{3} \text{ times more links}$$

This relation exists if we assume that each person is on the same power or authority level and is prepared to participate at the meeting.

- If a department is split in two, the level of disorder and energy wasted will very likely increase compared to the original organization. The reason for this is that two independent-minded managers will do things their own way, generally creating problems and inefficiencies for each other. Also a new interface is created with its need for maintenance. Now two minds must be informed by higher management as to goals and paths and their interpretation may vary based on each manager's experience. This is not to say that splitting a group into two or more units is not to be done, but other solutions should be sought out first.

Another benefit of the entropy theory is that it leads to a primary weakness in virtually all companies—the encouragement of unneeded growth by paying more to managers who run larger organizations. Pay is often tied to the complexity of the job and responsibility for others. Thus, a manager who can expand his department from 10 to 20 people can argue that he should earn more because of the added responsibility. In contrast, an exceptionally able manager could get a cut in pay or no increase because his staff has been reduced from 20 to 10, even if it is producing somewhat more than 50% of the work that the original group produced. It is recommended that managers be rewarded under two conditions:

1. When growth is needed and output keeps a reasonably close pace with staff increases.
2. When the staff is cut because of (1) greater efficiency or (2) the need for the group's products or services declined, but efficiency increased.

A method for calculating entropy is described in an article "Measuring Organizational Entropy," *Akron Business and Economic Review*, Summer 1973, p. 15–21. The equation provided has not been proven by experiment, but it still can provide a rough guide on an organization's trend toward increasing disorder when the change is too subtle to detect by observation.

> *Caution:* Since the entropy theory's success depends on its changing the staff's way of looking at the organization, their attitudes and their habits, changes in organization structure and operational systems are not necessary. Therefore, old systems do not have to be discarded for the theory to reduce disorder or wasted energy.

3

Organizing and Staffing for Effective Management

Before a project or job can be done, some form of organizing and staffing is needed. In some cases, as in very small companies, these elements of management are not formally analyzed and identified. The owner or general manager of the company develops the company's structure, operating systems, and staff mix only in his mind or on a few scribbled notes. While this approach can work for a small company, a more explicit method is needed to ensure a better organizational design and to help people understand the framework for doing business. Also, as an organization grows, it becomes impossible to keep all the information needed in one's head.

The following sections will help you in evaluating your present organization or in developing a new department, division, or company by providing:

- Criteria for an effective organization
- Methods for organizing people for effective performance
- Methods for organizing project work for greater output and on-schedule performance
- Organizational pitfalls to watch out for

3.1 Criteria for an Effective Organization

The aim of the organizational structure of a company is to integrate various people and activities so that the product of the company or department is made to required quality and performance standards as efficiently as possible. There is no one way to structure an organization; its design depends on a number of factors that need assessment and manipulation by the leaders. In designing the structure, these various factors are evaluated in terms of their importance in meeting the company's objectives, which presumably have already been defined by the owner, president and market. Table V (page 52) lists the various factors or criteria to be considered in achieving an effective organization.

The achievement of an effective organization is an iterative process. Most companies are constantly redesigning and refining the structure to account for oversights in the previous design, new products or market conditions, changing labor mix, new management philosophy, unforeseen problems, and disappointing performance. While openness to change is essential in today's dynamic and complex world, we should not lose sight of an almost 2,000-year-old observation:

> **Case in Point:** "We trained hard . . . but every time we were beginning to form up into teams we would be reorganized. I was to learn later in life that we tend to meet any new situation by reorganizing . . . and a wonderful method it can be for creating the illusion of progress while producing inefficiency and demoralization."[1]

This observation is as true today as it was in ancient times—perhaps more so. Therefore, managers must be constantly on guard against making organizational changes which do not offer significant benefits that are clear to everyone. Casual and cosmetic changes often create morale problems, confusion, and errors; lower production; and prompt the departure of good people.

> **Case in Point:** One medium-size company in the East with weak top-management control, revised its structure and associated operating systems every few years. As a result, over $500,000 in direct costs was spent in additional procedures and paperwork. The impact on the staff's time to relearn new systems and structural relations was not determined, but probably exceeded $2 million over a 10-year period.
>
> A new director was hired who made an explicit commitment to living with the existing system, except for some well-defined adjustments. This nipped a major organizational change that was being readied by some middle managers. This not only avoided wasting a lot of people's time, but saved over $70,000 in direct costs that would have been spent to have a management specialist develop and document the new organization and to revise the operations manual.

[1]Lawrence J. Peter, "Peter's Quotations—Ideas For Our Times," William Morrow, New York, 1977, p. 83.

In designing the organizational structure and related operational systems, the items in Table V should be reordered to reflect the prime needs of the company or organization to achieve its objectives. Once this is done, each criterion should be expanded to include the following:

- Source of criterion and its priority level.
- Key factors to be considered in meeting the criterion, such as authority level of implementor, special procedures or documents needed, and an objective method for determining whether the criterion is being met after design and implementation.
- Organizational and systems interfaces needed.
- Special resources, people, or techniques needed to achieve the criterion.
- Timing—when does it have to be implemented in relation to other organizational or operational elements.
- Potential problem areas in implementing the criterion.

TABLE V

CRITERIA FOR EVALUATING OR DESIGNING AN EFFECTIVE ORGANIZATION

- Meets overall needs of company, product, and customer
- Minimizes disorder and waste in human energy
- Provides adequate independence of critical functions; e.g., quality assurance does not report to directors of manufacturing or engineering
- Has a well-defined hierarchy and identification of responsibilities
- Is predominantly based on traditional, proven techniques
- Is logical in its design; e.g., related functions are under one vice president or director
- Is simple as possible in terms of the environment and product
- Provides design growth potential without requiring a major restructuring when minor changes are needed
- Provides for lateral, vertical, and diagonal communication
- Ensures that staff is trained in its structure and reasons for its selection
- Makes sure operating systems and procedures are consistent with the structure and needs of the company
- Makes sure that it is amenable to change when conditions or performance indicate deficiencies or potential future problems; e.g., deletion or addition of functions can be readily accomplished

- Identifies whom to go to if problems need resolution and cannot be worked out at lower levels.
- Broadly defines functions and work scope
- Minimizes levels of management
- Avoids blowing marginal functions out of proportion into separate groups, branches, or departments

3.2 Organizing Functions and People for Effective Performance

Once the requirements for the organization are defined and agreed to, the specific functions required to meet company objectives need to be expanded into a more detailed network. When all the key functions are listed, they need to be reviewed to assure that there is no overlap with other functions, or redundancy. Also they need to be re-evaluated to make sure their importance to the success of the company is great enough to represent a separate function (this is normally identified by a block on an organization chart).

After the list of functions is validated as being an accurate reflection of the company needs, each function has to be assigned a level of authority or responsibility within the company. Thus, the President's Office would be the highest level, then Contracts, Finance, Marketing, Engineering, and Production could be the next level, and then various subfunctions would be placed within each major organizational function. Where in the company's hierarchy each function goes, depends on a number of factors:

1. Importance of function to success of company.
2. Need of President, V.P., or Director to have direct and accurate inputs on the function's activities and performance.
3. Ability of President, V.P., or Director to exercise meaningful control of the function.
4. Availability of sufficient time for President, V.P., Director to provide regular in-depth review of operations and to exercise control of these operations when needed.
5. Type of organization: functional, matrix, or project: see Section 3.2.1.

After each function has been identified and assigned its position in the hierarchy, people need to be assigned to each function.

Caution: The hierarchal structure of an organization should not be misconstrued to mean overall importance of the manager or function, but to identify responsibility for policy making, decision making, priority identification, and power to control or change things when necessary. While status is often associated with the location of a manager in the hierarchy, it should be made clear to everyone that functions which create the products or services that are the lifeblood of the company are the most important and that all other functions, regardless of titles and position, exist to help these functions succeed. The conscious or unconscious belief of some managers that the lower echelons exist to serve them can lead to the early demise of an otherwise promising company—or at least it will never attain its maximum development and efficiency.

Selection of people for each function should be made on objective grounds. For example, the following checklist should be used:

TABLE VI

FUNCTIONAL MANAGER SELECTION CRITERIA CHECKLIST

Does the person . . .

- Have a solid background in the discipline involved; does he understand the needs, problems, systems, procedures, and hazards involved in achieving an effective function?
- Possess leadership qualities that will help him/her to unite people and to stimulate them to achieve objectives?
- Have a systems philosophy and approach; place the overall company's success over the activities performance?
- Interface and communicate well with others or tend to manage in isolation, removed from functions that provide free exchange?
- Exhibit the management qualities defined in Chapter 1?
- Display enthusiasm about the assignment?
- Accept responsibility and accountability for assignments?
- Appear creative and open to new ideas, or has rigor mortis set in?
- Work well with you or tend to ignore orders and go it alone?
- Does the person have skills or knowledge that complement yours?

In summary the procedure for developing an organizational system includes:

- Identify key objectives and needs of company based on market conditions.
- Identify major functions needed to meet objectives and needs.

- Establish hierarchy of relations.
- Define key qualities required of functional managers.
- Assign managers to each function.

In assigning people to each function, a pitfall that should be avoided is trying to find a home for a manager who is superfluous and doesn't really fit into the organization.

> **Case in Point:** In one Los Angeles company, a reorganization resulted in elimination of a manager's job and top management felt obligated to find him a new assignment. As a result of the reorganization, a new department had been created. It was decided to place him in charge of this group, even though he did not have any background in this area. Without knowing much about the problems, needs, and day-to-day operations of this function, he floundered for two years, creating problems, working on the wrong tasks and demoralizing the staff. Finally he was replaced.
>
> This example is not given to say that a competent manager could not have succeeded without an extensive background in the department's activities; only that someone shouldn't be put in a spot simply because he is available. It would have been better to put him in a temporary staff position with special assignments until the right job opened up for him.

The result of the organizational development process should be an organization chart similar to Figure 3-1, except that names are also assigned. (See page 56.)

Some people oppose issuing organization charts because people tend to get locked up with very constricted organizational attitudes, get their feelings hurt, isolate themselves from others, and focus inward at the subsystem level rather than viewing themselves as a part of a larger whole. This last reaction can be avoided by selecting systems-oriented managers and through training programs or management meetings that emphasize a broader perspective. The attitude: "This problem affects Bob's department so I'm not going to worry about it," will still exist even without organization charts if higher management doesn't work at infusing a broader view and responsibility in their people.

Figure 3-1 also shows subordinate breakdowns in the major blocks. Whether this is needed depends on the size of the organization. Some companies have separate organization charts for each major function and subfunction.

In addition to the organization chart, charters for each major function are needed. For smaller companies or when responsibilities and duties of the function are clear to everyone, a written charter may not be needed. However, with time, unwritten charters become fuzzy as people come and

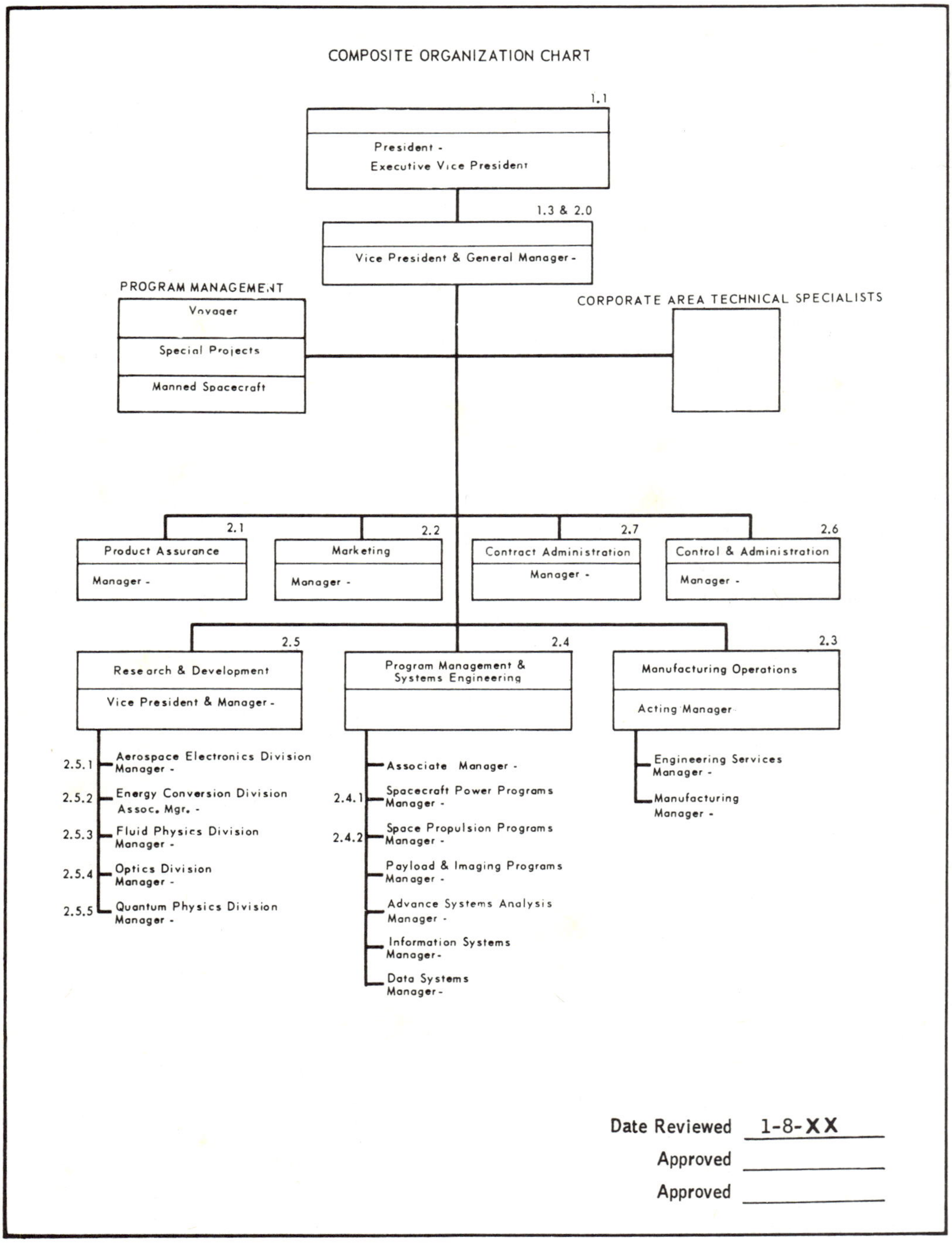

Figure 3-1. Company Organization Chart

Used with permission of Prentice-Hall, Inc.,
"Industrial Documentation Handbook," Thomas T. Samaras, 1978, p. 109

go. The entropy law can work its way here and create disorder when it is not expected. For example, when two organizations have closely related activities in certain areas, the responsibilities, authority, and duties of each group should be reviewed by all managers who work with the functions or might be affected by them in some way. If this is not done, one manager may institute operations that later come to the attention of the other manager who feels that the activities properly belong to his function. The arguments, ill feelings, wasted time, and confusion that result will drain considerable energy from both organizations as well as the entire company, and its entropy will increase.

3.2.1 Types of Organizational Structures

There are three types of organizational structures or systems commonly in use. These are functional or line, project, and matrix. Each structure has its advantages and disadvantages. Depending on the manager's experience, he/she may strongly support or oppose any one of these structures.

Brief descriptions of each type of organization follow:

Line/Functional: This organization is broken up into functional areas under the control of one manager, who directs people, makes assignments, and gives them performance appraisals, fires and hires. (A functional organization is also referred to as centralized.)

Project: People are assigned to a project manager as jobs come in. This individual has total responsibility for progress, cost, and schedule, as well as total control over the staff. The manager directs them, evaluates their performance, and takes corrective action when needed. The project manager and staff are reassigned, after the project is completed, to a new project or to a proposal effort.

Matrix: This organization is a combination of functional and project features. The functional managers provide resource people for the project managers who are responsible for the overall project success and schedule, cost, and progress. However, functional managers are responsible for specific tasks that they accept and for the day-to-day supervision of their people. The people assigned to the project still report to their functional managers and are evaluated and rewarded by those functional managers. Of course, the functional managers' evaluation of their people is strongly influenced by how the project manager feels about their performance and cooperation.

Written task plans represent internal contracts between functional and project groups. The plan defines the work scope, budget, schedule, and milestones that the resource manager commits to. These plans are described in Chapter 4.

The type of organization selected depends on top management's experience, company needs and mode of operation, and resources available. Table VII summarizes the advantages and disadvantages of each type of organization.

If a company is switching from a functional organization to a matrix, top management should take care to define responsibilities carefully and clearly. Otherwise the following could occur:

> **Case in Point:** A new matrix organization was set up in a company that had been previously a straight functional organization. As a result of the change, functional managers felt stripped of much power and some found ways to interfere with the smooth operation of the company. Interference methods included interminable meetings to discuss problems, numerous changes in procedures, ignoring of project management directions, opposition to planning and scheduling requirements, and generation of new requirements that diverted energy from getting the job done. Many of the new systems needed to make the matrix organization work were looked upon as unnecessary work, involving too much red-tape.
>
> The project people in turn got involved in work that the functional people were capable of handling and increased their entropy (degraded their energy) by causing delays, extra meetings, and raising technical problems that did not materially affect the product's quality or performance.

TABLE VII

ADVANTAGES AND DISADVANTAGES OF DIFFERENT ORGANIZATIONS

Type	Advantages	Disadvantages
Line/ Centralized	More effective control and use of staff.	Project authority and control is weak.
	Concentration of specialists increases use of collective experience and knowledge.	Strongest groups or project leaders outside organization tend to get better service.
	Standardized hiring, operations, and drafting criteria improve overall efficiency.	Responsibility for project progress and cost is difficult to pinpoint.
	Better development and application of new production design techniques.	Decisions on problems or needs related to a specific task or project take longer to make because the manager is concerned with many projects.

Line/ Centralized	Top flight manager can be recruited and rewarded for improved performance of the department.	Unless well managed, work output per person may be less than on a project basis.
	More opportunity for professional growth.	
	Greater versatility and flexibility.	
Project/team	Well-suited for tight organization and control and short schedules. Provides rapid reaction time.	Continuity of team personnel and technical developments will be poor unless teams can be immediately reassigned to a new job.
	Staff for project is hand picked for project based on experience and past smooth interaction with project team.	Technical exchanges are poor among personnel on different project teams.
	Strong control by one person having one objective to meet.	Personnel tend to get more involved in each others problems. In general, this dissipates energy which could be used more profitably in their own areas.
	Successful teams develop strong esprit de corps.	More difficult to time the transfer of staff to other work as one project ends and another begins.
	Better cost control because spreading of time among several projects is not required.	Growth/promotion possibilities are more limited when teams are dissolved after each project.
		Harder to balance work loads; e.g., personnel on Project 1 may be working 6 days a week while members of Project 2 are busy only three-quarters of the time.
Matrix	Provides better project control than obtained from a line organization.	More conflicts over priorities and assignments between department and project managers.

TABLE VII (Continued)

Type	Advantages	Disadvantages
Matrix	Provides more stable and continuous employment for staff than project organization.	Staff members are accountable to two bosses who may have conflicting demands and goals.
	Offers better exchange of information among projects than with project organization.	Accountability of profit and loss is more difficult; e.g., project and line managers blame each other for cost overruns or performance problems.
	Provides better continuity and use of technological developments when compared to pure project organization.	

3.2.2 Operational or Management Systems

A major part of the organizational process is the development of written policies and procedures. While the scope of these documents should be kept to a minimum, they are necessary tools for effective management.

The policy manual should be prepared early in the organizational process and should include the company's position in relation to personnel matters, commitment authority of company officers, consultant agreements, and conflict of interest considerations.

Systems and procedures should evolve as the organization is defined. Systems should be defined by flow charts (see Figure 6-1 in Chapter 6) and specification sheets so that the major elements of each functional operation are analyzed and identified. For example, a few procedures that would be important to define early in the engineering function include:

- Work planning
- Work authorization
- Work standards for performance measurement
- Engineering documents and their formats and requirements
- Release and document control system
- Document retrievability system
- Document retention schedules
- Design verification techniques

Systems and procedures should be defined in a hierarchy of documents which cover only those requirements or systems that are mandatory at that level of the organization. Other documents should deal with details below this level. A sample listing of documents in the order of their authority follows:

- Corporate Policy Manual
- Corporate Quality Assurance Manual
- Program Management Manual
- Divisional Policy and Procedures Manual
- Department Procedures
- Branch Procedures

Very often management underestimates the value of written policies and procedures. These documents may have to change frequently, but their benefits to the company are considerable. They can provide the following advantages:

- Crystallize ideas on how the company should operate
- Raise questions that would not have been asked until much later in the organization's life
- Ensure mutual agreement and understanding. (Companies that have operated without documenting their systems find all kinds of problems when they eventually put them in writing. Suddenly people start disagreeing with who's doing what and how, even though nothing has changed.)
- Provide a baseline for future changes. Unless you have your systems and procedures down in writing, it is difficult to change them formally and to assure consistent following of them by the staff.
- If problems are evident, the systems and procedures can be evaluated objectively for a solution if they are the cause.
- Help new people to get on board faster and minimize confusion as to how the company or function operates.
- Satisfy the government or a customer who may require written procedures before the contract is awarded.

3.2.3 Staffing the Organization

Once the major breakdowns of the organization are identified, each functional manager or director must specify the types of people he or she needs. The variety available is quite large. However, there is a fairly common set of classifications. These include:

President	Executive Vice President	Vice President
Executive Assistant	Director	Program Manager
Functional Manager (department, branch, section, or unit)	Supervisor	Leadman
Foreman	Administrator	Project Engineer
Manufacturing Engineer	Manufacturing Planner	Planner
Engineer	Designer	Draftsman
Scheduler	Estimator	Expeditor
Service Engineer	Salesman	Analyst
Programmer	Technician	Operator
Technical Representative	Coordinator	Purchasing Agent
Contracts Administrator	Machinist	Patent Administrator
Configuration Manager	Systems Analyst	Engineering Aide
Clerk	Document Processor	Illustrator
Editor	Materials Coordinator	Quality Assurance Engineer
Inspector	Maintenance Engineer	Public Relations Administrator
Personnel Administrator	Secretary	Scientist
Chemist	Physicist	Mechanic
Comptroller Representative	Assembler	NC* Operator
Systems Engineer	Accountant	Clerk
Typist		

The preceding list is only a small sample of job classifications. Because of the variety and levels of skills involved, many companies prepare a book of job descriptions to help define responsibilities, functions, skill needs, and pay ratings. (This book may be over 100 pages long.) Figure 3-2 is a sample job description for an administrative type job. Generally, the requirements for a professional and non-professional classification differ. Figure 3-3 shows a job description for a non-professional worker. Note that within each broad job classification, different grades may be needed to cover the entire function's needs. Thus, there may be a junior, intermediate and senior job description for a draftsman or other work category.

Many companies try to conform to standard practice for their industry in terms of job classifications. However, changes in environment, staffing, and organizational needs may require the invention of new classifications. While the proliferation of job classifications increases entropy due to more paperwork and processing effort, it is sometimes necessary. However, the need for new classifications should be evaluated and controlled by higher management, and industrial relations should cancel job descriptions when they no longer apply.

---

*NC = Numerical control

POSITION DESCRIPTION

Date:	July 19XX	Position:	Administrative Specialist
Written by:		Incumbent:	
Approved	(1)	Department:	Design
	(2)	Branch:	
	(3)	Reports to:	Manager

POSITION PURPOSE:

This position is accountable for investigation, creation, evaluation, preparation and implementation of new systems of operation for improved efficiency, control, and productivity. It also monitors the day-to-day operation of the Department and interfaces with various groups and individuals to improve operations and negotiate the resolution of problems before they can get out of hand.

DIMENSIONS:

Capital Equipment Expenditures: $70,000.
Value of Projects, Tasks and Subtasks: $200,000.

NATURE AND SCOPE:

This position reports to the Manager of the Design Department.
The incumbent works closely with the various Engineering Branch Managers on a variety of assignments involving design and drafting operations, evaluation of new techniques and equipment, and interfacing with section, branch and department managers. The incumbent fills in for the Manager of the Department when he is away from the plant.
This position evaluates and analyzes the operation of reproduction and microfilm equipment, records and drawing status report systems, and the cost effectivity of new systems. Inasmuch as no historical data is available for the type of work being done, these evaluations require assumptions that must be tested, and judgment as to the reasonableness of recommended plans.
The incumbent also prepares administrative system flow diagrams, feasibility studies, cost estimates, administrative and technical procedures, work statements, and recommendation reports. The incumbent develops solutions to interface or operational problems involving draftsmen, designers and engineers, quality control experts and manufacturing representatives. Regular principal contacts include branch managers, department managers, section leaders, manufacturing representatives, the controller representative and vendors.

Figure 3-2 Position Description

Used with permission of Prentice-Hall, Inc.
"Industrial Documentation Handbook," Thomas T. Samaras, 1978, p. 356

The greatest challenge of the position is to quickly develop optimum solutions to operational or administrative problems which serve the needs of all affected groups. Other challenges include:

(1) Having a systems viewpoint while still focusing on details.
(2) Finding ways to significantly improve department performance and reduce costs by devising and employing monitoring systems that do not cause extra burden on the workers.
(3) Providing management with reliable and timely facts in response to questions about department operations.
(4) Efficiently coordinating activities requiring the participation of people with diverse backgrounds.
(5) Promoting open communications within the department for improved morale, cooperation, and resolution of problems.

PRINCIPAL ACCOUNTABILITIES:

1. Complete assignments received from Manager with a minimum of supervision and a maximum of reliability by developing plans and follow-through of necessary actions.
2. Inform Manager of all important developments, problems, and activities by meetings, memos, procedures, and reports.
3. Select new techniques that will improve the design and drafting operation at minimum cost by accurate, objective analyses.
4. Expand the range of expertise in design and drafting organizational structures, procedures, controls, new methods/materials, behavioral analysis, cost estimating, and quantitative analysis through additional training, self-study, and schooling.
5. Detect potential problems before they develop and inform Manager of them by keeping in close touch with design and drafting activities.
6. Promote a service-oriented and cooperative image for the Department by helping people with problems or questions.

Figure 3-2 Position Description (continued)

Classification #3—Title: DRAFTSMAN A

Titles now in use in this classification:
Layout Draftsman, Draftsman, General Draftsman

Minimum education and experience required:
Preferred—2-year vocational technical school that meets AIDD Certification requirements for Draftsman" (See page 17), subject to a minimum of 1 year on-job experience in a temporary position at somewhat lower salary before fully qualifying for this position.

Figure 3-3 Sample Job Description

Used with permission of Prentice-Hall, Inc.
"Engineering Graphics Deskbook," Thomas T. Samaras, 1975, p. 60

("Page 17" refers to AIDD manual.)

Alternate #1—3-year high school training which meets AIDD Certification requirements for "Junior Draftsman" plus 3 years drafting experience.

Alternate #2—High school graduate with 1 year of mechanical drawing, 1 year of algebra, 1 year of geometry, plus 6 years drafting experience.

Fair Labor Standards Act status:
Non-exempt (from overtime pay)

Supervision received:
Under general supervision with considerable opportunity for individual action.

Work direction exercised:
Might guide and instruct other draftsmen occasionally in this and lower classifications.

Supervision exercised:
None

Level of duties and responsibilities:

1. Handles normal drafting assignments under regular supervision.
2. Is completely familiar with drafting standards, symbols, nomenclature, engineering terms, proper use of materials, reference books and catalogs in a specific area of work.
3. Discusses job requirements directly with persons for whom work is being done.
4. Gathers information and data for jobs.
5. Makes routine calculations using standard engineering formulae.
6. Is assisted at times by other draftsmen in this and lower classifications; instructs, guides and checks their work.
7. Takes field or shop measurements as required.
8. Does limited amount of design under close supervision.

Figure 3-3 Sample Job Description (continued)

Caution: While new jobs should not be established too easily, a rigid position can also lead to higher costs and entropy through the loss of highly qualified and productive people.

Selection and assignment of people within an organization is, of course, a critical step. Failure to properly match people to the right division, department, or project can affect virtually every aspect of the organization's performance. Consequently, a well-developed organization won't be worth much if good people don't fill most of the spots identified. Some guidelines for selecting people follow:

- Do they have the experience, qualities, education and talents you need?

- Do they consistently use their talents or skills to get their work done or do they tend to coast?
- Do they have personality problems that will antagonize and alienate others, reducing their effectiveness and output?
- Do they have growth potential if you are interested in putting them in positions as backups to their leaders?
- Do they appear to be committed to a long-term stay with the organization or company?
- Do they appear more interested in furthering their careers than in doing a good job?
- Do they constantly complain and interfere with other people's work and morale?

3.2.4 Communication Guidelines

Communication guidelines within and outside the company are useful for many organizations. If these rules are not defined early, problems and conflicts will occur. These problems and conflicts will require a lot of energy and time from management to unravel the communication network that was allowed to evolve without any plan or direction.

Some areas that should be defined include:

- Can functional people communicate directly with customers, vendors, and subcontractors or must their exchanges be processed through the functional or project manager?
- Can a functional person direct a vendor or subcontractor to change the work he is doing without a formal change authorization? For mature companies this may seem obvious, but experience shows that engineers and others often issue oral instructions to people outside the company that are completely unauthorized. They often commit the company to thousands of dollars without any management review or approval.
- Can company material and documents be given to a vendor, subcontractor, or customer by a project engineer or functional person without project manager or contracts administrator approval?
- Can a project or functional manager act on the oral or written instructions of the customer's representative? It is bad practice to allow your staff to do this without the contract administrator's approval.

Case in Point: The project manager of a $400,000 project had an excellent working relation with the technical representative of the customer throughout the project's life. However, after the project was half through it was found that the budget was being overrun. An investigation by higher management revealed that the project manager was responding to numerous oral requests for changes in work scope from the technical representative. No documentation was generated to identify the impact of these changes on schedule or cost or to authorize the new work. Since the contract assigned the authority for issuance of all approved changes in work scope or funding to the customer's procurement administrator, the company could not recoup its losses. However, a business-oriented project administrator was assigned to help the manager. The administrator was given strict orders to document and process all customer-requested changes through the company's contracts department. Within three months, the company received an additional $50,000 to cover new changes in work scope requested by the customer's technical representative.

- Can visitors attend company meetings, and what information may be given to them?
- Should documents given to a potential customer or supplier be marked with proprietary or private notices that restrict the use and dissemination of the documents?
- Do confidentiality agreements include the requirement to return proprietary or private data when the agreement is ended?

In addition to these types of communication problems, how should internal communications be handled? The following should be addressed by management to minimize problems:

- May someone communicate directly with his boss's boss? Under what conditions?
- May someone within one organization communicate with someone else in another organization? Under what conditions and at what management level?
- May higher level managers communicate directly with someone without going through his/her manager first?

Caution: Managers and supervisors often get uneasy when their bosses are seen talking with their people. The problem here is that the person may complain or criticize his boss without the boss having the opportunity to defend himself. Of course, if the boss's manager tells him everything the person discussed with him, open communication will cease. The solution is not easy, but an effective higher manager will use grass-roots information to help his managers do a better job rather than to punish them.

- When should memos be written instead of using oral communication?
- When should contact reports be written when someone from outside the company discusses a project with a person on the project?

The communication system need not be overly complex, but some guidelines and rules are needed. The scope of these rules depends on the nature of the company and the complexity of relations with the outside world, including foreign countries where exporting of information may violate the laws of the United States.

3.3 Organizing Project Work for Greater Output and On-Schedule Performance

While the functional organization must precede the project organization, how the project and work are organized is no less important. The project organization is usually specially created to meet a specific project's needs. It may consist of a project manager, administrative assistant, other support people, and a number of project engineers. The organization may change, depending on where in the life cycle of the product the project is. For example, during the conceptual phase, most people on the project will be technical while during the fabrication stage, manufacturing, quality assurance, purchasing, and test engineers will be the primary functional areas within the project.

Besides the project organization, a contract work breakdown structure is needed. The work breakdown structure (frequently referred to as WBS) is a product-oriented family tree of hardware, software, services, and other work that results from the project efforts during the development and production of a product. The WBS completely defines the project.

Figure 3-4 is a sample WBS. It is similar to an organizational chart for a company, except that it covers a larger variety of components or work elements. It also does not include the names of people or functional groups. Each level in the WBS is identified, starting with level 0 or 1 as the highest and increasing to 2, 3, 4, etc. as a path is followed down the tree to the lowest element identified.

The purpose of the WBS is to identify and organize all work into a pictorial diagram that ensures compliance with the contract work statement and clear-cut assignment of responsibilities and accountabilities to various task managers within the project. Another important factor is its use in the performance measurement described in Chapter 6.

Once the WBS is approved, a WBS dictionary is prepared down to some level of the WBS as defined by the customer or project manager. A

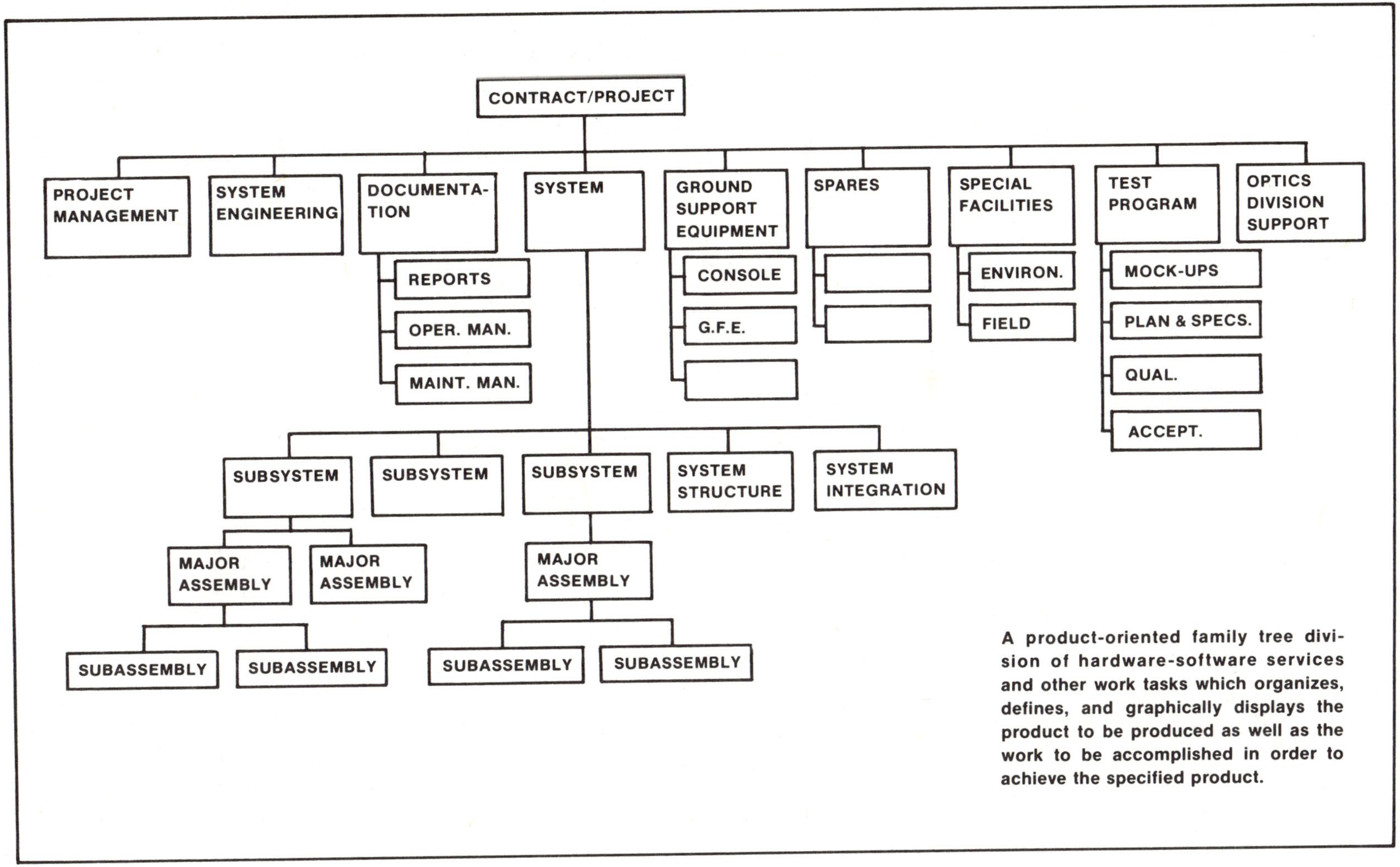

Figure 3-4. Work Breakdown Structure

Courtesy of Paul R. MacDonald Procurement Associates, Inc., Covina, CA

WBS dictionary is a collection of work descriptions for each element that define the purpose, scope of work, and other pertinent information. The purpose of this document is to make sure that the customer and project staff have a common understanding as to what is required to complete each WBS element. It also acts as a baseline so that when changes are needed, they are reflected in revised dictionary sheets to assure that the new requirements are understood and worked into the project.

Another tool for organizing the project is the WBS organizational matrix. This document lists all the organizations within the company that are responsible for a specific work element defined by a block in Figure 3-4. Next to each organization, a WBS work element number is recorded to assure proper identification and interconnection. The value of this matrix is that it allows questions or problems within a particular WBS element to be traced to the responsible organization so that they can be resolved quickly.

Work breakdown structures, dictionaries, and matrixes are normally used for fairly large projects. However, they can be useful for any size project if tailored to fit its work scope and needs. These documents can help the project manager identify and organize his work before having his kickoff meeting and even before he has gotten the staff on board. They can be useful in guiding the design of his project organization also. These documents can save much lost time in getting staff members oriented and working toward their goals. They also ensure that the manager is in control and is in fact leading his/her people. Of course, the first cut of these documents may be based on sparse or tentative information, but for a small project they can be easily revised after the first kickoff meeting.

For large projects, the manager may not be capable of doing this job on his own. In this case, the project engineer(s) and functional managers can work on this task with the assistance of the planning and scheduling group.

3.4 Organizational Pitfalls

Beware of entropy generators within your specific organizational elements; e.g., people who create problems and work for themselves and others without a net gain in productivity or quality. In attempts to implement a manager's policies and objectives they can create ill feeling, unnecessary work, and delays. They can also make things more complicated than they need to be and alienate people outside your organization with a reduction in cooperation. Some guidelines for detecting these promoters of disorder include:

- Do they lack social graces and become offensive when someone disagrees with them?
- Do they threaten people when they don't agree with them?

- Do they reflect a condescending attitude toward people in other groups?

Case in Point: Two people in an engineering services department were discussing problems in implementing a new operating system. An engineer walked in to ask a question about the new system. One of the service department people looked angrily at the engineer and said: "You engineers can never follow instructions unless someone twists your arms." The engineer turned red and left the office. It took two months before he would cooperate with the services department."

- Do they lock into ideas or systems and rigidly avoid considering other's needs?
- Do they frequently make fun of people or managers in other groups?
- Do they lose their tempers when disagreed with?
- Do they have a "I know what's best for you attitude"?

Hopefully the answers to these questions are "no" for people who have to interface with other departments or groups.

Other pitfalls that can create entropy within an organization include:

- Superficial top management support and interest in organizational changes; lack of follow-up to make sure they are working.
- Frequent organizational changes without significant improvements in performance or efficiency.
- Lack of clear-cut responsibilities and authority assignments.
- Allowing new managers to initiate changes when operations and performance are good to demonstrate that they are doing something useful.
- Too many managers have near-equal power and no one manager has enough to make timely decisions and to see that they are implemented.
- Too many layers of management prevent information from going up or down the hierarchy without getting lost or distorted and slowing down responses to new objectives and instructions.
- No operating charters developed for each major function.
- Work is not defined and organized in a systematic way.
- Span of control is too great. A maximum of five is often given in the literature. However, it depends on the situation and up to 40 people may be effectively managed in certain cases.
- People report to more than one boss. The lack of unity of command can be distressing, confusing, and demoralizing.

4

Planning, Scheduling, Budgeting, and Accounting for Successful Projects

Few industrial managers would think of doing a project without including some degree of planning, scheduling, budgeting, and accounting effort. The problems with these areas of industrial management revolve about two questions: "What methods shall be used for planning, budgeting, etc.?" and "How much effort should be expended in these areas?" Answers to these questions cannot be given a cookbook treatment because they depend on a blend of the following factors:

- Scope and complexity of the project
- Manager's experience with past projects
- Types and attitudes of project staff
- Requirements of higher management and the customer
- Need to improve future performance
- Schedule requirements
- Penalty or incentive clauses in contract
- Risks in achieving cost, technical, and schedule objectives
- Real benefits or payoff to be obtained from increasing resource investment in planning, scheduling, etc.

Planning, scheduling, budgeting, and cost accounting experts will usually urge the manager to establish comprehensive and sometimes elaborate systems. This is normal because these people exist to supply these functions and their experience indicates that lack of planning, budgeting and other procedures often lead to unsuccessful or disastrous projects. Phillip Metzger reports that the most recurring cause given for project failures is lack of adequate planning. He says that projects fail because the manager doesn't consider the job from all angles, sometimes has no plan at all, and sometimes the plan is a fairy tale.[1]

While planning, scheduling, and budgeting are absolutely necessary for most projects, no hard rules exist to specify how much work in these areas is required to assure success. It is clear that more is not necessarily better for it is possible to wind up spending more time and money in the planning and scheduling of a project than in designing and building the product.

> **Case in Point:** At one company in Northern California, a project manager found the planning, budgeting, and scheduling work of his staff unsatisfactory and kept recycling their plans until they met his standards for format, style, and content. As a result, the staff spent the first three months of their time in work not directly related to the design and fabrication of their product. This not only delayed progress but consumed labor not budgeted for in the contract and also demoralized the staff, who rightly felt that they were getting bogged down in paperwork that was intended to improve performance, not retard it.

The preceding example illustrates how important it is for the project manager to plan his own work first so that his/her staff can provide adequate detailed plans, budgets and schedules the first time. This example also shows the need to let the staff know that non-technical work needs are an intrinsic part of the project and that the contract budget includes a certain number of dollars for planning and scheduling.

The percentage of labor devoted to planning, scheduling, etc. varies considerably from project to project. Therefore providing a figure such as 5% to 20% is only a value for ballpark purposes. Obviously, accurate definition of work scope and needs can help reduce this effort by eliminating repetition of the planning process until the objectives of the project manager are met. There are several steps that the project manager can take to minimize the cost and time required for planning, scheduling, and budgeting. These include:

- Use proven, established systems that are also useful to the project staff and not just to management.
- Clearly identify real needs for effective project management.

---

[1]Phillip W. Metzger, MANAGING A PROGRAMMING PROJECT, Prentice-Hall, 1973, p. 13, 14.

- Make sure staff understands the planning requirements and why they are needed.
- Establish requirements firmly before asking for inputs from the staff; this will minimize the number of iterations required.
- Insist on a firm contract baseline before requesting detailed planning from the staff.
- If a firm work scope baseline is not available, but planning, scheduling, and budgeting are required by the customer or higher management, tailor the requirements to minimize need for detailed work that is very likely going to change.
- Prepare staff instructions that are simple and unambiguous.
- Insist on uniformity of preparation before work is begun by staff.
- Hold kickoff meeting to review requirements, time expected to be devoted to planning and other guidelines.
- Avoid changing the methods or system for each project. Routine saves time and labor even if the system or methods are not ideal.
- Have project engineer do first cut, subject to fine tuning by the cost account or task manager.

It is the project manager's responsibility to remember the need for activities related to planning, scheduling, budgeting, and accounting. They exist for three reasons: the first reason is to allow the project to be conducted efficiently and in a business-like way; the second reason is to provide records or reports for performance measurement, evaluation, control, and reporting; and the third reason is to provide official (legal) records of costs spent and commitments made so that invoices are correct and the accounting department has the capability of providing data on charges from the staff and vendors or subcontractors.

The following sections of this chapter provide an overall look at key planning, scheduling, budgeting, and accounting functions. For detailed methods and other systems, refer to books[2] devoted to these specific areas.

4.1 Start of Planning Process—Review Contract and Proposal

The contract is the first document that a project manager should study to determine the type and extent of planning, scheduling, budgeting, and accounting effort required. In some cases, the customer may call out very specific requirements and these will limit the manager's freedom of choice.

---

[2] e.g., Archibald & Villoria, "Network Based Management Systems," Wiley and Sons, New York, 1968.

However, most contracts do not deal with these areas because it is assumed that the company meets minimum management standards if it was selected to submit a bid or proposal. Also, a management plan is often included in the proposal.

For most projects, a proposal or bid has usually been prepared in competition with other companies to win the contract. (In some cases, the proposal was submitted to management for obtaining company funds to conduct the project.) If this document was prepared with the intention of really winning the contract, it will contain much valuable data that can be used by the project manager to initiate his/her planning work. Of course, things change and the proposal manager may not be the project manager. Therefore, the method for conducting the project may be subject to new ground rules and management requirements. However, even if subject to change, the proposal is a most valuable tool for planning, scheduling, etc., the project and should be studied carefully.

The proposal should provide the following information:

- Project objectives
- Original scope of work (may be different from contract)
- Overall schedule
- Summary work breakdown structure (discussed in Chapter 3)
- Preliminary budget breakdown
- Project organizational structure
- A list of the key staff members
- Need for special facilities and equipment
- A management plan that defines how the project is to be controlled, reporting requirements, and strategies for solving potential problems
- Review of expected difficulties or special product or project requirements

However, much of the proposal material is subject to revision based on new insights, changed work scope, resource availability, completion of new facilities, receipt of new production equipment, changes in overhead rates, and availability of new vendors or subcontractors.

The project manager should identify any conflicts between contract requirements and the original proposal. For example, a lower price or shorter delivery schedule may have been negotiated without a reduction in work scope. If the manager feels that the funding or schedule cannot be met, this is the time to discuss it with higher management to obtain additional company funds or to develop a strategy to minimize losses. In some cases, nothing may be changed, but at least management will be aware of the problem. However, this is an undesirable situation because it will demoralize the manager and staff if they feel that they are in a no-win situation or have no plan to get well in terms of schedule or budget.

4.2 Set and Communicate Objectives, Constraints, and Assumptions for Project

Completion of the proposal review process should then be followed by an explicit identification of project objectives, constraints, and assumptions which should include the following characteristics:

Objectives

- Must be consistent with contract, customer, and company requirements
- Must be tangible and measureable; e.g., first 20 units will be delivered to customer's facility by March 5, 19__.
- Must be attainable—otherwise people will not take them seriously or may give up before starting
- Must be accepted or agreed to by the staff—studies show that mutual goal-setting with voluntary staff commitment to meet goals or objectives produces the best results
- Must not be excessive in numbers—the more objectives there are, the more the prime ones will be diluted

Constraints

- Must be consistent with contract, customer, company and end product
- Must be explicit and clearly defined or qualified
- Must be explained to staff as to why they exist
- Must be consistent with what is realistically attainable with current technology; e.g., "material waste during the production process should not exceed 1 percent" may not be feasible for your company's old equipment and facilities.

Assumptions

- Must be consistent with project needs, company conditions, and external environment

- Must include consequences if the assumptions are not realized; e.g., if 3 additional N/C machines are not in operation by March 10, the project schedule will slip 1 week for each day in excess of March 10
- Must be communicated to management

After refining these elements, communicate them to the staff. This may be done by memo or by a meeting. Both methods may be needed if the project manager's experience indicates that the staff tends to forget or underemphasize objectives, constraints, and assumptions.

4.3 Prepare Project Plan

After evaluating the contract and proposal, the project manager should prepare a written plan describing the objectives, organization, constraints, resource requirements, approach, strategy, schedule, and budget required to complete the project.

Written plans are important even for small projects. Their benefits include:

1. Help overcome procrastination, confusion, stagnation, loss of purpose and floundering. Crystallize thoughts.
2. Help keep manager and staff on the right path in terms of where they are going and how they are going to get there.
3. Help block out distractions that can divert everyone's energies from the primary project aims.
4. Provide checkpoints during the project to make sure the staff is on course. These checkpoints allow the staff to get back on course when they deviate from the right direction.
5. Allow manager and staff to measure their progress and to obtain valuable feedback on their performance.
6. Improve communication between the project manager and staff.
7. Provide deadlines that create a challenge for the staff to meet and mobilize their energies toward specific accomplishments.

Figure 4-1 is a sample outline for a project plan. Note that for a small project, this plan may be sufficient to reach the desired objectives. However, for a large project, this plan will only be a starting point for development of much more detailed plans, schedules, and budgets. These are described in subsequent sections of this chapter.

1. INTRODUCTION
   - Statement of purpose
   - Overall objectives
   - Justification for project
   - Constraints and assumptions
   - Project Organization
2. WORK SCOPE
   - Work Breakdown Structure
   - Narrative Work Element Descriptions
   - WBS Assignment Matrix or Assignments List
   - Lists of deliverable hardware and software (documents)
3. SCHEDULE AND MILESTONES
   - Overall schedule
   - List of key milestones
4. BUDGET
   - Required funding by year
   - Committed funding by year
   - Funding curves
   - Manpower curves
   - Scarce material requirements
5. CAPITAL EQUIPMENT AND FACILITY REQUIREMENTS
6. ALTERNATIVES AND CONTINGENCIES

APPENDIXES

Figure 4-1 Sample Outline for a Project Plan

4.4 Prepare Summary Schedule and Long-Term Network

A summary schedule and long-term network are needed even if a project plan has been prepared. Of course, their requirements must be consistent with the objectives, constraints, and assumptions mentioned before. In the process of schedule and network development, some modifications of objectives and goals may be needed. This is a normal process and ensures consistency between schedules and project objectives and needs. (See Figures 4-2 and 4-3.)

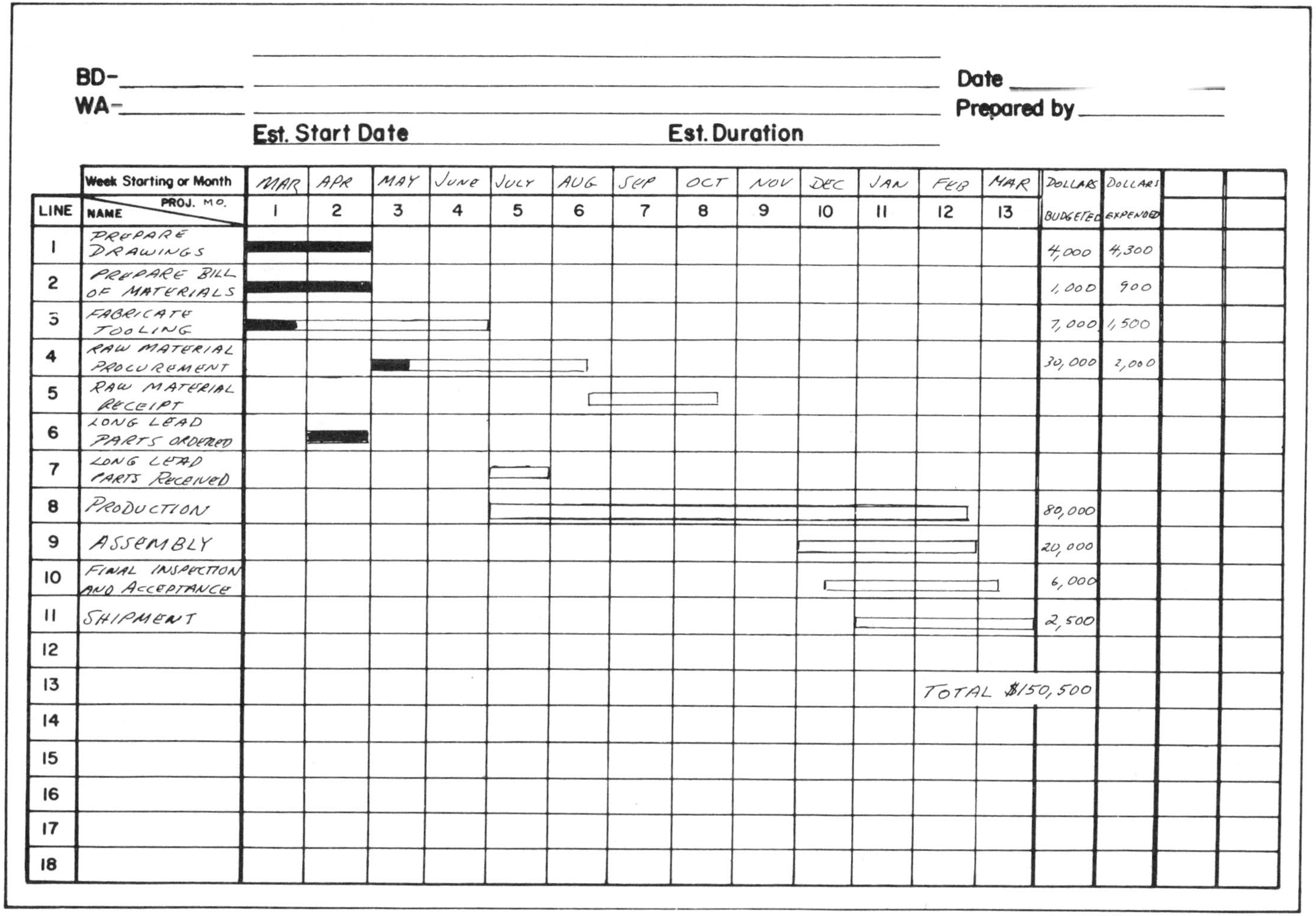

Figure 4-2. Production Schedule and Progress Report

Used with permission of Prentice-Hall, Inc., "Industrial Documentation Handbook," T. Samaras, 1978, p. 309

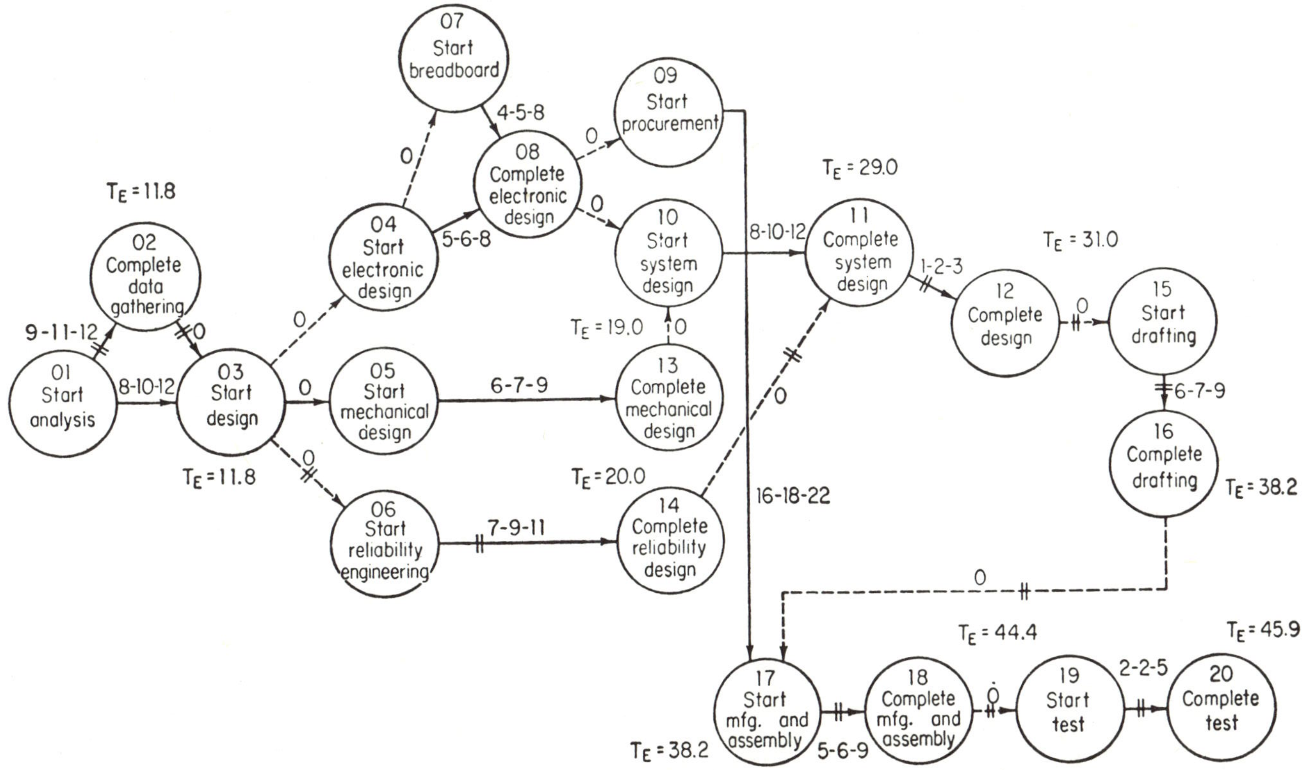

Figure 4-3. PERT Chart

Used with permission of McGraw-Hill Book Company, V. G. Hajek, "Project Engineering," 1965, p. 73

The summary schedule (which may have already been prepared for the Project Plan) should identify the key or major tasks to be done. Each task requires a start and stop date and one or more milestones. Milestones should be events of major importance to the overall project and customer. Figure 4-2 shows a sample summary schedule. When a WBS exists, this schedule should list level 2 and 3 work elements.

From the summary schedule, a network may be required for more detailed scheduling and planning of a fairly large project; e.g., $1 million or more. Networks are diagrams that interconnect various work activities to accomplish the project's objectives. Activities are shown by lines with circles at each end called events. Figure 4-3 is a typical network. Most often networks are called PERT (program evaluation and review technique) for the manufacturing industry and CPM (critical path method) for the construction industry. The benefits of these networks are that they allow:

- Planning to be done first; thus work items are identified and interrelated before they are scheduled.
- Time and cost requirements can be easily added to each activity line.
- The longest work path can be identified and monitored to avoid schedule slippage.
- A complex effort can be monitored and evaluated for corrective action when conventional bar charts can't do it effectively.

Detailed schedules at the immediate supervisor's level are also needed. These are described in Section 4.10 on work plans.

For more detailed presentation of schedules and networks refer to Samaras & Yensuang, "Computerized Management Techniques for the Manufacturing and Construction Industries", Prentice-Hall, Inc., Englewood Cliffs, NJ, 1979.

4.5 Identify Elapsed Time for Each Activity

Whether a network or detailed bar schedule is prepared, each activity must be assigned an elapsed time for completion. This time depends on the activity, labor and equipment available, waiting periods, experience, and the judgment of the person responsible for completing the activity. With schedules, the time required is indicated by a line drawn under a calendar heading in weeks, months, or years. For networks, a number indicating weeks is recorded above the line between two events. PERT uses three time estimates, pessimistic, most likely, and optimistic. An equation is then used to compute the most probable time statistically required to complete the activity. CPM uses only one time estimate.

4.6 Identify Estimated Cost and Manpower for Each Activity

Once the time required for each activity is specified, estimates for labor and cost are also made. These may also be added below the line or in any form helpful to the manager. When this step is completed, each activity now represents a self-sufficient work package or item that is defined by:

- Start and end events or points (and special events called milestones)
- Activity duration
- Cost to complete activity
- Number of hours or people needed to do job

In some cases, the types of skills needed for each activity may also be identified for better resource management and planning. Very often this type of information can be put into a computer. This keeps the network from getting cluttered with various categories of manpower and other data already recorded. Of course, the same thing can be done manually by preparing a special manpower category summary list for each activity.

Note that after work plans are completed (see Section 4.10), the estimates may be converted to firm budgets for each activity.

4.7 Identify Constraints

An important part of network scheduling is the identification of constraints. This means that certain events are picked out for special attention because if they do not occur on time, other work will not be able to start or be completed. Obviously, this information plays a major strategic role in managing the project; e.g., the manager can track these constraining events more carefully so corrective action can be taken when a slip appears to be developing. Thus, resources can be temporarily assigned from activities that are not on the critical path or are ahead of schedule to restore the activity to its original schedule.

Constraining events are usually identified by a dashed line connecting this event to the event dependent on its completion. When computerized management techniques are used, a printout can be obtained of all constraining events so that management can review all of them for possible trouble.

4.8 Identify Critical Path

The longest work path for completing a project is called the critical path. There is only one critical path (CP) for a project and a delay in the completion of any item on this path will inevitably cause a delay in the completion of the project unless a strategy can be developed to make up the lost time somewhere else in the path. Therefore, activities on the CP normally require the greatest amount of attention and control.

4.9 Identify Cost Accounts

Cost accounts should have already been developed at this point in the planning process or must be done now—before the work packages or plans are completed.

A cost account is a meaningful management control point for cost, schedule, and work scope requirements. It is also a basis for doing the following:

- Assigning responsibility for a significant work area
- Assigning accountability for a work area
- Preparing a budget for the work
- Accumulating costs or charges against the work area
- Measuring performance for the work area
- Reporting progress and taking corrective action

Cost accounts are often converted into documents[3] that include:

- Definition of work scope
- A firm schedule
- A budget
- Cost element identity (e.g.,labor, material, and subcontractors)
- Single organizational responsibility
- Monthly performance data (see Section 6.5 in Chapter 6)
- Variance analysis when needed (see Section 6.4 in Chapter 6)
- Corrective action planning

Cost accounts are identified by job order numbers assigned by the accounting department, based on the account structure worked out with the project manager.

4.10 Prepare Work Plans and Detailed Schedules

A work plan should be prepared for each major area of work. It may cover one or more cost accounts. This depends on the project manager's

[3]also referred to as work/task plans.

philosophy and needs and the size of the cost account. If there are a lot of cost accounts, and a work plan for each, a lot of paper work will be generated with subsequent increased review and maintenance costs and delays. A rough guideline for preparing labor-intensive work plans is $200,000 to $300,000 of direct costs. However, for a materials or subcontract effort, $1 million or more may be adequately covered by one work plan. The primary basis for planning work should be to prepare the minimum paper work required to assure successful achievement of project objectives.

Figures 4-4 through 4-7 show one type of work plan. It consists of three parts:

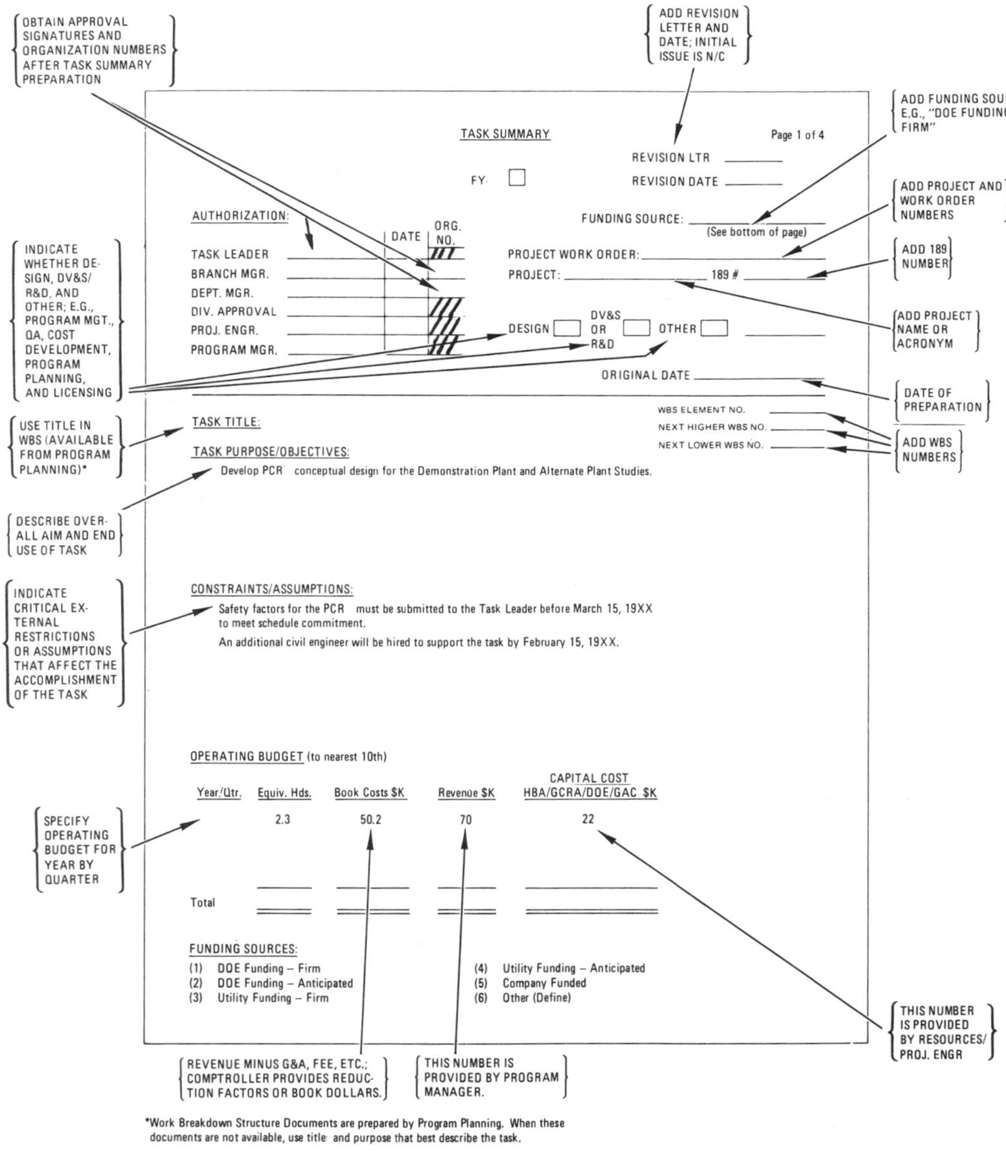

Figure 4-4. Task Summary

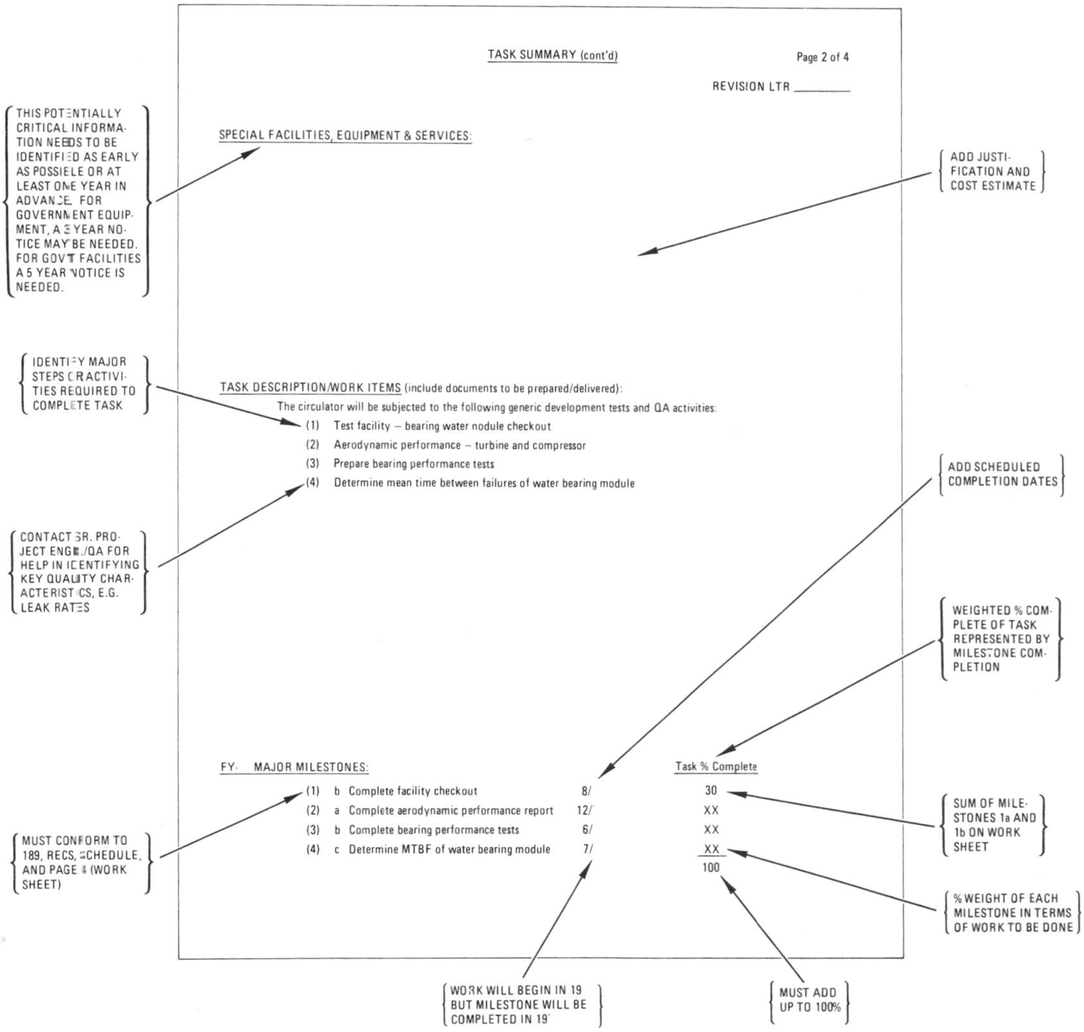

Figure 4-5. Task Summary (continued)

- Summary of work plan objectives, constraints, work elements, and milestones
- A detailed budget estimate or requirements summary
- A detailed schedule for the work required

The responsible cost account manager should oversee the preparation of the document or prepare it himself. He/she should then review it with the staff to make sure they can do the work described.

After the work plan is completed, it is approved by management and becomes a mini-contract between the cost account (task) manager and project manager.

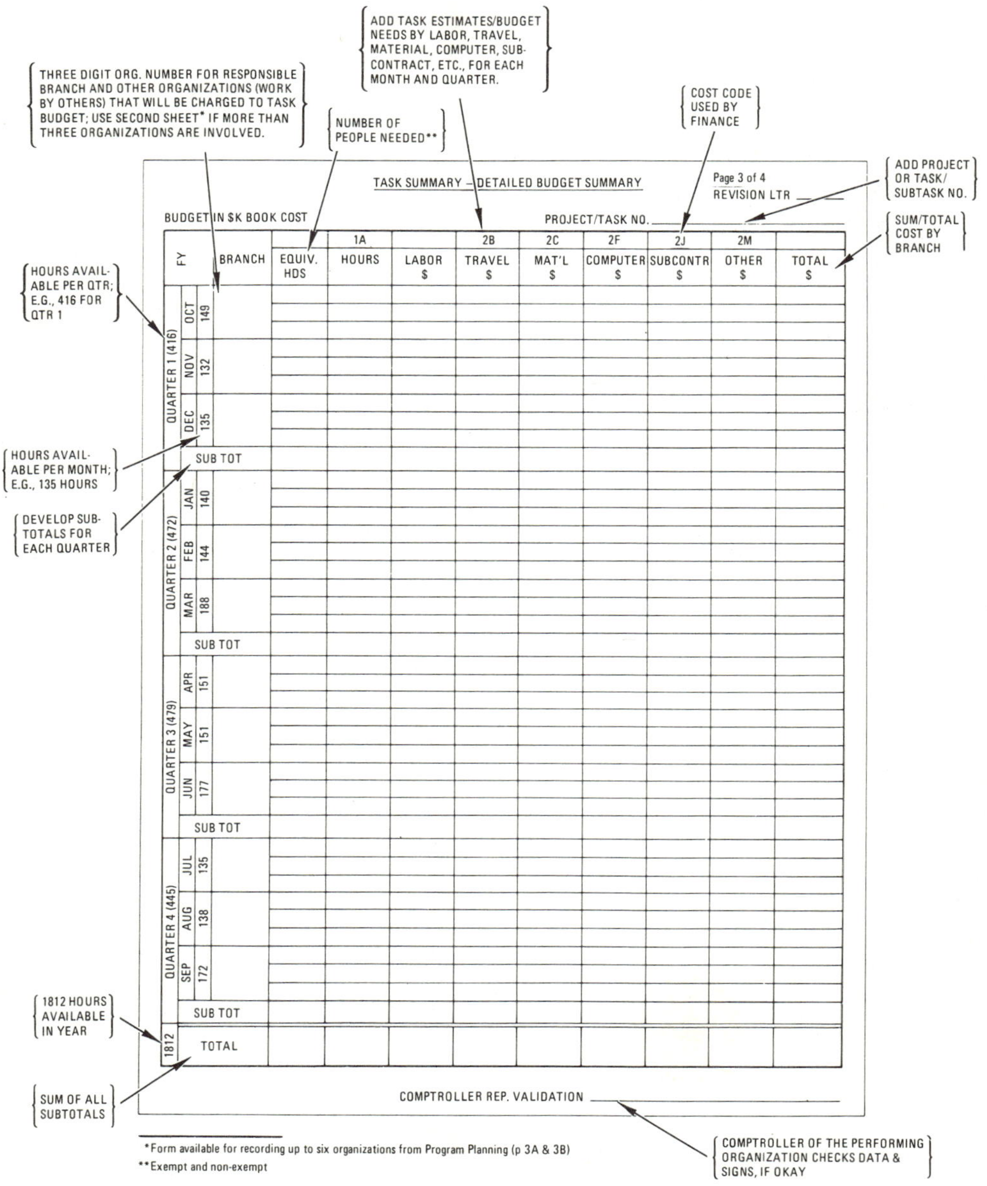

Figure 4-6. Task Summary—Budget Summary

4.11 Assign Industrial Budgets

The work plan is the basis for budget assignment. The approval of the work plan by the project manager represents a commitment of the project to support the task manager with funds up to the amount specified in the plan. Once this budget becomes frozen by mutual agreement, there are certain rules that are followed when management desires an effective performance measurement system. These rules or constraints are listed next:

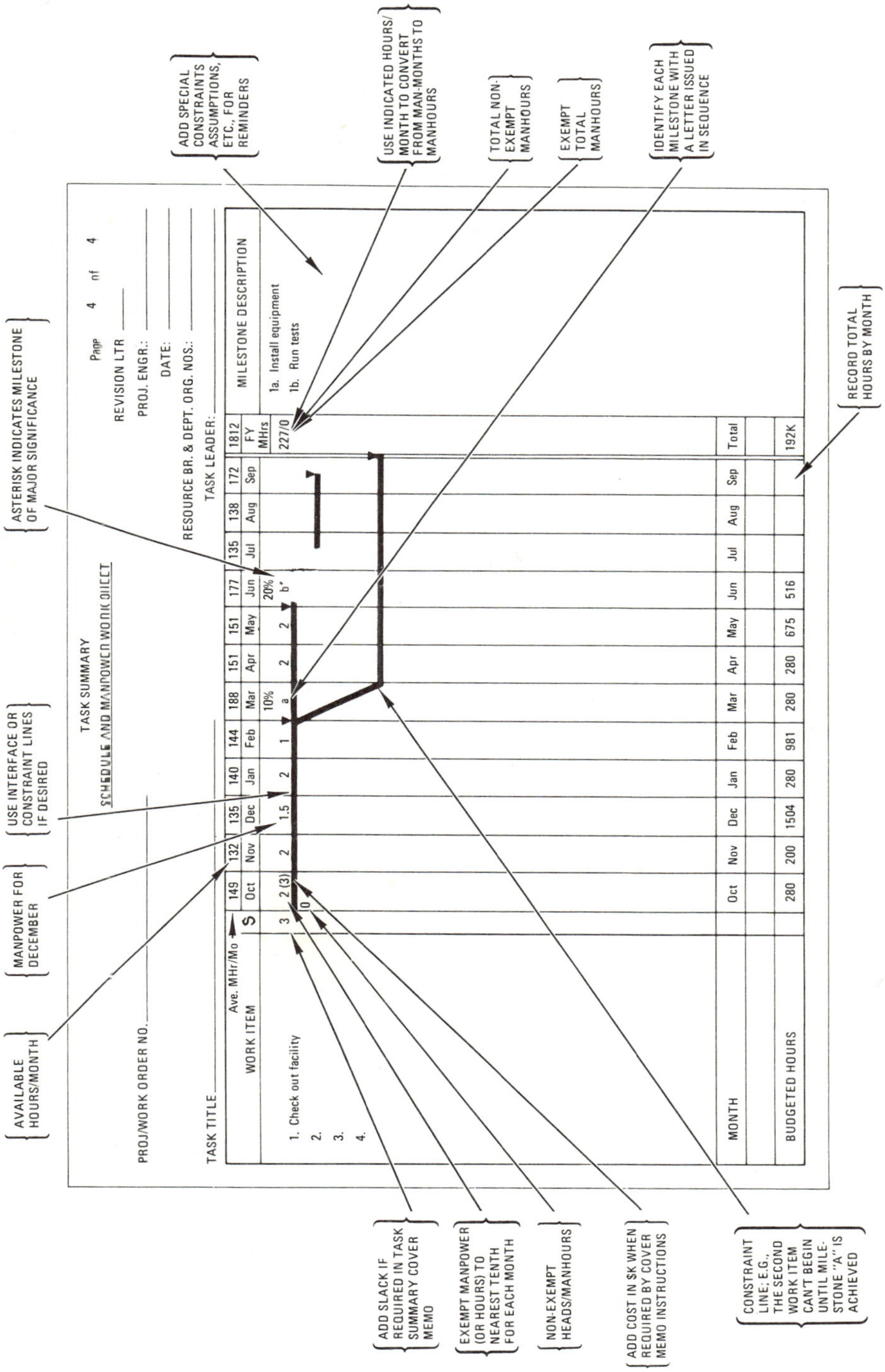

Figure 4-7. Task Summary—Schedule and Manpower Work Sheet

- Retroactive changes to budgets or costs of completed work are not permitted
- Work cannot be transferred to another manager or task without transferring its associated budget
- In-process work cannot be rebudgeted
- Closed work packages or tasks cannot be reopened

The above rules provide for objective measurement of the task manager's performance by avoiding frequent changes in budgets and work plans because the manager did a poor job of planning or didn't control his/her people's activities. While this approach is not generally followed strictly in commercial work, the Government's Cost/Schedule Control System or Performance Measurement System require contractor's to follow these rules (see Chapter 6).

4.12 Negotiate Budgets and Redefine Work Plans

As with any contract, a certain amount of negotiation may occur before the budget and work plan are approved by both the project and task (cost account) manager. This is a healthy process and helps assure a clear understanding by everyone as to the requirements that apply and the results expected upon completion of the task.

The cost account/task manager must be careful not to accept a budget and work scope that cannot possibly be met. Since this individual is responsible and accountable, failure to perform will look bad to higher management and may affect the manager's progress and future with the company. Therefore, the cost account/task manager should be confident that the requirements agreed to in the work plan can be met.

The project manager is also responsible for not programming the task manager for failure by persuading or forcing him to commit to unrealistic budgets and work scopes. If the cost account manager cannot live within the current budget, then some creative thinking is needed to identify a reduced work scope that can produce desired results.

A forceful or persuasive manager should recognize the danger of gaining a reputation for cutting proposed budgets. This may force cost account managers to estimate high or they may not want to work on assigned projects because of fear of failure.

4.13 Open Job Numbers and Authorize Work

Before work can begin, charge or job numbers are required. The accounting function should work with the project manager to develop the job number structure and issue job numbers to the staff.

In some companies, the issuing of job numbers is considered equivalent to authorizing work to begin. However, this is not always true. It is possible that the issuance of job numbers is needed to allow proper definition of work and assignment of these numbers to work elements in the WBS (described in Chapter 3) before any work is ready to begin. In this case, a separate document may be required to authorize work to start. This document could selectively allow the staff to begin work on certain work elements. Only these job numbers would be opened in Accounting and any others added to time cards or invoices would be bounced. (The Comptroller usually issues a memo to Accounting directing it to accept charges against the job numbers listed.)

Stop work orders are also needed for medium and large companies. These documents are issued by the project manager, subject to review and appeal by the cost account manager, when work must be stopped on a task. The need for these documents is illustrated below:

> **Case in Point:** One company used an oral order from the project manager to stop work on a task. At the end of the week, the comptroller reported that 240 hours had been charged to the task. An investigation by the project manager revealed that the cost account manager did not agree with the stop order and had failed to communicate it to his staff. He argued that since the work plan was a mini-contract, it could not be abrogated unilaterally or without formal paper work.

When a formal stop order system is not used, the cost account/task manager can find a number of ways to avoid stopping work. These include:

- Didn't understand the oral order
- Couldn't tell his people because he/she had to go to a meeting out of town
- Doesn't remember being asked to stop work
- Thought the project manager was going to send a memo to stop work
- Was in the middle of a critical task and couldn't stop without wasting a lot of work
- His/her people didn't understand that they had to stop working immediately

While the project manager may be able to get the charges backed out of the accounting system, the ill feeling and trouble involved are harmful to everyone. Therefore, a simple, but formal, agreement to stop work is desirable.

4.14 Collect and Summarize Costs

Once work is authorized, charges must be collected and summarized so that management can keep track of expenses in relation to company or contract funding. Charges should be kept separated into various categories for effective monitoring and decision making. These cost collection and summarization bins include:

- Exempt labor
- Nonexempt labor
- Materials
- Computer time
- Subcontracts
- Travel
- Other direct costs
- Overtime

This breakdown allows the manager to focus on specific areas of the project and this in turn allows different strategies or corrective action plans to be implemented. The degree of breakdown of course can vary; e.g., costs by each labor category may be accumulated. Whether this separation of labor costs is needed depends on the company, past experience, and the project itself.

Accounting or the Finance Department is responsible for collecting and summarizing costs incurred during the project. The actual inputting of these costs is by time card or by invoice, depending on whether it is internal labor or purchased labor and material.

Summarization of costs should also be available by organization and by WBS element, regardless of its level in the WBS. This allows the manager to trace variances or cost problems to a particular organization or WBS element for corrective action.

If a WBS is not used, it is important that the cost accumulation and summarization system allows costs to be gathered and reported for individual components or parts so that spares and replacements can be accurately priced or for more accurate estimating of future projects.

4.15 Reporting Costs

For many projects, a formal method for reporting costs to the customer is needed. The data required includes both costs incurred for the preceding month and cumulative costs for the entire project up to and including the preceding month. A sample cost report is shown in Figure 4-8.

Page

____ of ____
Form Approved
OMB No. 38R-0190

COST PERFORMANCE REPORT — WORK BREAKDOWN STRUCTURE (Format 1)

Contractor:	Contract Type No.:	Project Name / Number	Report Period	Signature
Location:				Title
				Date

Quantity	Negotiated Cost	Est. Cost of Auth. Unpriced Work	Target Profit/Fee %	Target Price	Estimated Price	Share Ratio	Contract Ceiling	Estimated Ceiling

Item	Current Period					Cumulative to Date					At Completion		
	Budgeted Cost		Actual Cost Work Performed	Variance		Budgeted Cost		Actual Cost Work Performed	Variance		Budgeted	Latest Revised Estimate	Variance
	Work Scheduled	Work Performed		Schedule	Cost	Work Scheduled	Work Performed		Schedule	Cost			
(1) Work Breakdown Structure	(2)	(3)	(4)	(5)	(6)	(7)	(8)	(9)	(10)	(11)	(12)	(13)	(14)
General and Administrative													
Undistributed Budget													
Subtotal Without G&A													
Management Reserve													
TOTAL													
Reconciliation to Contract Budget Base													
Variance Adjustment													
Total Contract Variance													

Figure 4-8. Cost Performance Report

Similar reports can be used internally for cost account, project, functional, and top management.

Both customer and internal cost reports require variance identification from plans, including underruns and overruns.

4.16 Planning and Budget Changes

In spite of the budget restrictions described in Section 4-11, conditions beyond the project manager's or cost account manager's control may require revision of the work plan. These conditions include:

- Customer's funds have been cut requiring a revision of the contract work scope
- Unexpected changes in material, labor or subcontracts require renegotiation of new work plans
- New technical developments require redirection of the contract

The method for revising budgets and plans varies. A separate planning and budget change sheet may be sufficient to alter the work plan or the work plan may be revised directly and re-issued. The altered plan should be approved by the same people who signed the original document. In some cases, minor changes may only require the cost account and project managers' approvals. Whatever system is used, the change must be documented and transmitted to all affected parties for revision of their plans, schedules, and budgets.

4.17 Zero Base Budgeting (ZBB)

Zero base budgeting (ZBB) is a technique for taking an objective and fresh look at each organization's budget based on the goals and contributions of that organization. With ZBB, management examines organizational budgets each year or oftener by setting the budget at zero and building up in a step-wise fashion comparing the benefits that the company will derive with each step increment of the budget. This process, of course, is much different for the traditional procedure, which takes the previous year's budget as a baseline and then determines whether the budget will be increased, reduced, or kept the same. Very often this procedure does not take a very close view at what the organization is producing for the money it is spending.

A few hundred companies have tried this system which was developed by Peter Pyhrr, Budget Director at Texas Instruments, Inc. Its primary application is with service-oriented organizations within the company rather than with production activities. For example:

Case in Point: Southern California Edison saved money when a vehicle maintenance manager insisted as a result of the ZBB process that adding 20 people to the company's 357-person maintenance staff was cheaper than having an outside agency handle it. Because of a hiring freeze, middle management rejected the idea. But based on the ZBB process, top management overrode middle management objections and the additional people were hired. The company saved $300,000 a year.[4]

The American Management Association conducted a survey of organizations using ZBB. The survey found that many companies felt ZBB helped them improve their allocation of resources, decision making, and planning. Most companies reported that their aims in implementing ZBB were "extremely well to fairly well achieved;" 6% of the companies reported that the results obtained were poor or not achieved at all.

Donald N. Anderson, Vice President of Executive Action, Inc., reported the secret behind ZBB's success was that it ignores common unconscious assumptions that most managers make when they plan and budget work. These include:

- If we need 4 people to do this job, we can do it twice as fast or in half the time with twice as many people.
- If we need 4 people to do jobs A, B, and C, we'll need an additional 4 people to do three other jobs, D, E, and F, which are about the same size.
- If we spend $50,000 to get certain product quality, we can double the quality by spending $100,000.
- If we cut our staff by 20%, we'll have to reduce our services to other organizations or the customer by 20%.

The above assumptions are based on the belief that a directly proportional relation exists between the number of people or dollars used for a project and the quantity or quality of the output produced. Experience shows that it is rare to get a directly proportional output with increases in people and budget. And then only in young, growing organizations. As an organization grows, the adding of people and spending more money produces an output curve that gradually turns down as shown in Figure 4-9.[5]

What these concepts tell the manager is: "Don't automatically assume that your organization's output will decline by 20% because you have to reduce the staff by 20%. The output reduction could be much less than 20%. Likewise, increasing staffing and budget by 20% will often result in

[4]What It means to Build a Budget From Zero," *Business Week*, April 18, 1977, p. 160.

[5]Donald N. Anderson, "The Secret Behind Zero Base Budgets," Executive Action, Inc., Santa Ana, CA (no date).

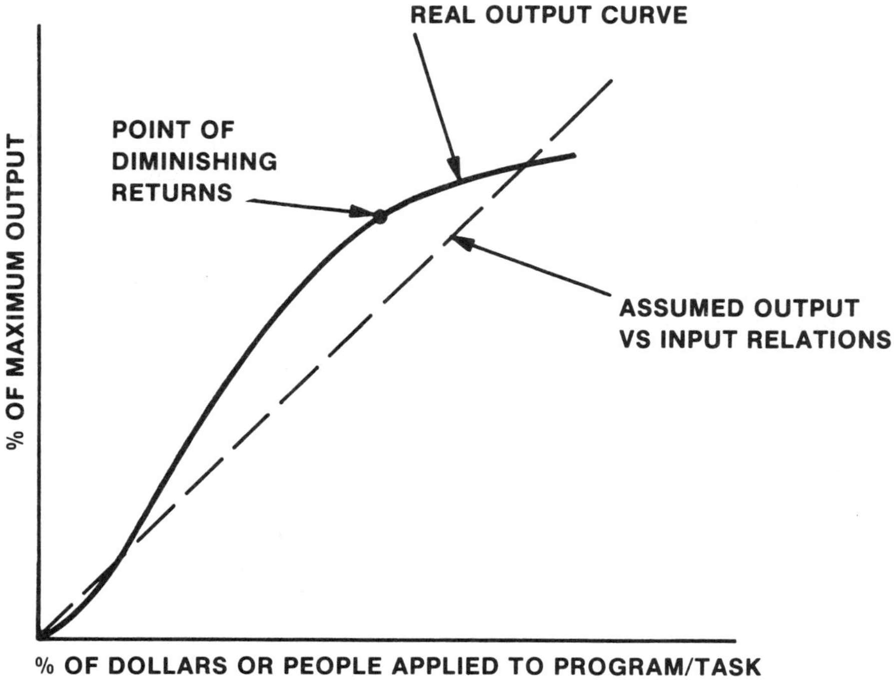

Figure 4-9. Organization's Output

less than a 20% increase in output. Refer to Case In Point in Section 2.13, Chapter 2.

Anderson's experiences are consistent with the entropy theory described in Chapter 2 where it was pointed out that entropy (disorder or inefficiency) increases as the number of people and budget in the organization increase. (See Rules 4, 7, and 8.) Thus an increase in people will often produce a smaller increase in output than expected.

The detailed procedure for implementing ZBB should be obtained from books (e.g., Pyrrh's "Zero Base Budgeting," Wiley-Interscience, 1973) or manuals on the subject. However, an outline of the key steps involved in preparing what are called "decision packages" for each organization involved is given next:

- What are the primary sources of work for your organization? Who requests services or products provided by group?
- How does the output of the organization benefit the organization or company?
- How is performance measured?
- What are the processes, procedures and methods involved in taking inputs from other organizations and converting them into outputs or products or services that are used by the company or customers?

- How many people are needed to do this work?
- What determines how the work is done? Law, top management policy or department policy?
- What other ways of doing the work are possible? Via another organization, different processes or equipment, or outside contractor?
- If staffing and budget must be cut by 25%, how would you reorganize your function, including reassignments?
- With the reduced staffing and budget, what outputs or benefits would cease or be reduced?
- How would you reduce the impact of reduced organizational output on the company as a whole?
- How would you be able to measure the impact on the company of your reduced or eliminated output.

Another step that should be worked into a ZBB plan is the listing of each output or service of the organization in a ranking order of importance to the company, with its associated cost. Thus an overall picture can be provided that compares each service or output with its relative cost. This simplifies the culling of services or outputs that aren't worth their cost or are of marginal value.

How long ZBB will stay on the scene is hard to tell. It may become a permanent part of the business world's standard practices or it may be limited in use only to large companies—following the path of other systems, such as PPB (Planning, Programming, and Budgeting). However, small and medium size companies can benefit from the valuable ideas of ZBB and apply them in a less formal way than recommended. Very often, if supervisors and managers understand the basics involved they can apply them to some extent in the traditional budgeting procedures followed by the company. Certainly, they must recognize that because a department had a budget of $500,000 this year is no reason that it should be the same or more next year, unless it is directly related to the outputs and benefits needed by the company.

5

Controlling Activities and Operations to Avoid Misdirected Efforts, Delays, and Cost Overruns

Control is making things happen the way you want them to happen. It includes any activity that leads to corrections of deviations from objectives, plans, specifications, policies, rules, and standards. The techniques for achieving control depend on the manager, staff, company, product, and customer. Therefore, there is no fixed set of control measures that apply to all companies. However, the majority of the control techniques described in this chapter can apply to most companies, small and large. The degree of sophistication in implementing the controls will vary with the size of the company, product complexity, and safety considerations.

The key features of an effective control program for a project or company include:

- Clear identification of what really needs to be controlled.
- Specification of the harmful results or risks in not having formal control over these areas.
- Determination of the extent and complexity of control needed for each area of control identified in the first step.
- Estimation of the cost and time required to implement and maintain controls.

- Elimination of control requirements when the benefits are not worth the cost and time requirements.
- Design of control systems or techniques that meet minimum needs at minimum cost to the company or project.
- Evaluation of the workability of the control systems selected.
- Review of control systems and techniques with staff and their modification.
- Active management support of control systems and techniques.
- Periodic reassessment to eliminate unneeded control systems and to fine-tune existing techniques based on experience acquired in their use.

The following sections include control requirements in relation to work authorization, stopping work, baseline control, design reviews, project status reviews, and change control. Management by objectives is also discussed.

The techniques given are basically independent of each other. Therefore, they are not presented in any particular order.

5.1 Work Authorization

For a small company, work authorization control may be simply a direct order to begin work on a project from the project or general manager. For medium and large companies, a more formal system is normally used to avoid the following problems:

- Start of work when proper job/charge numbers have not been established. As a result, people incorrectly charge work done on new project to overhead or another project.
- Start of work when adequate planning has not been completed first.
- Start of work based on go-ahead from customer's representative when company has not received a formal contract or other written authorization to expend funds.
- Start of work on the wrong tasks.

The authorization of work is controlled as follows:

1. Contract signed by officer of customer is received by company.
2. A contract receipt notice is issued to resource (functional) and project management.
3. A planning budget for the new contract is approved by management.

FROM ______________________ ____________
NAME OF PREPARER ORG.

DATE: ______________, 197 __
OPEN ☐ CLOSE ☐ DELETE ☐
BUDGET ONLY ☐ REOPEN ☐
NEW PROJECT ☐ NEW TASK ☐
NEW SUBTASK ☐ CHANGE BUDGET ☐
ONLY TO OPEN

TO: PROJECT ACCOUNTING

SUBJECT: PROJECT, TASK, SUBTASK, WORK ORDER REQUEST

PROJECT	TASK	SUB-TASK	WORK ORDER	RESP. ORG.	DESCRIPTION	USED FOR CLASS 5 ONLY		
	CLASS 5 JOB NO.					PROJECT	TASK	SUB-TASK

INFORMATION REQUIRED FOR OPENING A NEW PROJECT, TASK, SUBTASK, OR JOB NUMBER: INDICATE SPECIFIC REASONS FOR REQUEST, IDENTIFYING A MAJOR WORK STATEMENT OR SCOPE OF WORK TO BE PERFORMED. (INCLUDE EXPLANATION FOR EACH LEVEL REQUESTED)

* ✓ = INPUT LEVEL CODE (I.E. WORK ORDER)
BLANK = SUMMARY LEVEL ONLY (NOT FOR INPUT)

APPROVALS:

APPROVAL - DIVISIONAL COMPTROLLER (ALL REQUESTS) DATE

APPROVAL - (CLASS O/NEW TASKS) ASST. COMPTROLLER-BUDGETS/REPORTING ANALYSIS DATE

CONCURRENCE (ALL "OPEN" REQUESTS) PROJECT ACCOUNTING SUPERVISOR DATE

INFORMATION REQUIRED FOR NEW PROJECT:

RCN ____________
COMPANY I.D. ____________
PROGRAM AREA ____________
PROJECT TYPE ____________
ALLOCATION CODE ____________
TAX CODE ____________
CUSTOMER ____________

Figure 5-1. Authorization to Open New Project

4. Project manager organizes planning effort of staff and issues directive specifying the planning requirements that must be met before work can begin on the project.
5. Staff prepares work plans defining work to be done, schedule, budget, milestones, and special needs for equipment or facilities.
6. Work plans are approved by management and Finance (verifies that budgets of all work plans do not exceed total project budget).
7. Project manager authorizes Comptroller/Finance to open job numbers. (See Figure 5-1.)
8. Project manager issues work authorization notice to staff. This notice identifies the tasks that can be started and their associated job numbers.

Some companies require a separate work authorization notice to be issued before the staff can begin work (see Step 8). However, the approved work plan may be used to perform this control function although it does not provide the positive control of a separate authorizing document. When the risks of having people start work on the wrong tasks are low, the elimination of the work authorization reduces the paper work required.

5.2 Stop Work

Once work is in progress, it may become necessary to stop it before the project is completed. Events requiring work stoppage include:

- Customer's funding availability has changed.
- Customer desires a change in direction, work scope or product requirements.
- The customer or top management (if an internally funded project) has decided that the project is not going to succeed and needs to be canceled.
- Project is having scheduling or cost overrun problems that require replanning of the work.
- A particular task has been completed early and no further charges are to be accumulated against it.
- A design change is in process and parts ordering, fabrication, or testing work must be stopped until the new design is implemented.
- Funds for the current year have been used up and a temporary stop is needed until additional budget or funds are approved.

A stop order should be written to assure effective communication to the staff. Reliance on verbal instructions can result in the following:

Case in Point: In one 300-person organization, the project manager called the controller and requested him to notify the staff that work and charges against a specific task be stopped. The controller immediately notified the task manager by phone. The next week an

EARTH SCIENCES

NUMBER 315

PAGE 1 OF 1

STOP ORDER

ESTIMATED DATE OF LIFT 11/5/XX PART NUMBER	NEXT ASSEMBLY NUMBER	MODEL AND EID / EFFECTIVITY	CIN (DCR NO.)
80206-10	80107	AL-200 1#UP	2102

REASON FOR STOP:
CUSTOMER REQUEST TO CHANGE MATING CONNECTOR TO AIRLOCK FROM FEMALE TO MALE.

ENGINEERING NOTES:
THIS STOP ORDER AFFECTS DRAFTING, PUBLICATIONS, AND TEST EQUIPMENT.

COGNIZANT ENGINEER:	DATE	PROGRAM MANAGER:	DATE
F. [illegible]	10/14/XX	S.C. Hoffman	10/13/XX
		PROJECT ENGINEER: D. Howard	DATE 10/14/XX

MFG. NOTES:
TOOLING, PROCUREMENT, FABRICATION, AND ASSEMBLY OPERATIONS ARE AFFECTED BY THIS CHANGE.

MFG. REP.	DATE	CHANGE COORDINATOR	DATE
R. [illegible]	10/16/XX		
REVISIONS:		DATA CONTROL RELEASE:	DATE
DATE:			

Figure 5-2. Engineering Stop Order

Used with permission of Prentice-Hall, Inc., "Industrial Documentation Handbook," Thomas Samaras, 1978, p. 267

additional 120 hours were found charged against the task and the charges had to be backed out of the accounting system. As a result of the confusion, discussions, and accounting labor involved, the company wasted about $600. The controller noted that this was not an unusual occurrence when verbal stop orders were used.

A stop order can take two forms. One type is simply a memo from the project manager specifying the job number, task title, and WBS number of the work to be stopped. When the order applies to items in procurement or manufacture, a more formal document is normally used as shown in Figure 5-2.

A stop order lift date is also given on the form. This date is useful for procurement, manufacturing, quality assurance, and inspection manpower allocation and scheduling.

5.3 Baseline Development and Revision

A baseline is a reference point that provides a firm basis for moving onto another phase of a project. Failure to use baselines can result in a continual back-and-forth shifting from one project phase to another with great impact on progress and costs (e.g., the project may vacillate between the conceptual and preliminary design phases).

Baselines are established at key points in a project's life cycle. For the development and fabrication of a new product, these baselines are established when:

- The conceptual design and product definition are completed
- The preliminary design is completed
- The final design is completed
- The prototype or qualification model is tested and found acceptable.
- The first production model comes off the assembly line
- The product is installed and tested at customer's facility or site

Baselines are defined by various documents, such as specifications, drawings, test data, and procedures. The specific documents that define each baseline are identified early in the project planning phase. When these documents are approved by a special meeting or design review as bona-fide baseline documents, they are listed by exact document number and revision letter on a baseline index.

With each baseline established, the staff has a firm foundation to move forward to the next step or phase with assurance that nothing of importance will be changed without careful review and impact evaluation by all concerned.

As the project progresses from the conceptual to production stages two things happen:

1. The baselines that define the product's configuration (specifications, drawings, etc.) become increasingly more complete and detailed.
2. Changes to these baseline documents become progressively more difficult to get approved to minimize changes that cause backsliding, higher costs, delays, and lower staff morale.

For more complete information on baseline management, see Samaras & Czerwinski, "Fundamentals of Configuration Management," Wiley-Interscience, N.Y., 1971.

5.4 Project Kickoff Meeting

The project kickoff meeting is an important initial control device. Of course, its communication function is also a key feature. It plays an important role in orienting the staff as to the purpose and constraints of the project. However, a kickoff meeting provides the setting for future control actions by:

- Identifying objectives and who is responsible and accountable for various tasks.
- Providing a review of control techniques that will be followed on the project.
- Establishing variance thresholds which, if exceeded, will require corrective actions.
- Requiring variance reports to assure proper analysis of problems and development of a corrective action plan.
- Identifying corrective strategy techniques available for use on the project.

Since an understanding of controls to be used on the project is essential for their effective implementation, the kickoff meeting is a valuable method for getting the staff acquainted with the project manager's requirements.

5.5 Design Reviews

Design reviews are control devices for assuring that the product design is on schedule and meets contract requirements, customer specifications, and project technical objectives. These reviews may be held to evaluate specific subsystems within the product or the entire product.

Review meetings should be held near the completion of the conceptual, preliminary design, final design, and prototype/qualification model testing phases of the project.

Key features of a design review are:

- Independent evaluation of the design by qualified systems, design, manufacturing, licensing, safety, and quality engineers.
- Careful comparison of the design with previously established baseline requirements.
- Identification and elimination of designs that are not responsive to customer requirements, are unreliable, or use parts that have been found too expensive, unsafe, difficult to install, or have high failure rates.

An effective design review provides management with the following assurances:

- The design is really what is needed.
- The design is evolving on schedule and ready for the next phase.
- The design is documented according to project requirements.
- The staff, management, and customer are informed as to project design status and understand that failure to challenge the design will lead to its firm establishment as a baseline for moving onto the next phase of the project's life cycle.

A cautionary note applies here. Management should be careful to avoid unneeded changes or to impose their personal preferences upon the designers. If the design meets originally defined requirements, then managers should restrain themselves to avoid the following problem:

> **Case in Point:** Design reviews at one company in the West Coast were held regularly. However, the designers found the meetings very trying because their designs were picked over by their managers without really improving them and resulted in considerable redesign work even though the proposed designs would work as submitted. This lowered their morale and productivity and caused schedule slippages.
>
> When the impact of these changes was brought to the managers' attention, they disciplined themselves to focus on design defects or major cost-cutting revisions. As a result, the meetings were completed in half the time and required much less design revision by the engineers. The savings exceeded many thousands of dollars and improved designer morale and productivity because their work was not criticized as much.

To achieve effective design reviews, take the following steps:

1. Plan the review a few weeks in advance.
2. Issue a memo defining the review requirements and scope. Be sure to guide the reviewer's focus on the major aims of the review so that unnecessary comments and changes are minimized.
3. Send each reviewer a design package for his review before the meeting.
4. Assign one person to coordinate the meeting and to keep minutes.
5. Keep an accurate record of what action items are required and who is responsible. Also specify the date the action should be completed.
6. Review action items at end of meeting and issue to staff.
7. Follow up to make sure action items are implemented. (This is usually done by the design review coordinator or project manager.)

5.6 Project Status Reviews

Project status reviews are another control technique for effective management. These reviews are held periodically (monthly or quarterly) to examine the non-technical aspects of the project so that problems can be identified and corrective actions taken by management.

The areas subject to project status reviews include:

- Major task status in terms of schedule, budget, milestones, and work done.
- Summary of major accomplishments.
- Description of any significant changes from original plans or requirements; e.g., contract changes, new specifications, and different product configuration.
- Problem areas and recommendations for correction.
- Plans for period leading up to the next review.

Project status reviews can be held for three levels of management. The first is when the staff reviews project status for the Project Manager. (This review may not be required for small projects when the manager is working closely with his staff.) Written reports may be used instead of meetings.

Project status reviews are also held for higher managers, such as Program Directors, General Managers, and Vice Presidents or Presidents. The purpose of these meetings is to keep these people informed of status and to assure that actions are being taken by the project manager and others to correct any undesirable deviation from plans.

A third level of review involves the customer. Here the project manager and key staff members present an overview of the project status and answer any questions the customer has in relation to progress, problems, and misunderstandings.

Project status reviews should be documented and copies of the memo or report sent to attendees for review and possible identification of misunderstandings of what was discussed or concluded.

5.7 Corrective Action Requests

A corrective action request is a formal means for returning an abnormal situation or activity to normal. Generally, Quality Assurance prepares this document when it discovers a department or person who is not following prescribed company policies or procedures.

Figure 5-3 is a sample corrective action request (CAR). This document describes the problem, prescribes a solution, and requires follow-up by the originator to assure that the corrective action has actually been taken. While a CAR is normally used for manufacturing problems, it can be employed in virtually any area of company operations.

5.8 Change Request and Review

Changes to key project requirements and baselines must be controlled to avoid administrative and technical anarchy. Before the project is set into motion, the project manager and his/her administrative staff need to define the method for proposing and approving changes and the criteria for whether a change must be formally submitted for review and approval.

A sample change request (CR) form is shown in Figure 5-4. Sample criteria for having people prepare a CR follow:

- A change in the basic work structure (e.g., WBS) is required.
- A change to an interface between major systems or between the company and an outside organization is involved.
- The change will increase or decrease the cost of the project or product by 10% and at least $20,000.
- The change will affect the schedule by 10% and at least 2 weeks.

Of course, the values specified, such as $20,000, must be consistent with the project/task scope and budget. For large projects, $100,000 or more may be the threshold for requiring a formal change request.

The change request should contain the names or functions within the company and project that must review the change before it can be implemented. In many cases, the change may give rise to a change proposal that is sent to the customer for his approval and possible allocation of more funds and time to complete the project.

CORRECTIVE ACTION REQUEST AND REPORT № 1659

TO T.K. YENSUANG

FROM H. G. GUZMAN

SUBJECT OR REFERENCE: ATL MECHANICAL CONTROL SYSTEM SYSTEM/MODEL TE-500A

CWOR/P.O. 4022

DISCREPANCY OR CONDITION: THE SUPPLIER'S FAILURE TO COMPLY WITH DOCUMENTATION REQUIREMENTS IS THE 5th OCCURANCE IN THE PAST 7 MONTHS.

RECOMMENDATIONS: CLOSER REVIEW OF OUR REQUIREMENTS IS NEEDED WITH WEEKLY FOLLOW-UP BY SUPPLIER UNTIL CONDITION IS CORRECTED.

ACTION REQUIRED BY DATE 9/19/XX SIGNED [illegible] DATE 9/12/XX

REPLY (If more space is needed, attach additional sheets.)

CAUSE OF DISCREPANCY OR CONDITION: INADEQUATE INSTRUCTIONS AND TRAINING

CORRECTIVE ACTION (NOTE EFFECTIVE DATES AND REFERENCE DOCUMENTS): NEW PROCEDURE ACQ-22, "DOCUMENT REQUIREMENTS INDEX," HAS BEEN ISSUED. A SERIES OF TRAINING SESSIONS, WITH EMPHASIS ON DISTRIBUTION AND ROUTING OF DATA, WAS CONDUCTED. ALL AFFECTED PERSONNEL ATTENDED THESE SESSIONS. THE NEW PROCEDURE HAS BEEN ADDED TO THE AUDIT SCHEDULE FOR PERIODIC VERIFICATION OF COMPLIANCE.

SIGNED J. Miller DATE 9/18/XX

DO NOT WRITE BELOW THIS LINE—FOR ORIGINATOR ONLY

EVALUATION OF CORRECTIVE ACTION

CORRECTIVE ACTION	FOLLOW-UP	NEW C.A.R.R. NO.
SATISFACTORY YES NO	YES NO DATE	

REMARKS:

SIGNED DATE

SEND PARTS 1, 3 AND 4 WITH CARBON INTACT—PART 3 WILL BE COMPLETED, SIGNED AND RETURNED TO ORIGINATOR. PART 4 TO BE RETAINED BY CORRECTIVE ACTION ENGINEER.

Figure 5-3. Corrective Action Request

Used with permission of Prentice-Hall, Inc., Industrial Documentation Handbook," Thomas Samaras, 1978, p. 346

Change request reviewers have a great responsibility because a bad decision can create problems downstream that may cause the project to miss schedule or overrun its budget. Each reviewer must consider these factors before he/she approves the CR:

CHANGE REQUEST NO. 12

ABC COMPANY | PROJECT NO.: SEA DEFENSE | DATE 4/21/XX

SUBJECT CORE CAVITY FOR SEA DEFENSE SYSTEM

DESCRIPTION OF CHANGE

Increase the height of the upper plenum in the core cavity by 15 inches; this will be accomplished by increasing the height of the core cavity assembly by 15 inches. The PORT exterior height will not be increased; the thickness of the PORT lower head will be decreased. This change will result in an increase in the length of the control rod assembly, the reserve shutdown assembly, and the in-core instrumentation.

The page for the 6000 unit in DO-700 will be changed to include the requirement that "the PORT upper plenum shall be high enough to allow the installation of the fuel elements in the third row of a fuel region."

CHANGE SUMMARY SCOPE CHANGE	DESIGN CHANGE	BUDGET EFFECT	SCHEDULE EFFECT
☐ INCREASE	☒ MANDATORY	☐ INCREASE	☐ LENGTHEN
☐ DECREASE	☐ IMPROVEMENT	☒ DECREASE	☐ SHORTEN
☒ NO CHANGE	☐ RECORD	☐ TRANSFER	☒ NO CHANGE
	☐ NO CHANGE	☐ NO CHANGE	

EFFECT OF CHANGE

	Manhours	Cost
Engineering	100	1,504
Drafting	30	248
Capital Cost	-	- 40,500
TOTALS	130	- 38,748

*Note: An additional savings in operating costs of $270,000 per unit will be realized assuming 8 reflector reloads in the life of the unit. See details on attached sheet.

SCHEDULE No change in schedule.

JUSTIFICATION FOR CHANGE

If the core cavity in the 6000 model unit is increased by 15 inches, the 6000 and 8000 units would have:

a) The same distance between the cross ducts.
b) The same angle to the bottom cross duct.
c) The same length CR assembly.
d) The side reflector could be full length instead of half size blocks.

CHANGE REQUESTED BY Structures ORG. #21 THIS CHANGE $-38,748 (REDUCTION)

CHANGE CONTROL BOARD ACTION

________ NOT APPROVED ________

CCB CHAIRMAN ________ DATE 5 June 19XX

CCB MEMBERS

APPROVALS

PREPARED BY	DATE 4/24/XX
BRANCH MGR.	DATE 4/25/XX
DEPARTMENT MGR.	DATE 6/1/XX
REVIEWED	DATE 6/6/XX
REVIEWED	DATE

Figure 5-4. Sample Change Request

Used with permission of Prentice-Hall, Inc., "Industrial Documentation Handbook," Thomas T. Samaras, 1978, p. 262

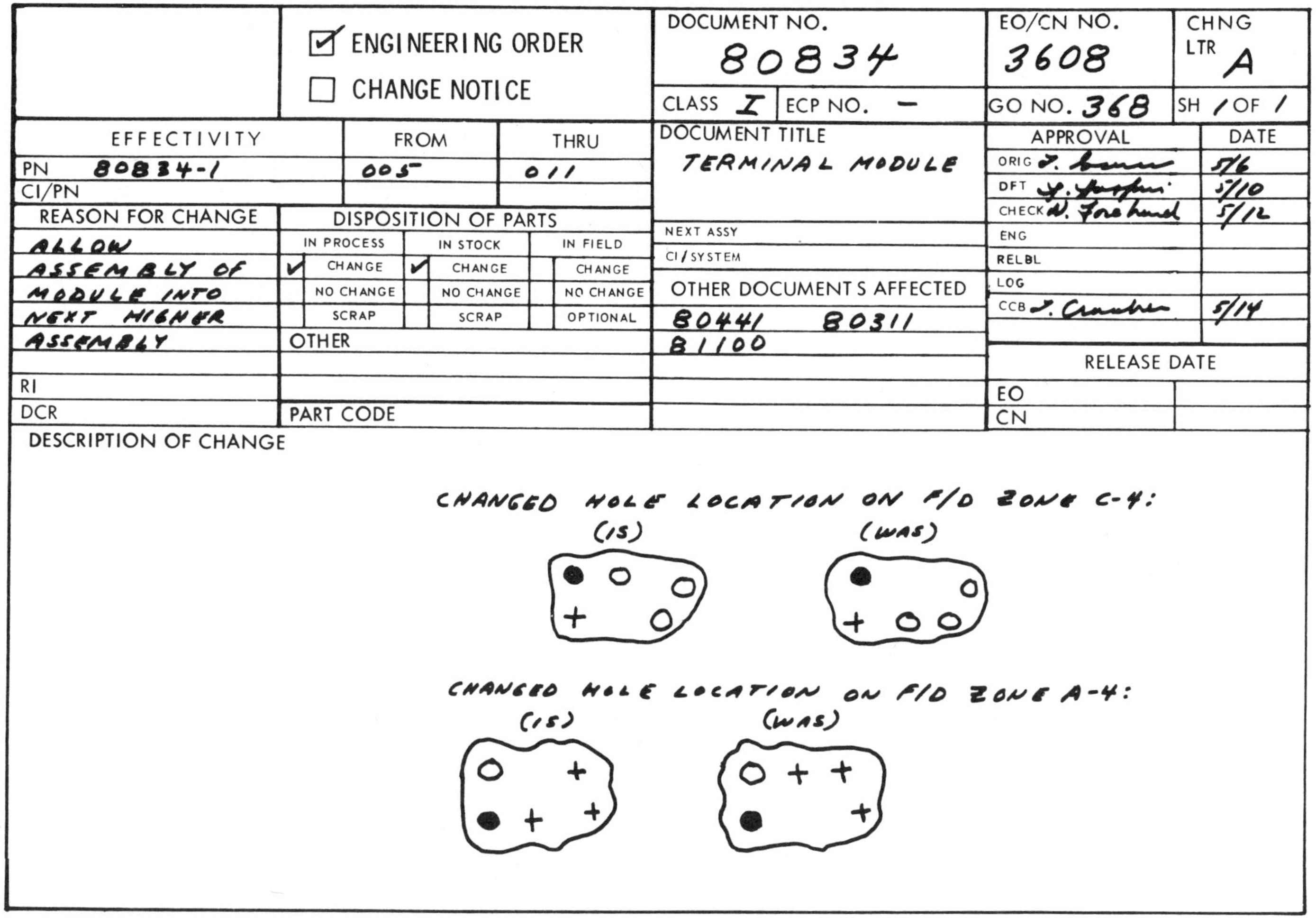

☑ ENGINEERING ORDER
☐ CHANGE NOTICE

DOCUMENT NO. 80834
EO/CN NO. 3608
CHNG LTR A
CLASS I ECP NO. –
GO NO. 368
SH 1 OF 1

EFFECTIVITY	FROM	THRU
PN 80834-1	005	011
CI/PN		

DOCUMENT TITLE
TERMINAL MODULE

APPROVAL	DATE
ORIG J. [signature]	5/6
DFT J. [signature]	5/10
CHECK W. [signature]	5/12
ENG	
RELBL	
LOG	
CCB J. [signature]	5/14

REASON FOR CHANGE
ALLOW ASSEMBLY OF MODULE INTO NEXT HIGHER ASSEMBLY

DISPOSITION OF PARTS

IN PROCESS	IN STOCK	IN FIELD
✓ CHANGE	✓ CHANGE	CHANGE
NO CHANGE	NO CHANGE	NO CHANGE
SCRAP	SCRAP	OPTIONAL

OTHER

NEXT ASSY
CI/SYSTEM
OTHER DOCUMENTS AFFECTED
80441 80311
81100

RELEASE DATE
EO
CN

RI
DCR
PART CODE

DESCRIPTION OF CHANGE

CHANGED HOLE LOCATION ON F/D ZONE C-4:
(IS) (WAS)

CHANGED HOLE LOCATION ON F/D ZONE A-4:
(IS) (WAS)

Figure 5-5. Engineering Order

Used with permission of Prentice-Hall, Inc., "Industrial Documentation Handbook," Thomas T. Samaras, 1978, p. 265

- Will it compromise the product's safety, reliability, availability, and performance?
- Will it increase the cost of the product beyond what the customer is willing to pay?
- Will it increase indirect operating costs not directly related to the product, such as greater service or maintenance costs by another department after the product is sold?
- Will it delay the product's market entrance so that a competitor will be the first to reach the customers?
- Is the risk in successful implementation worth its desirable features?
- Is the technical staff in full agreement on the change? (Strong disagreements on its feasibility or desirability indicate a high probability of failure exists.)
- Is the change really needed or wanted by the customer?

Because of the high risk of rejection, the staff should be clearly instructed that no work on the proposed change is allowed before the CR's approval, except in preparation of the CR and its supporting data. If timing is critical, the CR should be expedited by special meetings or actions.

5.9 Design Change Notice or Engineering Order

Changes in released design or engineering documents are of critical importance from a technical viewpoint. These changes may be quite simple or extensive, with serious ramifications. These ramifications could be significant increases in engineering and manufacturing costs, schedule slippage, or non-compliance with customer specifications. Therefore, a well-defined change control system is needed, regardless of the company size or product complexity.

The mechanism for documenting, proposing, and distributing engineering or technical changes to previously approved design documents is the change notice. (See Figure 5-5.) This document (8½ × 11) is attached to the drawing or other design document after its approval. It is considered an integral part of the drawing and items built must conform to its requirements.

Most companies allow up to 5 CN's to be issued against a drawing until they are required to be incorporated and the drawing revised and reissued containing all the changes.

5.10 Contract Change Notice

No changes should be made in the contract objectives, requirements, budget, and schedule without a formal contract change notice (CCN) from the customer. The CCN should be signed by an officer of the company or contract administrator authorized to change the contract for the customer.

Verbal and written directions by people unauthorized to modify the contract or purchase order can lead to payment problems and legal entanglements. While the need for formal CCN's is readily understood by higher management, lower level managers and the project staff are often ignorant of this requirement and create many problems as a result. (See Case in Point, Section 3.2.4.)

5.11 Management Directives

A management directive is a specific type of memo that allows the project or functional manager to direct his/her staff to change an operational requirement, product specification, do additional work, establish a baseline, waive a requirement, or revise the work plan or budget.

The staff should be informed that memos entitled "Management Directive" have greater significance and authority than memos not so identified.

It should be pointed out that the project manager cannot use a management directive to change company policies or contract requirements without written authorization from higher management, the contracts administrator or the customer.

5.12 Exception Reports and Review Meetings

Because of the complexity and depth of project activities, complete reports summarizing all work tend to overwhelm many managers. To reduce this paper work, only exceptions to plans should be reported to managers. This allows them to evaluate the significance of deviations and to focus on corrective actions. In addition to exception reports, meetings should be held periodically to review each behind-schedule or overrun item. At these meetings, the responsible managers discuss what corrective actions are being proposed and how effective they are in restoring progress to its original plan.

5.13 Oral Reports

Oral reports can be effective control devices because they provide greater motivation to keep work on schedule and within budget. People find it more unpleasant to make bad reports in front of a group than to write them down in a report. Oral reports also give the manager an opportunity to probe further and to get a sharper picture of the real impact of a delay or problem than from a simple statement in a report. Very often a face-to-face discussion of program problems will reveal significant information not covered in a written report.

5.14 Commitment List

A commitment list deals with work items not normally covered by schedules and work plans, such as action items, agreements to send a letter to the customer or a vendor, and the completion of a short study on a special problem. Commitment lists briefly describe the commitment, who is responsible for it, who needs the information, and the dates of assignment, planned completion, and actual completion.

For large projects, the commitment list may be put on a computer.

A commitment list and action items list are similar. A sample commitment list is shown in Figure 5-6 (page 112).

5.15 Priority List

A priority list gives the staff guidance on what to work on when jobs overlap and cannot be done at the same time to meet commitments. Without this list from higher management, lower echelon supervisors will make their own decisions, which often are not based on an appreciation of the work needs and their impact on the overall company objectives. For projects or companies that have a fairly routine, stable and even workload, priority lists may not be useful.

The advantages of priority lists are:

1. They represent the best reasoned decisions of higher management as to which jobs have the greatest impact on the company's success and future.
2. They eliminate discussions, arguments and wasted time when a problem is discovered. Thus, supervisors can make faster decisions.
3. They provide a document that can be revised and reissued allowing the staff to keep informed of changes in management priorities.

Some managers refuse to issue priority lists because they believe the staff will ignore lower priority work and it will never get done. Certainly, this is a real possibility, but if staff has so much work that it can't get to lower priority work, then corrective action is needed by management.

5.16 Audits of Operations/Products

Audits are a control device for assuring that the staff is following standard company or project policies, procedures, and standards. Without

PAGE 1

ENGINEERING DIVISION
STEAM GENERATOR DEPT INTERNAL COMMITMENT LIST
REPORTING DATE 09-14-xx

SORTED BY ORG

STATUS CODE

NEW	1
CONTINUING	2
COMPLETED	3
CANCELLED	4
LATE ITEM	*

SEQ NO.	ORG NO.	COGNIZANT ENGINEER / COGNIZANT MANAGER	REQUESTOR TYPE-NO. / RESP ORG	REQ DOC TYPE-NO. / DATE	RESP DOC TYPE-NO. / DATE	REQD DATE / ESTIM DATE	STATUS / CODE	PRIORITY	DESCRIPTION	DEBC LINE NO.	C D H P
0357	370	EVANKON	HUNTER	306-1469 03-11-xx		ONGOING *	2	10	SULZEB INTERFACE CHECK	01	U
0642	370	HUNTER	WEBSTER	306-1897 08-19-xx		09-17-xx	1		PRELIM SIZING OF BF BAYONET FOR OPTIMIZED SYSTEM PERFORMANCE CONDITIONS	01 02	C

Figure 5-6. Commitment (Action Items List)

periodic audits, people tend to get lax in following operational systems when they require extra work or cause delays, such as in preparing change requests or releasing design documents. Even the threats of audits help keep people within the system because they don't like to be written-up in corrective action reports by management or quality assurance.

Product audits involve comparison of the as-built product configuration with the drawings, change notices, and specifications that the product was built from. Deviations between the two can indicate inadequacies in the drawings or in manufacturing and quality controls. A careful product audit may reveal 10 or more percent discrepancy between the hardware and paper work (even with a quality control program in effect). Product audits will help motivate manufacturing and quality assurance to send change requests to engineering when designs are found inadequate or difficult to build and will thus keep the product and its paper work matched so that rework or maintenance will be more readily accomplished.

5.17 Project Manual

A project manual provides a common set of requirements that have been found necessary to run effective projects. This manual saves the project manager a lot of time by avoiding re-inventing the wheel for each project. It also sets a common set of policies and procedures that everyone can learn once. If each manager has to invent his/her own management and control systems, the staff will have to spend more time learning them and more mistakes and deviations will occur.

A project manager's manual may contain instructions on the following:

- Accounting
- Contract Administration
- Proposal Coordination
- Facilities
- Information Services
- Machine Shop
- Operations
- Property Administration
- Purchasing
- Publications
- Security
- Shipping and Receiving
- Technical Support
- Quality Assurance

5.18 Communication Guidelines and Policies

Lack of controls in communication with the outside world can lead to many problems, including legal ones. Therefore, the project manager must outline do's and don'ts for his/her staff when the staff have opportunities to talk or write to people outside the company.

Some areas that need to be addressed were already covered in Section 3.2.4. Other control points should deal with:

- When must the project manager notify the customer or higher management of impending changes?
- When is resource manager approval needed of a communication to be issued by the project manager?
- When is a written contact report to the project manager needed?
- When, if at all, can the staff send documents to an outsider without processing them through the project manager?

In establishing these rules it should be remembered that there are several major types of communication areas (restrictions set may vary with each type):

1. Project or administrative related; e.g., schedule, funds, or work definition and scope
2. Technical related
3. Subcontractor related
4. Vendor or supplier related
5. Associated contractor related
6. Government or customer related
7. Foreign related

Besides identifying the channels of communication permitted, other rules applicable to most projects should also be defined:

- Proprietary or private data may not be released to customers or potential customers unless they have signed a formal confidentiality agreement with the company.
- Government classified information or documents cannot be given to anyone without proper clearance and authorization by the responsible Government agency.
- No one may alter the terms of a contract or purchase order without contract's or purchasing's approval. (This restriction applies to project managers unless they have been delegated this authority.)
- No one may release any other party from its obligations to the company without contracts department/administrator approval.
- Certain information may not be given to foreign citizens. Controls are needed to prevent written or oral information from being given to foreigners which would violate the Export Control Act, or other Federal regulations.
- Documents that contain potentially patentable designs must be reviewed by legal function or patent administrator before they can be given to anyone outside the company. Also a restrictive notice is

needed to caution people not to abuse the information presented and to return it when no longer needed.

While higher level management will set controls on information flow to the outside world, the project manager is the key person for controlling the external distribution of company or project information/documents.

5.19 Deviation or Waiver Requests

Company or project requirements cannot always be followed. When a justifiable reason for not following a requirement exists, a mechanism is needed for reviewing and approving the deviation and communicating it to the staff. These deviations may apply to operational or to product requirements.

Deviations or waivers[1] should be recorded on a special form for this purpose to allow ready identification of its nature. Also management and quality assurance approvals should be provided.

A loose set of standards for authorizing deviations can lead to many variations from standard practices. These variations can create confusion among the staff and inevitably lead to more work and destruction of existing systems. Therefore, deviation requests should not be approved too easily. Ground rules for approving a deviation or waiver are suggested below:

- The schedule cannot be met if the change is not allowed.
- The project is too small to follow the requirements of the project manual and will overrun its budget.
- The product is acceptable to quality assurance and customer and would require additional costs and delays to rework it to required standards. Future units will conform to engineering or quality requirements.

A sample deviation or waiver request for a product change from approved requirements is shown in Figure 5-7 (page 116).

5.20 Control of Computer Programs

Computer programs are critical items that are sometimes not controlled as carefully as drawings and specifications. However, they need as much control as design documents to prevent compromising their contents

[1]A deviation request is prepared before a change is made; a waiver is usually prepared after the change has occurred, such as for an unintentional change in manufacturing practice.

WAIVER/DEVIATION
WIND SPECTROMETER
W. A. 70690

IDENTIFICATION OF PART AFFECTED

Nomenclature: All Welded Modules
Part Number: Embedment Specification EP-50270GA and Weld Spec. GMO-50571-GEN
M. O. Number: ________ Serial Number: ________
ISR Number: Blanket

DEVIATION

Reason:
1. Hardness test to be omitted because tester not available yet.
2. RTV 502 or other silicone rubber found unsuitable.
3. Wax coating found unsuitable for this application.
4. Epoxylite shrinkage during cure greater than stycast.

Description:
1. Hardness test to be performed at JP using control sample. (Lack of immediate test data not to hold up fabrication.)
2, 3. Substitute Dow #7 silicone grease in place of RTV and paste wax.
4. Delete 030 embedment allowance.

Approved: Jim Amiss
OS Project Manager — Date

Approved: J. Luzio
OS/Q. A. — Date

Approved: R. Swartz
JP Q./A. — Date

Approved: A. Zimmer
JP Cogn. Engr. — Date

Figure 5-7. Waiver Deviation Form

Used with permission of Prentice-Hall, Inc., "Industrial Documentation Handbook," Thomas T. Samaras, 1978, p. 341

and validity. Computer programs can be controlled similarly to design documents. The steps include:

1. Define the types of program to be controlled.
2. Assign a unique identification number to the program.
3. Prepare a release or approved-for-use record for each program.
4. Obtain evidence that the program works as intended.
5. Submit tape, cards, and other data entry material to data processing with the release record.
6. Add program to released program index.
7. Prepare a program change notice to revised program and get it approved.
8. Submit approved change notice to data processing.
9. Add revision character (letter or number) to program to indicate that it has been revised or modified. (If the program has had a major alteration, a new number should be issued, especially if the old program will be used by others.)
10. Verify validity of revise program and revised program index.
11. Retain the old version of the program for historical information.

The scope of control used depends on a number of factors that need to be evaluated by the project or functional manager. These include:

- How critical is the program to product success?
- What potential safety hazards exist?
- What contract or government requirements apply?

5.21 Corrective Action Approaches

Effective controls require a repertoire of possible corrective actions or strategies. A list of actions that may be taken to return a project or task onto its original path or an acceptable substitute follows:

1. Add more people to task.
2. Add more shifts.
3. Temporarily move people from a task ahead of schedule or not on critical path to expedite one that is in trouble.
4. Send some work outside.
5. Hire job shoppers.
6. Hire consultant.
7. Install new, faster production equipment.
8. Reassign your best people to the task until it is caught up.

9. Request customer authorization to slip schedule or overrun budget.
10. Revise work scope.
11. Rearrange sequence of work if it will expedite its completion.
12. Offer bonus for on-time completion.
13. Replace slow people.
14. Search for and eliminate unnecessary work.
15. Search for and eliminate roadblocks.
16. Buy parts instead of making them.
17. Offer special fee if parts or assemblies are delivered on schedule when their late delivery will create an unacceptable impact on the overall project schedule.

5.22 Improving Control with Management by Objectives

Over 25 years ago Peter Drucker coined the term "Management by Objectives," which has become known as MBO. This concept has spread to industry and government and most medium and large companies have some form of MBO in effect. While there have been failures, its success has generally been good. The reason for this is that it provides clear and tangible guidance as to where people are going so that the company will achieve its overall goals.

While goal setting is a primary aspect of the planning process, goals, or objectives are also critical elements in the control process. When concrete, measurable goals or objectives are set, then performance can be tracked and any deviations or delays detected so that the individual or management can take corrective active to get back on the track and timetable.

The process of setting objectives starts with establishment of top level goals. Then more specific and numerous objectives are developed within the organization until the lowest echelons of the organization have identified and agreed to various objectives that are consistent with higher level objectives. The aim of these objectives is to ensure the successful attainment of the overall company goals.

Establishing these goals and objectives involves writing them down in terms of measurable achievements, such as "To complete 90% of production estimates for special sales orders within two work days after receipt." or "To install new product line by Oct. 12, 19___." In setting these objectives. the manager and each of the staff must sit down in a face-to-face meeting to discuss and agree to the various objectives for the coming next 6 to 12 months. Only by mutual agreement can the objectives ensure that the work will be done to promote individual and company success. Of course, during the process of reaching agreement, problems and results will be more clearly identified and some changes to the ideas of the manager and staff member will occur. Hopefully, these new ideas will bring both people closer to reality with a greater probability of mutual growth and success.

Anthony P. Raia summarized the MBO process shown in Figure 5-8.[2]

Essential Elements	Major Steps
Set goals and objectives	• Develop long-range goals and strategic plans • Identify specific overall organizational objectives • Develop departmental objectives • Establish individual job objectives
Plan actions	• Develop action/work plans: define what, who, when, where, and how much is needed to attain a given objective
Self-control	• Implement controls and take corrective action—individual, not his manager, will control his/her own behavior and the work required to meet his/her objective.
Periodic reviews	• Review progress in terms of meeting objectives; identify problems and remove obstacles • Evaluate performance, person's behavior, and increase motivation by: —Management training and self-development —Financial rewards —Career planning

Note: Raia uses the term "goal" to identify broad desired future condition with a long-term intent. Objective is a desired accomplishment. It is a specific, measurable, short-term target.

Figure 5-8 MBO Process

[2]A. Raia, "Managing By Objectives," Scott Foresman, Illinois, 1974, p. 16.

5.23 Performance Measurement System

A performance measurement system provides control of a project's work scope, schedule, and budget. It is a total control system in terms of the business and technical work scope requirements of a project. However, it does not deal with design changes. Refer to Chapter 6 for a description of the control features of this system.

6

Performance Measurement Techniques for Better Control and Visibility

Accurate measurement of performance on a project or task is usually achieved after the fact by comparing the product, when it was delivered, and its cost with contract specifications, the planned schedule, and approved budget. Of course, rough progress assessments are obtained from milestone attainment and on-going estimates of percent of work complete from task managers. However, the manager appraising this performance picture must mentally integrate the various accomplishments, problems and schedule or cost overruns to derive an overall assessment of performance. While this method is by far the most common, another method exists that provides managers with more objective performance status during the entire project period.

This chapter gives an overview of a performance measurement approach that is similar to those used by over 150 companies in the United States.

6.1 What Is Performance Measurement? Is It Really Needed?

A Performance Measurement System is a formal, highly structured approach for providing timely and accurate cost, schedule, and technical progress data for management planning, evaluation, and corrective action.

PERFORMANCE MEASUREMENT SYSTEM FLOW DIAGRAM

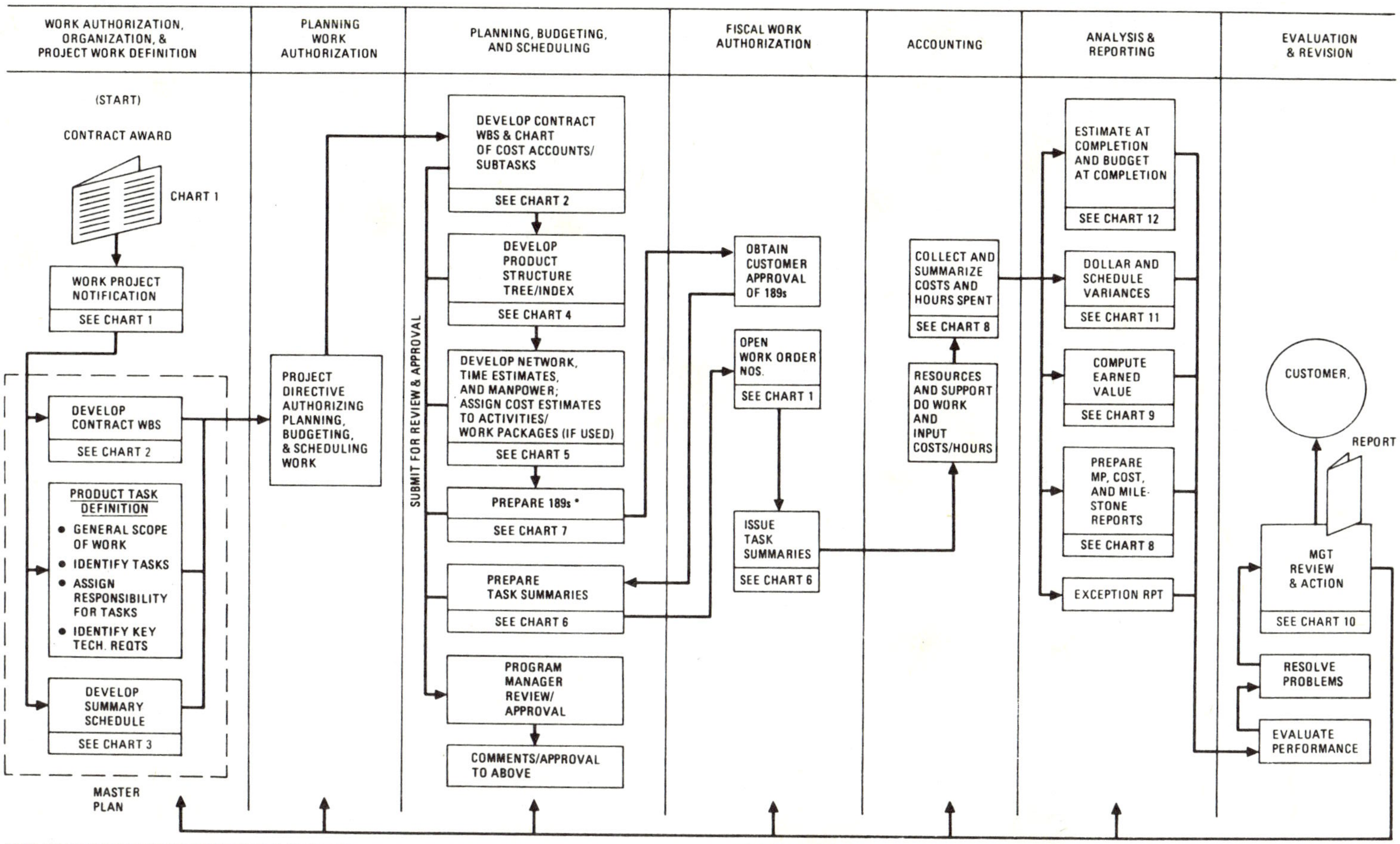

NOTE: CHART NUMBERS REFER TO DETAILED FLOW CHARTS.

*189s MAY BE PREPARED EARLIER IN SEQUENCE, AS REQUIRED.

Figure 6-1. Performance Measurement System Flow Diagram

If the system aspect of this term is omitted, then the term "performance measurement" is defined as: The calculation of the value of work done in terms of the plan for work accomplishment and its comparison to the work done and the actual cost incurred. The resulting comparison provides the manager with quantitative values of schedule and cost performance. (This comparison process is described later.)

The functions of a Performance Measurement System (PMS) are summarized below and Figure 6-1 shows the various elements needed to make the system work.

Function Title	Description
Work authorization	Method for formally authorizing work to proceed.
Organization/program definition	Definition of contractual effort and assignment of responsibility for work to functional organization elements.
Planning, scheduling and budgeting	Development of WBS[1], cost accounts, product structure trees, cost proposals, schedule networks, and task/work plans.
Accounting	Collection and summarization by WBS elements of charges to task and programs.
Reporting and analysis	Project status is reported in terms of work planned, work done, and value of work done. Budget and schedule variances beyond a certain level and estimates at completion are also reported.
Evaluation and revision of and access to data	Study of variances by management, with corrective actions for staying within budget and schedule constraints (baselines). Project manager has access to cost, schedule, and performance data for evaluation. Authorizations to change work scope, budget, and schedule result in revised baselines.

The aims of a Performance Measurement System are:

1. To define and organize all contract work.
2. To assure that internal management techniques and operations are sound.
3. To establish a performance measurement baseline for the contract and to control work and document all changes in the baseline. (This baseline is an integration of project work scope, schedule, and budget.)
4. To use earned value (cost value of work done) as the basis for performance measurement.

[1]See Chapter 3.

5. To make sure that the contract status and trend data are valid and traceable to problem areas.
6. To make effective management decisions easier.
7. To document all work and functional (resource) requirements necessary to complete the project.
8. To integrate cost, schedule, and technical parameters.
9. To assign specific responsibility and authority for accomplishing work to the individual who performs the work.
10. To provide timely and auditable reports of cost, schedule, and technical results.

Most of the elements of PMS have already been discussed in previous chapters, such as work breakdown structure, assignment matrixes, work plans, schedules, budgets and reports. Therefore, this chapter will focus primarily on how performance is actually measured.

Before proceeding, however, a critical question needs to be raised. "Is a formal PMS really needed?" This is a difficult question to answer. Every new system costs money, drains labor and diverts attention from objectives and end products. Therefore, the benefits must be clearly visible and attainable to justify embarking on the design, implementation, and maintenance of a highly structured PMS. At this time, there is not a set of concrete data that can clearly demonstrate that the implementation of a PMS saves money or reduces the schedule. However, people who have

TABLE VIII

PMS IMPLEMENTATION CHECKLIST

- Is all work on projects being defined and organized so that no surprises occur later on during the work?
- Is management provided with accurate visibility as to work progress or is it often surprised at the so-called end of project when much work remains to be done and no budget is available?
- Does the present management system integrate cost, schedule, and technical results?
- Are people assigned specific responsibility and accountability for getting tasks done?
- Are problem areas traceable to their source?
- Does your customer want you to install PMS and is his business worth the effort?
- Is management satisfied with the present system's effectiveness?
- Is top management ready to provide full backing for its implementation? If not, the PMS will likely turn out to be a failure.

worked with PMS report that it is worth the investment. But when it comes to a comparison between two similar projects—one using PMS, the other using traditional techniques—it has not been shown that the PMS project did significantly better in meeting its cost and schedule objectives. Therefore, each manager, or company must use other criteria for determining whether PMS will more than pay for itself. It should be noted that PMS is based on good business practices and its value should not be underestimated because scientific data proving its cost and time saving benefits are not available.

In determining the value of PMS, the manager should keep in mind that its implementation in a medium-size company could cost $200,000 and much more. Once installed, additional costs specifically related to PMS could be 5% or more of the total project cost.

Table VIII is a checklist that can help the project manager or functional manager determine whether PMS should be implemented.

6.2 When Should PMS Be Used?

PMS in its highly formal, structured form should be used for large programs; for example, greater than $50 million and no lower than $2 million. However, smaller projects may use some of the features of PMS to their advantage as a part of their normal project organization and planning, monitoring, and corrective action activities. Therefore, the following sections will cover only some salient aspects of performance measurement that can be applied to small, medium, and large programs without invoking the entire PMS structure.

> *Note:* If a thorough study of PMS is desired, the Department of Energy publishes eight volumes of procedures and requirements on the subject. These manuals are identified as PMS-1 through PMS-8. The Department of Defense also has a number of documents under the heading CSCS (cost schedule control system). The Institute of Industrial Engineers, Decision Planning Corporation, and others conduct seminars on PMS in industry.

6.3 Earned Value Methods for Measuring Progress

A key aspect of PMS is the determining of the real or earned value of project or task as it progresses from the start to the end dates. This feature can be worked into a project during its planning, budgeting, and scheduling activities without a great disturbance.

Computation of earned value works this way:

1. Each major task is scheduled on a separate bar chart.

2. Each work item or line entry on the chart is identified with one or more milestones representing measurable completion events, such as issuance of drawings, completion of tests, or delivery of material or finished hardware into stores.
3. Each milestone is evaluated for its contribution to the completion of the task and assigned a weighted percent value. The sum of the weighted percents for all milestones will equal 100% of the task.
4. These milestones and percent values are reviewed with the project manager for concurrence or revision.
5. As the project progresses, each manager reports status for each work item in his/her task based on these milestones as follows:

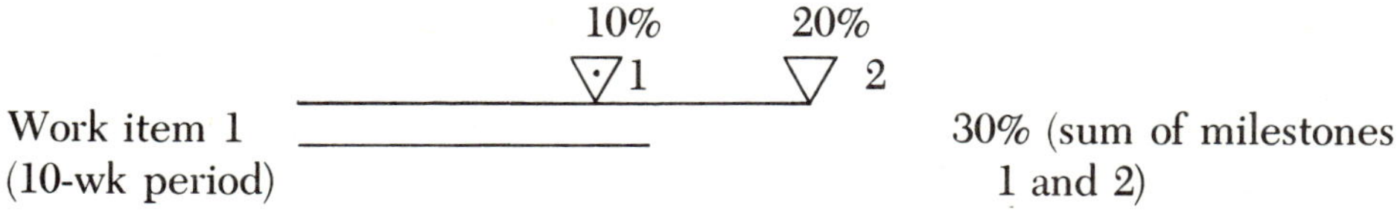

The top line gives the work plan for a 10-week period. The bottom line indicates work completed. The period in milestone 1 indicates that it was completed. The bottom line shows that the work between milestones 1 and 2 is halfway complete. This part of the percent complete estimate is somewhat subjective and the task manager may report an optimistic status. Thus, the total percent complete would be calculated as:

Milestone 1:	10%
Milestone 2:	50% of 20% = 10%
Total progress:	10% + 10% = 20%

If the task manager has been overly optimistic in assessing progress between fixed milestones, the error will show up when the second milestone is scheduled for completion (Some PMS experts recommend the use of numerous milestones to reduce the subjective elements in estimating progress.)

Now that the actual percentage completion status of the work is known, the manager can compute the earned or real value of the work done. This is done by multiplying the percent complete value and the task budget.

$$\text{Earned value} = \%\ \text{complete} \times \text{task budget}$$
$$20\% \times \$50{,}000 = \$10{,}000$$

This means that the project manager has received $10,000 worth of work for the period covered for task XX. By itself, this figure doesn't mean too much. However, when combined with the following items, it gives a substantial measure of task status:

Earned value:	$10,000
Actual cost of work (from accounting)	8,000
Budget scheduled for milestone 1 and half of milestone 2:	15,000

With this information in hand, the project manager can compute the cost and schedule variances for the task as follows:

$$\begin{aligned}\text{Cost variance (CV)} &= \text{earned value} - \text{actual cost}\\ &= \$10{,}000 - \$8{,}000\\ &= \$2{,}000\end{aligned}$$

Since the variance is positive, the manager has gotten more for his money than planned. A minus sign would mean the opposite.

The schedule variance is computed next.

$$\begin{aligned}\text{Schedule variance (SV)} &= \text{earned value} - \text{scheduled budget}\\ &= \$10{,}000 - \$15{,}000\\ &= -\ \$5{,}000\end{aligned}$$

The minus sign indicates a behind-schedule condition equivalent to $5,000. Schedule variance is often measured in dollars. However, a percent may be more useful. In this case, the schedule variance is divided by the scheduled budget to get:

$$\begin{aligned}\%\ \text{SV} &= \frac{\text{earned value} - \text{scheduled budget}}{\text{scheduled budget}} \times 100\%\\ &= -\frac{\$\ 5{,}000}{\$15{,}000} \times 100 = -\ 33.3\%\ \text{behind schedule}\end{aligned}$$

Thus the manager is getting his/her money's worth but the work is taking too long. He/she thus needs to consider whether corrective action is required and what should be done to speed up progress.

The percent cost variance is computed in a similar way using the following equation:

$$\%\ \text{CV} = \frac{\text{earned value} - \text{actual cost}}{\text{earned value}} \times 100\%$$

The preceding calculation was based on discrete work measurements. Other work exists that cannot be measured in the same way:

Level of effort (LOE): this work cannot be broken into discrete milestones and assigned percent completes. Project management and administration are examples of LOE. Earned value in these cases is collected based on the passage of time. Thus, if a budget of \$30,000 is allocated for project management and half the project is over, then the earned value is computed as follows: \$30,000 × 50% = \$15,000.

Apportioned Effort: this is associated with the completion of other work, such as inspection or testing of a product. Thus, earned value is obtained by assigning a standard budget value to each item produced, such as 10%. For example, if 400 products worth \$40,000 were manufactured and shipped, quality control would earn 10% × \$40,000 = \$4,000.

Material: the problem with materials is determining the weighted percent complete. What percent should be given to issuance of the order, receipt of the material, and use of the material in final products? These values must be determined based on the experience of each manager.

For a large project, the computation of earned value for each task can be a time-consuming process. Therefore, many companies use the computer to calculate earned value, schedule and cost variances each month on an automatic basis. Of course, percent completes and milestones attained must be inputted to the computer.

6.4 Variance Analysis to Explain Deviations

Once it has been established that a task is in trouble, the task manager should evaluate his/her problem and submit a plan for getting the task back on schedule or within budget.

Since it is impractical to require the task manager to prepare a report each month for each task under his/her responsibility, variance thresholds need to be set early in the project to ignore minor variations. A possible set of thresholds for cost and schedule variances at the task level is:

Cost variance threshold = ± 10% and \$5,000 per month or
± 10% and \$20,000 cumulative to date
Schedule variance threshold = ± 10% and 2 weeks per month or
± 10% and 1 month cumulative to date

A variance analysis report would not be required for our example. While the CV exceeds the threshold percent (\$2,000/\$10,000 = 20%), it is less than \$5,000. However, the schedule variance is 1/3 of 10 weeks or 3.33 weeks, which exceeds both the 10% and 2-week variance limits.

The variance report should include the following information:

- Summary of variances (cost and schedule)
- Estimate to complete the work in terms of budget and time

- Estimate at completion
- Reasons for variances
- Possible solutions for correction of the problem and the solution recommended by the task manager

Upon receipt of this report, the project manager may discuss it with the task manager or merely acknowledge agreement on the corrective action recommended.

Note that variances in materials are a function of the amount of waste and difference between estimated costs and actual costs.

6.5 Performance Reports

Two types of performance reports are shown in Figures 6-2 and 6-3. Figure 6-2 provides performance measurement data for the current month and year to date as well as projected completion variances. The codes used are fairly standard and are defined below:

BCWS—budgeted cost of work scheduled (budget)
BCWP—budgeted cost of work performed (earned value)
ACWP—actual cost of work performed (actual charges)
SV—schedule variance (—indicates an undesirable condition)
CV—cost variance (—indicates an undesirable condition)
BAC—budget at completion
EAC—estimate at completion
VAR—variance

Figure 6-3 is a combination tabular and graphical report. The acronyms are the same as for Figure 6-2. The efficiency or performance ratio shown in calculated by dividing the earned value (BCWP) by the actual cost of the work (ACWP). (See pages 130 and 131)

BRANCH REPORT PAGE 1

PERFORMANCE MEASUREMENT SYSTEM
DOLLARS {$000}

REPORT NO. 2
REPORTING DATE: 07/28/__
INFORMATION CURRENT AS OF: 07/28/__

123 QUALITY ASSURANCE

ORG PROJ TSK	CURRENT MONTH					YEAR - TO - DATE					COMPLETION		
	BCWS	BCWP	ACWP	SV	CV	BCWS	BCWP	ACWP	SV	CV	BAC	EAC	VAR
123 3227 013 QUALITY ASSURANCE	3.0	5.6	.0	2.6	5.6	22.8	14.0	12.0	8.8-	2.0	.0	.0	.0
123 4275 005 QUALITY ASSURANCE PROGRAM	6.3	.0-	6.7	6.3-	6.7-	59.1	48.0	56.4	11.1-	8.4-	.0	.0	.0
123 4370 005 QUALITY ASSURANCE PROGRAM	4.0	.0-	.0	4.1-	.0-	45.7	33.2	54.9	12.5-	21.7-	.0	.0	.0
TOTAL QUALITY ASSURANCE	13.4	5.6	6.7	7.8-	1.1-	127.6	95.2	123.3	32.4-	28.1-	.0	.0	.0

CODE:
ORG = ORGANIZATION
PROJ = PROJECT
TSK = TASK

Figure 6-2. Variance Report

PROJECT MANAGEMENT REPORT
COST $ (000)

PROJECT = 300 MWe

PROJECT MANAGER: R.H.

▽ MILESTONE SCHEDULED
▼ MILESTONE COMPLETED
WORK IN PROGRESS
WORK SCHEDULED
ACTUAL COST WORK PERFORM (ACWP)
BUDGET COST WORK PERFORM (BCWP)
BUDGET COST WORK SCHEDULE (BCWS)

WORK ORDER NO.			TASK DESCRIPTION	BUDGET COST (BCWS)	EARNED VALUE (BCWP)	ACTUAL COST (ACWP)	PERCENT SV	PERCENT CV
			PRIMARY COOLING SYST.					
13XX	211	XXX	MAIN HE. CIRCULATOR	7497	7833	5460	104	143
13XX	212	XXX	MAIN LOOP ISOLATION VALUE	1362	1228	749	90	164
13XX	213	XXX	STEAM GENERATOR	11701	10314	6601	88	156
13XX	214	XXX	PRIMARY COOLANT INSTRUM.	888	997	688	112	145
13XX	215	XXX	MAIN CIRC. SERVICE SYST.	1632	1632	996	100	164
13XX	216	XXX	MAIN CIRC. HANDLING EQUIP.	1287	1326	756	103	175
			TOTAL	24367	23330	15250	96	153
			REACTOR VESSEL					
13XX	111	XXX	PCR	7262	7484	4865	103	154
13XX	112	XXX	LINERS & CLOSURES	3310	3112	2334	94	133
13XX	113	XXX	COOLING SYSTEM	1915	1835	1101	96	167
13XX	114	XXX	THERMAL BARRIER	3868	4622	2819	119	164
13XX	115	XXX	ELECTRICAL PENETRATIONS	1312	1210	726	92	167
13XX	116	XXX	STRUCTURAL INSTRUMENTATION	924	924	628	100	147
13XX	117	XXX	WIRE WINDING	526	498	309	95	161
			TOTAL	19117	19865	12782	104	155
			REACTOR CORE					
13XX	171	XXX	FUEL ASSEMBLY	6255	6192	5015	99	123
13XX	172	XXX	CONTROL & SHUTDOWN ASSEMBLY	5993	6128	4228	102	144
13XX	173	XXX	BLANKET ASSEMBLY	4728	5034	3272	106	154
13XX	174	XXX	IN-CORE THERMAL PROBE	1314	1282	769	98	167
13XX	175	XXX	PRE-OPER. CORE COMP'S	0	0	0	0	0
			TOTAL	18290	18636	13284	102	140
			GRAND TOTAL	61774	61830	41316	100	149

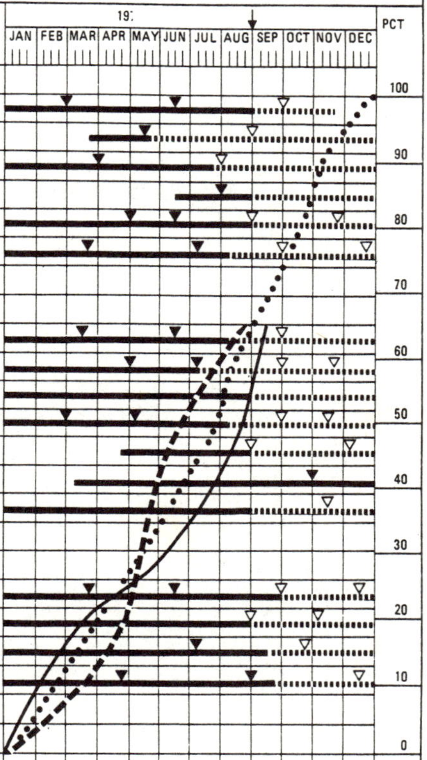

	JAN	FEB	MAR	APR	MAY	JUN	JUL	AUG	SEP	OCT	NOV	DEC
BUDGET (BCWS)	4660	4685	4770	4820	4990	5250	5290	5340	5490	5525	5554	5400
EARNED (BCWP)	4513	4617	4726	4867	5180	5275	5272	5356				
ACTUAL (ACWP)	4712	4725	4790	4805	4862	4987	5045	5315				
SCHEDULE VARIANCE (SV)	(147)	(68)	(44)	47	190	25	(18)	16				
COST VARIANCE (CV)	199	(108)	(64)	62	318	287	227	41				
EFFICIENCY/PERFORMANCE RATIO	99	99	99	100	103	105	105	100				

••••• SCHEDULE VARIANCE, %
—— COST VARIANCE, %

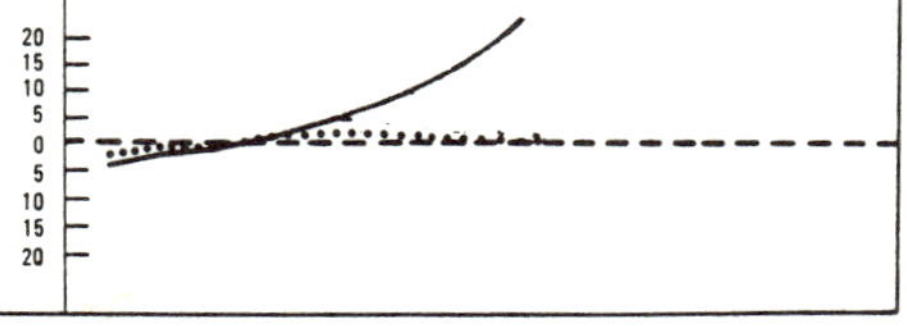

Figure 6-3. Project Management Report

7

Tools for Decision Making

A number of tools or techniques for making decisions exist. These include analytical, quasi-scientific, scientific, intuition, and experience. While scientific or quantitative tools are the most desirable, there aren't many that can be readily used by managers. These tools are difficult to apply because they require specialized mathematical knowledge or are based on assumptions and projections that if wrong can lead to erroneous decisions. Therefore, non-mathematical techniques are the predominant mode for decision making.

This chapter reviews a variety of decision-making tools or techniques and evaluates their strengths and weaknesses. The chapter concludes with a summary of pitfalls to avoid.

7.1 Information and Sources of Information

The primary basis for decision making is accurate information about the problem or various courses of action. When the manager has accurate, relevant, and timely information he/she is in a strong position to make a good decision—that is, to select the best course of action out of two or more possible paths. However, information alone does not guarantee the best selection because logic and judgment must be brought into play to assure correct evaluation, interpretation, and application of the information. The qualities of logic and judgment vary from manager to manager and depend on his/her intelligence, creativity, experience, attitudes, and knowledge. While an assessment of these characteristics is beyond the scope of this chapter, some criteria for assessing the quality of the information available are given in Table IX, Information Quality Checklist:

TABLE IX
INFORMATION QUALITY CHECKLIST

- Is the information complete?
- Are the information sources reliable?
- Is the information accurate?
- Is the information relevant to the area or problem requiring a decision? How much is redundant or superfluous?
- Is the information current?
- How fast is the information changing; e.g., will this information be obsolete in 1 week, a month or a year?
- Does the information need processing; e.g., should it be multiplied by a factor to compensate for the passage of time or a changing aspect of the environment to which it applies?

Information can be obtained from numerous sources. The quality of this information varies considerably and should be evaluated objectively whenever possible. A matrix for helping the manager assess the quality of the information source follows:

	QUALITY OF SOURCE			
Source of Information	Poor	Good	Excellent	Qualifications/Remarks
Your staff	____	____	____	____
Staff assigned to other managers	____	____	____	____
Higher management	____	____	____	____
Associates and peer managers	____	____	____	____
V.P., President	____	____	____	____
Board of Directors	____	____	____	____
Customer	____	____	____	____
Salesmen	____	____	____	____
Consultants	____	____	____	____
Experts	____	____	____	____
Professional associations	____	____	____	____
Trade organizations	____	____	____	____
Union	____	____	____	____
Other companies	____	____	____	____

	QUALITY OF SOURCE			
Source of Information	Poor	Good	Excellent	Qualifications/Remarks
Computer data base				
Company records				
Newspapers				
Reference documents				
Advertisements/catalogs				
Memos-correspondence				
Studies/reports				
Books				
Government publications				
Seminars				
Conferences				
Briefings				
Project kickoff meetings				
Finance/Comptroller				
Marketing				
Advance planning				
R&D				
Engineering				
Product support				
Purchasing				
Manufacturing				
Quality assurance				

Since each manager's experience will vary, it is impossible to provide an accurate rating of each information source. Therefore, the manager should add his/her own X's in the matrix to crystallize his/her thoughts for future reference in decision making.

7.2 Personal Experience and Experience of Others

Personal experience is by far the most common basis for making decisions. After all, effective management is developed through learning what actions or decisions have led to failure and which ones have succeeded. While not infallible, personal experience and good-quality information are probably the best tools for effective decision making. However, a few cautions must be considered when making decisions in this way. The manager should ask himself the following questions:

- Is there a missing element that makes this situation or problem different?
- Has the environment changed so that the solution or approach will not work again?
- Is there a critical timing factor involved that could defeat the approach which didn't apply in the past?
- Is there a new element involved that could prevent the approach from working?
- Is there a different mix or style of people in the company who would not react the same as in the past?

In today's competitive and complex environment, most managers must depend on others for help in making decisions. It is often impossible for the manager to know every operational detail; consultation with the staff will very likely be necessary before making a decision. The experience of others can thus lead him into failure or success based on the quality of this experience and its correct application to the present situation. A few guidelines for assessing the reliability of other people's experience include:

- Is the individual's experience extensive?
- Has previous information supplied been accurate?
- Does the person have a personal reason for favoring a specific decision; e.g., an interesting job or an opportunity for promotion or a raise?
- Is the individual's experience current or based on conditions that existed 5, 10, or 20 years ago?
- Is there corroborating information from other sources to support recommendations made?
- Is the person's recommendation based on an understanding of the total picture or based on a narrow perspective?

7.3 Intuition

Intuition in decision making is probably used more often than many managers would care to admit. However, if intuition is recognized as a "non-verbalized awareness of a situation that is based on one's total experience and assessment of the problem" then it isn't as unscientific as it would appear. Our subconscious minds often contain information that is not available in decision making. Of course, this method should be either avoided or supplemented with more explicit and objective information when available.

A manager's past success with intuitive decisions is a reliable method for evaluating the risk involved in relying on this technique. But it should be remembered that intuition, even if highly successful, is subject to error and if a critical decision is involved should be corroborated by some other method when possible.

For a detailed discussion of illogical thinking, refer to Roger A. Golde's "Muddling Through," (Amacom, New York, 1976).

7.4 Staff Reports

Staff reports are a common tool for decision making in industry. The procedure involves assigning a competent researcher to study and collect data in a particular area or problem so that the manager can have a documented source of information for decision making.

When the manager has considerable trust in the person preparing the report, the author's recommendations will be followed with only a cursory review of the report. In other cases additional information may be required from other sources before making the decision.

The value of staff reports is that problem requirements are defined carefully, information is gathered systematically, and results are analyzed carefully before a decision is made. The report also provides a permanent record for the basis of the decision. It can thus be referred to and reexamined at a future date by others or the manager to determine the effectiveness of this type of decision-making tool and its value for future decisions.

7.5 Decision Trees and Tables

A decision tree is a highly organized way of reaching a decision. It uses a pictorial display of the choices available to the manager when it is not clear which choice is best by less structured techniques. The sample decision tree shown in Figure 7-1 involves three choices with two possible outcomes per choice (page 138). It is developed by the following steps:

1. Identify the decision to be made; e.g., should we bid on delivering 10,000 barrels of product X to the Bartees Company in Des Moines, Iowa?
2. List possible courses of action; e.g., submit one of three bids for $5.80/barrel, $5.00/barrel, or $4.20/barrel.
3. Identify the possible outcomes for each course of action. In this case there are only two: win or lose for each bid.
4. Compute the payoff; e.g., if the cost per barrel is $3, then the profit from

each barrel is: \$2.80 for the \$5.80 bid, \$2.00 for the \$5.00 bid, and \$1.20 for the \$4.20 bid. The payoff for each case is obtained by multiplying the profit by the number of barrels to be sold; e.g., \$2.80 × 10,000 = \$28,000.

5. Estimate the probability of winning the contract for each bid. Obviously, the lower the bid, the greater the chances of winning, and the lower the chances of losing. Figure 7-1 shows the various estimates made by the manager based on experience. (The 20% for the \$5.80 bid indicates the manager feels that there are 20 chances out of 100 that the company will win the contract. There are 80 chances out of 100 that the company will lose it.)
6. Determine the expected value of each outcome to the company. This is done by multiplying the payoff by the probability of the event occurring. Thus, \$28,000 × 20% = \$5,600. The expected value of losing is zero because no income will be derived in this case. The resulting expected values from Figure 7-1 are:

\$5.80 bid	Win: \$5,600 Lose: 0
\$5.00 bid	Win: \$10,000 (Highest expected value) Lose: 0
\$4.20 bid	Win: \$9,600 Lose: 0

7. Select the best course of action, which is "Submit bid of \$5,000 per barrel." However, other conditions may affect the manager's choice. For example, if the company is operating at close to maximum capacity, the \$5.80 bid may be submitted since it would yield a profit of \$28,000 if received. With the company near its capacity, it can afford to gamble here because the loss of the bid will not hurt it seriously, but its receipt would increase profits considerably. If the company business is off and most of the facilities are not being used, the lowest bid of \$4.20 may be submitted because it has a higher chance to win.

While decision trees are not infallible, they do provide a quantitative basis and systematic approach to choosing among various alternatives.

Decision matrixes or tables are also used to help the manager make a choice among various alternative actions. The principles involved are basically the same as for the decision tree just described. However, the information needed is organized in tabular form rather than as shown in Figure 7-1. A sample decision table is given next.[1]

[1]Martin K. Starr, "Management: A Modern Approach," Harcourt, Brace, Jovanovich, 1971, p. 127–128.

DECISION TREE

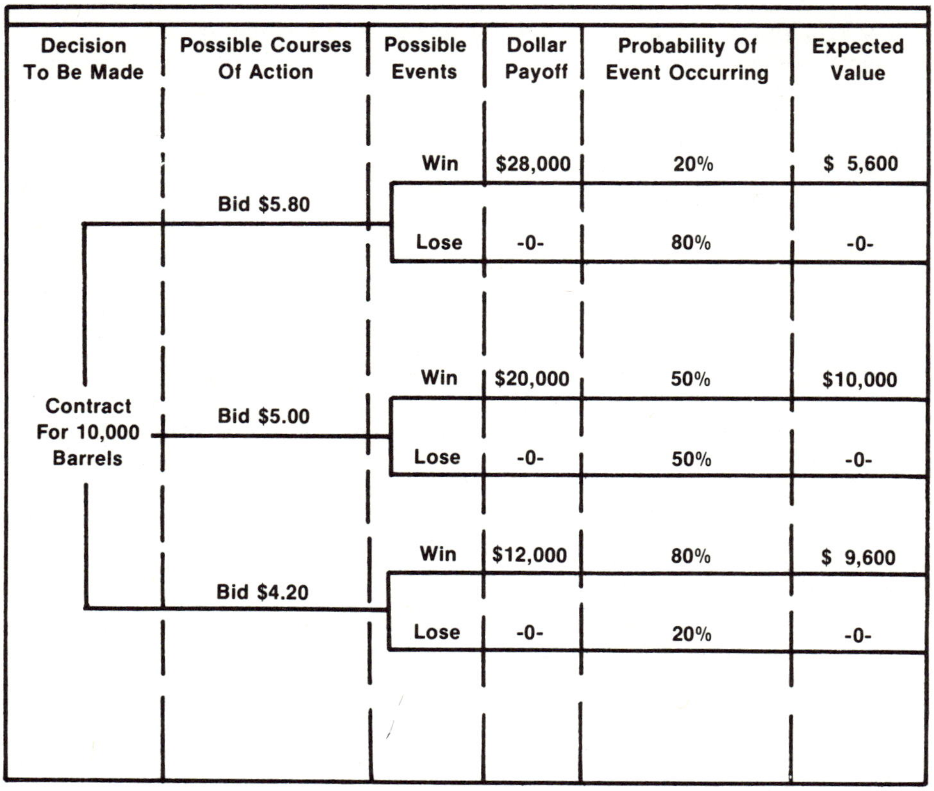

Figure 7-1. Sample Decision Tree

Used with permission of *Small Business Report*, 550 Hartnell Street, Monterey, CA 93940. "Steps of Decision Making." October 1978, pp. 12–13

Different conditions or environment that may exist	Z_1	Z_2	Z_3	
Probability of occurrence	p_1	p_2	p_3	Expected Value (EV) or Cost (EC)
Strategy/alternative x_1	R_{11}	R_{12}	R_{13}	$EV(R_1)$
Strategy/alternative x_2	R_{21}	R_{22}	R_{23}	$EV(R_2)$
Strategy/alternative x_3	R_{31}	R_{32}	R_{33}	$EV(R_3)$

The symbols used in the table are:

R = results or outcome; e.g., money saved or cost per part.

p = probability of environment/condition occurring; e.g., 35%, 50%, or 80%.

Z= condition or environment; e.g., people are available to make parts, extra people will have to be recruited, or all people will have to be recruited.

x = strategy or approach to best achieve result; e.g., x_1 = make parts, x_2 = buy parts from local company, or x_3 = make some and buy some.

Once the table has been constructed, with appropriate values recorded for p's and R's, the expected value for each strategy can be computed using the equation below:

$$EV(R_1) = p_1R_{11} + p_2R_{12} + p_3R_{13}$$

The process is repeated for $EV(R_2)$ and $EV(R_3)$. Then the strategy associated with the highest EV or lowest expected cost (EC) is selected, assuming other considerations don't apply, such as an impending strike at the company, or supplier is at capacity and cannot deliver the parts to your schedule.

7.6 Operations Research (OR)

Operations research refers to the application of scientific methods from several disciplines to problems related to the functioning or operating of a business unit. When management needs help in decision making, it asks an operations research specialist to provide a quantitative basis for making the best operating decisions and to determine the optimum solutions to operating problems. The operations research specialist does the following:

- Analyzes managerial problem which involves the organization's operations or systems
- Collects data on the problem and system involved
- Interprets the data
- Builds one or more models of the system
- Makes recommendations about future operations

It should be emphasized that the operations research specialist is not the decision maker. His/her function is to provide the manager with the information needed to make the final decision. In some cases, the manager may ignore the direction being pointed to by the data and rely on past experience, intuition, and common sense to make the decision. However, the information provided may help the manager to take preventive actions that will minimize the chances for failure or prepare for it should the OR specialist's analysis turn out to be correct.

The mathematical techniques used by OR specialists do not have to be understood by the managers using OR results for decision making. However, an overall awareness of the types of techniques or tools and what they involve can be helpful in improving communication. (For further information see "Quantitative Approaches to Management" by Richard I. Levin and Charles A. Kirkpatrick, McGraw-Hill, 1975 and "Operations

Management," Houghton Mifflin, 1972 by R.A. Johnson, W.T. Newell, and R.C. Vergin.) Brief descriptions of the techniques used by OR specialists in helping manager's make decisions follow:

Cost, Volume, Profit Analysis: Deals with variables that affect the economic viability of the company. Cost, volume, and profit are necessary inputs for various models that can be used for decision making. Graphic and algebraic techniques are used for this analysis, such as a break-even chart or mathematical determination of the optimum product or sales mix.

Probability Concepts: Deal with methods of making decisions based on the likelihood of various events occurring. Thus the OR specialist needs to know what the chances for these events occurring or not occurring are in numerical values. The manager usually has to provide these numbers based on his/her experience and knowledge.

Expected Monetary Value and Utility: Probability theory is united with financial data to produce valuable decision algorithms. (An algorithm is a set of ordered procedures, steps, or rules that lead to the solution of a problem in a finite number of steps.) The utility of a decision/action is sometimes examined instead of its monetary value.

Inventory Models: Mathematical models are used to reduce the total cost of purchasing inventory, carrying inventory, and being out of stock of inventory. Methods are also available in dealing with discount evaluation and joint ordering of items from the same vendor.

Linear Programming: Allows the determination of the optimum combination of resources to meet an objective. Graphic and algebraic techniques are used.

Determinants and Matrix Algebra: These mathematical techniques are used to help determine optimum business strategies and the behavior of marketing and financial systems over time.

Games and Competitive Strategies: Provide insights into conflict situations. Allow determination of the best responses when competitors take certain actions.

Markov Analysis: Permits prediction of changes over time when information about the behavior of the system is available. It is used to predict brand loyalties, movement of credit customers from one classification of collectability to another and movement of companies from one state of financial viability to another.

Queuing Theory: Used to examine random arrivals at a servicing or processing facility of limited capacity. Queuing models permit managers to calculate lengths of waiting lines, average time spent in line by a person, and need for adding more facilities.

Networking Theory: Provides diagrammatic and computer and tabular networks of a project to allow the manager to handle complexities normally beyond control with other planning and scheduling techniques.

Computer Simulation: A technique for simulating sales or other conditions that vary randomly or according to some pattern, such as the Monte Carlo process. The Monte Carlo process is a method of selecting numbers randomly from a probability distribution. Computer simulation is described in the next section.

7.7 Computer Simulation[2]

Computer simulation is another tool of OR. It is a method for imitating reality. Its basic feature involves asking: "If this happens, what will result?" A number of these questions are asked under various conditions and computer simulation provides the manager with courses of action that would not be readily available by other means.

Computer simulation is often used to provide a decision tree analysis similar to the manual method described before. For example, let's assume that a new textile plant is to be built for an estimated $200 million. Under ideal conditions, the plant could cost as little as $150 million. However, under adverse conditions. such as bad weather, unexpected increases in materials costs, strikes, and technical problems, the cost could reach $300 million.

The company's revenues from the new plant are based on population growth and income in the area, competition, developments in synthetic fabrics, and textile import quotas. In addition, operating costs will be a function of production efficiency, energy costs, labor and material costs, taxes, and other elements. Because sales revenues and operating costs are uncertain, annual profits are also in doubt.

By assigning probability distributions[3] to each of the major cost and revenue factors, a computer program can be designed to simulate what would happen with the new plant. The computer can select one value at random from each of the probability distributions, combine it with other values selected from the other distributions, and create an estimated profit and net present value or rate of return on investment. This profit and rate of return will result only for the specific combination of values selected during each trial run.

The computer automatically selects other sets of values and computes profits and rates of returns for each. The process is repeated for perhaps

[2]J. Fred Weston and Eugene F. Brigham, "Managerial Finance," 5th edition, Dryden Press, 1975, p. 334–336.

[3]A graph that compares the chances that a particular value will be achieved as it varies between its two greatest extremes of occurrences.

several hundred trials or cases. The computer retains the number of times each rate of return is computed. At the end of the computation, the frequency with which the various rates of return occurred are plotted as a frequency distribution curve.

Computer simulation is not always practical. The process involves determining probability distributions about a number of variables, such as market size, unit sales, investment costs, product prices, operating costs, and asset lives. Also considerable cost is involved with programming and computer usage. Therefore, only fairly large and expensive projects can justify the effort and investment. However, if decisions are needed for plant expansion or new product development, which require million-dollar investments, computer simulation can give the manager greater decision-making visibility into the relative benefits of various strategies.

Case in Point: A chemical company with sales above $250 million tied its operating forecasting directly into a computerized cost control system using model simulation. Data on product consumption, the previous year's shipment pattern, projected finished product needs, and projected levels of operation were fed into the system. As a result of this forecasting system, the company saved over $140,000 a year in bulk chemical products alone.

These savings were due to:

- Reduced monthly inventories
- Reduced production labor by smoothing out work needs and reducing premium pay
- Reduced need for constant coordination between sales and manufacturing due to fewer late deliveries[4]

7.8 Integrated Project Status Reports

Figure 6-3 (page 131) shows a sample integrated project status report. This report provides an overall assessment of progress on a task or project. It presents the manager with a comparison of planned and actual achievements, staff efficiency, and future achievements.

The accuracy of this information depends on the staff's discipline in providing up-to-date status and its incorporation into the report on a timely basis.

Before making a decision on information provided in these reports, the status should be checked with the responsible task manager to obtain additional information or clarification.

---

[4]Jerome H. Fuchs, "Computerized Control Systems," Prentice-Hall, Inc., Englewood Cliffs, N.J., 1976 p. 20.

7.9 Trend Plots

A trend plot gives the manager a graphic or tabular presentation of some parameter versus time or some other factor within a project, department, company or industry. Trend plots include cost versus time or error rates versus units produced or profit versus volume of business.

By viewing the past pattern of changes, the manager can make a projection into the future and thus detect a worsening of the trend, a tapering off, or an improvement.

The problem with trend plots is that there is no assurance that the trend will follow the present pattern or slope of the graph provided. Unexpected or modifying factors may occur that cause a steep increase in funds spent because of subcontractor payments or the purchase of new equipment or materials. Thus, much more information is required by the manager when he/she makes a decision based on a projection of the trend plot.

7.10 Variance Analysis Reports

Variance analysis reports were covered in Chapter 6. These reports provide managers with direct line supervision's best estimate of the problem and its recommended solution. A written report of this kind is superior to a verbal report because it gives the manager a chance to think about the problem before sitting down with the responsible task manager to make a decision on the best corrective action to take. It also allows him/her to gather additional information from other sources before meeting with the task manager. Figure 7-2 is a sample variance analysis report.

VARIANCE ANALYSIS REPORT

Project: ALPH-BT ____ Task Summary Title Fuel Element Des. ____ Report Period
8/5/____ WBS No. 6432635020 ____ Mo. 7 Yr. XX

	Current Month				Cumulative			
Cost Variance	BCWP	ACWP	VAR	%	BCWP	ACWP	VAR	%
	8.6	14.6	−6.0	70	116.9	133.2	−16.3	14
Schedule Variance	BCWP	BCWS	VAR	%	BCWP	BCWS	VAR	%
	8.6	14.1	−5.5	39	116.9	139.4	−22.5	16
Completion Variance	BAC	EAC	%					
	175.0	175.0	0					

Figure 7-2. Variance Analysis Report

Problem Analysis
Cost Underspending due to redirected manpower.
Schedule Behind schedule due to PDL priorities.

Program/Task Impact
One milestone has been delayed 2 months. The others are on schedule.

Proposed Solution
Cost Spending will catch up by Sept. when schedule is accelerated.
Schedule Intend to double manpower in Aug. & Sept.

EAC Impact None

Comments No major problems with task.

Cost Acct. Mgr.	Approvals	
Name T. M. Troy	Funct. Dept. Mgr. B. M. Daley	Date 8/5/XX
Date 8/4/XX	Program Mgr. R. O. Hurt	Date 8/5/XX

Figure 7-2 Variance Analysis Report (continued)

7.11 Risk Analysis Reports

A risk analysis report provides the manager with the staff's assessment of the risks involved in meeting a particular schedule or budget. These reports are prepared in a highly systematic fashion and rely on quantitative assessments of various task managers as to the percent probability of meeting a time or financial commitment.

This information is valuable to the manager who can then assess the potential profit to be earned against a future bid and the chances for failure. For example, if the staff's inputs indicate that the project has only a 50% probability of meeting the customer's schedule and the contract invokes a $1,000-a-day penalty for every day completion is delayed beyond a certain date, a potential profit of $50,000 may not be as good as originally thought. A 50/50 chance for not meeting the schedule for a 1-year-long project could easily extend, for example, to 1 year and 2 months. At a penalty of $1,000 a day, this would cost the company $60,000—$10,000 more than the expected profit.

The manager can use this kind of information to keep higher management informed as to the risks involved and this information can be helpful in establishing ground rules for negotiation with the customer or on how the project will be run and the priority rating it will be given.

7.12 Value Analysis

Value analysis involves examining a product or operation to eliminate any cost elements that are not essential to the effectiveness or marketability of the product or operation.

For a product, this involves simplifying the design, substituting lower cost materials, improving reliability or durability where the company is subject to warranty costs, or eliminating unneeded parts. A value analysis report can help the manager to decide whether a re-evaluation or redesign of a product will be worth the time invested. Also, when a number of different products are being evaluated, the value analysis reports can provide a basis for focusing on products that will provide the greatest payoff if redesigned to reduce material and labor costs.

When applied to company or project operations, value analysis can provide ways to eliminate unneeded or expensive steps that do not contribute worthwhile benefits. (This is similar to zero base budgeting described in Chapter 4.) As a result, the manager can implement changes that speed up work, eliminate paper work, and improve morale. Thus, value analysis can be an effective aid in deciding how to lower operational costs.

Case in Point: In one large company in San Diego, a value analysis of a supplier document processing system was subjected to a rigorous analysis. A number of unnecessary steps were eliminated as a result. The cost of the analysis was $1,120. The implementation cost of the changes was $2,850—for a total cost of $3,970. The annual savings to the company were roughly $150,000. The savings were achieved by the following measures:

- Simplified system for processing resubmitted supplier documents.
- Eliminated unneeded people from the review and approval cycle.
- Provided buyer with form letters and used carbon sheets instead of copying originals.
- Eliminated satellite files and reduced copying requirements.

7.13 Internal and External Factors in Decision Making

Decisions, regardless of the tools or methods used, can be affected by numerous environmental factors. While it is extremely difficult for the manager to be aware of all of them, they can have a significant impact on the success or failure of a decision. A checklist of factors that might be useful to consider before making a final decision is given in Table X.

TABLE X

CHECKLIST OF ENVIRONMENTAL FACTORS THAT MAY AFFECT A DECISION

- Will public attitudes affect your decision's success?
- Will present or proposed laws impact the decision?
- Will changes in the economic picture over the next year, 5 years, or 10 years affect the decision?
- Will changing social customs or attitudes apply to the decision?
- Will changes in foreign policy affect the decision?
- Will increasing/decreasing costs of special equipment, materials, processes, etc. affect the decision?
- Will changes in the labor market affect the decision?
- Will availability of needed materials impact the decision's success?
- Will the unavailability or poor reliability of suppliers undermine the decision?
- Will competition get stiffer or will actions being taken by competitors impede the success of the decision?
- Will transportation characteristics impact the decision?

  Case in Point: A management decision at a small company in Pasadena to have its staff engineer design a shipping crate for a sensitive instrument resulted in expensive repair work because the instrument was damaged during shipment three times out of five shipments. Also, demonstrations to potential customers on the East Coast were canceled because the instrument could not be operated due to the in-transit damage.

  Finally a professional designer of shipping containers was used to provide a container that would protect the instrument from damage. Also, a company experienced in transporting sensitive equipment was used. No further problems in shipment occurred.

- Will the size of facilities affect the decision? For example, one company found that it couldn't get a large storage vessel out of its manufacturing facility because its doors were too low. Someone forgot to consider the added height of the vehicle used to move the vessel to the railroad car.
- Will weather conditions affect the decision? Sometimes high humidity, extra cold temperatures, or strong winds can affect successful implementation of a decision?
- Will earthquakes, rock slides, or floods affect the decision?
- Will strikes, riots, boycotts, or revolutions affect the decision?

7.14 Decision Making When Answer Was Predetermined

Sometimes a manager makes a decision and then assigns someone on the staff to prepare a study to determine if the decision is right. Obviously, this can be a problem for the researcher if it is already known what the manager wants to do and the results conflict with the decision. If unaware of the manager's decision, the researcher may find the report trash-canned and be assigned to less demanding work or short-changed when raise or promotion time comes.

Unfortunately the manager or administrator who gets involved in this situation needs to be extremely skillful in changing the higher manager's mind or in finding an alternative path that can be successful without overriding the original decision. Possible strategies include:

- Concentrate on identifying some steps that can overcome the defects of the decision, and sell them effectively.
- Avoid taking the assignment if possible.
- Persuade the manager that the decision should be changed because of changes in the environment that could not have been accounted for at the time the original decision or assignment was made.
- Present an overwhelming array of objective reasons that indicate the decision will not succeed.
- Have someone else talk to the manager and explain why the decision won't work (a close associate or friend of the decision maker).

7.15 Overview of Decision-Making Process

There is no scientific technique that exempts decision making from the need to use intuition and common sense. However, subjecting each decision to a standard fact-finding procedure reduces factors to their essentials and presents them visually. This process not only helps avoid errors, but allows for later evaluation of the decision-making process to avoid repeating mistakes.

An overview of a systematic decision-making process that draws on the various techniques mentioned before follows:

1. Set specific objectives involved in the decision.
2. Collect information.
3. Identify alternative solutions.
4. Identify benefits to be obtained from each solution.

5. Determine when the benefits will be realized. For example, $1 earned 5 years from now may only be worth 50¢ then, due to its depreciation with inflation.
6. Determine costs of each solution.
7. Identify risks involved in each solution.
8. Consider a compromise decision; e.g., union constraints or people's attitudes and feelings must be evaluated. Their positions and reactions must be weighed against the benefits before a decision is made.
9. Evaluate degree of uncertainty in the decision. (A decision tree may be helpful here.)

7.16 Matrix of Decision-Making Tools

A matrix of decision-making techniques is provided to allow evaluation of the technique or tool to be used.

Method	Advantages	Limits/disadvantages
Tapping available information	Reliable; usually accurate.	May not be complete or timely.
Personal experience	Reliable and firm; doesn't rely on others.	Experience is limited; tend to assign too much weight to your own observations. Rapid closure on conflicting data or alternative solutions.
Experience of others	Provides broader base for evaluation. Expands manager's information bank considerably; depends on number of people available.	Hard to account for personal bias, superficial observations, and environmental considerations.
Intuition	Rapid; requires little research or examination; often right for successful managers.	Not objective or based on analytical techniques; could lead to disaster on a major decision if not supported with other means.
Staff reports	Generally more thorough and objective than superficial or off-the-cuff methods.	Staff member may be biased, used unreliable information sources, or be too inexperienced to identify flaws in the data.

Decision tables and trees	Objective, more scientific, more thorough.	Take expertise in their development and use; false assumptions or ignored factors may completely negate what appears to be valid decision. May require longer to make decision.
Integrated project status reports	Complete; accurate, visual, and easy to use; automatically supplied to a schedule.	May be late or data may have been incorrectly recorded; inputs may provide misleading information.
Trend plots	Simple, visual data to base decisions on.	Sharp changes in trends may occur because of unexpected events or activities.
Variance analysis reports	Accurate, reliable information from people doing work; allow manager to think about problem before taking action.	Staff may do a superficial job on them and thereby mislead higher management.
Risk analysis reports	Allow manager to assess potential schedule and cost problems in terms of potential benefits; e.g., profit or winning a new customer or keeping shop busy during a dry period.	Staff may not be expert in this kind of analysis and data may be unreliable. Also computer program may have defects that produce incorrect results. Computer program development costs can be high.
Value analysis	Provides manager with concrete data on how to improve a product or operating system. Data should be accurate and reliable.	Delays and cost of implementing changes may not be properly addressed or assessed.
Simulation studies	Provide information on a variety of "What if" conditions not readily available by other means and within a short time.	False or poor assumptions can lead to conclusions or decisions that are unrealistic. Can be an expensive approach. Need help of specialists.

Method	Advantages	Limits/disadvantages
Operations research	Scientific, mathematical approach provides results not readily available with other means.	Same as for simulation studies.

7.17 Avoiding Traps in Decision Making

A number of traps exist for the manager when he/she makes a decision. A list of the common causes for poor decisions follows:

- Incomplete or inaccurate information.
- Personal bias causes distortion or ignoring of facts.
- False confidence in staff members who present a facade of absolute certainty or confidence without real experience or knowledge to back up their recommendations (for example, depending more on who is right rather than what is right).
- Improper selection of people to research problem. They may be biased or have closed minds that can affect their data-gathering ability.
- Improper selection of information sources.
- Ignoring experience of other projects, companies, or industries.
- Failure to account for future changes in business, quality or mix.

Case in Point: A manager avoided purchasing sophisticated equipment that would have increased the productivity of his department because he had doubts about the demand for his staff's services in the next few years. As a result, he did not spend the $150,000 budgeted for this action. Two years later, the department staff had been reduced from 125 to 35 people and the nature of the work had changed so that the new equipment would not have been able to be utilized more than 10% of the time and its payoff with the 35-man staff would not have been achieved.

- Bad assumptions about the staff, product or conditions.
- Ignoring constraints set by the environment and higher management. For example, if top management has set a hiring freeze and the decision involves hiring two technical specialists immediately, then it is not likely that the decision will be successful.
- Generalizing an experience that may not be applicable to other situations.

- Unrealistic expectations; e.g., one director decided that no one should come to work late. With a staff of 1,300 people, he failed to recognize that a certain percentage of the staff will be late no matter what measures are taken and that a certain number of people will have accidents, family problems, flat tires, and other exigencies which are beyond their ability to predict or avoid.
- Overinvolvement in decisions that are someone else's responsibility. While cooperation is important, excessive involvement in others' problems depletes energy and can compromise your decision-making ability.
- Trying to make more than one decision at a time. (Breaks up concentration and can cause confusion.)
- Being pressured into a snap decision before all the information has been gathered and analyzed.
- Failure to develop an alternate plan of action if the decision turns out badly. Every decision has an element of risk in it. Therefore, the assumption that there is no chance of failure will prevent preparation of a plan to correct a bad course of action.
- Waiting too long to implement a decision. Once the decision is made, it should be put into effect right away. Wavering or delays increase its chances for failure by weakening your resolve and your staff's confidence in its correctness.
- Failure to accept a bad decision and to change it. While no one likes to admit a mistake, a strong leader can do it and gain respect at the same time.
- Ignoring the implementation of a decision can also lead to disaster. A half-hearted attempt can undermine an excellent decision because the dedication and energy needed by the staff will not be mobilized toward its implementation.

8

Increasing Productivity and Efficiency of Your People

Most organizations are between 30% and 60%[1] efficient. The reasons for this low efficiency or productivity are numerous. They include poor leadership, demotivated workers, poor organizational structures, undefined objectives, loose discipline, poor equipment, excessive or unrealistic rules and regulations, absence of work standards, ignorance, and apathy or complacency.

This chapter is devoted to reviewing a variety of techniques for improving productivity. The techniques covered here are only a sampling and many other methods are available from other books or from the minds of the manager and his/her staff.

8.1 Set Clear Objectives

Although the importance of objectives has been discussed before, it is important to emphasize that two basic types are necessary: the first type deals with the external aspects of the project or task; e.g., "To deliver 26 gas spectrometers that meet specifications to customer X by March 26, 19XX"; the second type is an internally oriented objective for the company or project that deals with improving productivity or efficiency. Thus, internal objectives include:

1. Increase manufacturing's productivity by 10% during the next 12 months.

[1]One book on management reports the average person is 10% to 25% efficient.

2. Reduce overhead costs in engineering by 15% during the next 6 months.
3. Use existing designs in up to 50% of the new projects to speed up work and reduce engineering and manufacturing costs.

Once management has set objectives, whether internally or externally oriented, these must be documented, discussed with the people expected to meet them, and revised to match reality when necessary. This, of course, includes reviewing and communicating objectives with all levels of the staff, not just managers.

Another aspect of objectives that is often overlooked is the need for their periodic review. Some managers think that the presentation of the next year's objectives at a staff meeting is sufficient to achieve them. This, however, seldom works because as people get involved in their work and associated problems, they forget what higher level objectives were, or may interpret management's silence as a lack of interest in attaining the originally stated objectives. Thus, frequent review of objectives and assessment of progress in meeting them are highly beneficial.

8.2 Give Precise, Specific Task Assignments

Failure to issue precise, specific assignments often leads to confusion, misunderstandings, greater costs, and wasted effort. This observation applies to both small and large assignments in small and large companies.

One of the reasons for poorly implemented assignments is the manager's attempt to save time by assuming that the staff understand what he/she wants without too much detail. Experience, however, indicates that unless the manager or supervisor outlines the key details of the assignment in his/her own mind, the person receiving the assignment is likely to do something wrong.

The best way to avoid this is for the manager to think through the main requirements of the assignment and identify what is not wanted as well as what aspects are especially desired. While this is difficult to do and does take some time, in the long run less manager and worker labor will be wasted.

8.3 Write Down Instructions and Requirements

Closely related to giving precise, specific assignments, is the practice of writing them down. Written assignments are more efficient because they increase the productivity of the person doing the work by a considerable amount.

Case in Point: Studies have found that a designer/draftsman can complete an assignment 25% faster when a sketch instead of verbal instructions is provided with the assignment. If a layout drawing is supplied, the draftsman can do the work with 80% less labor.

Another advantage of the written assignment is that it forces the manager to think through the assignment before discussing it with his staff. It also allows the person given the assignment to study it before beginning work and to avoid going back to the manager if he/she forgot a detail.

A manager found out that efficiency was not the only casualty from oral instructions, but that the end result was not what was wanted. He assigned a senior staff member to develop a scheduling and tracking system for his department. After months of effort, the staff member returned with his system. The department manager immediately rejected it because the level of detail control had been set much too low for practical implementation. Had he defined the system requirements on a piece of paper and reviewed these with the staff member, less work would have been needed and the control system would have needed only minor revisions.

8.4 Show Interest in Your People's Progress

Even if objectives are clearly set, requirements explicitly identified, and a written task summary or outline provided, productivity may not meet expectations. It is natural for people to work at a relaxed or low-stress pace and less work will be done than the person is capable of producing. This situation can be improved by the manager periodically checking on the progress of the job, asking if any problems exist, or offering to get help if needed. Direct management attention can often work miracles in increased productivity.

Case in Point: A contract was won by a company in California which involved modifying 200 items previously delivered to the customer. All items were to be modified and returned to the customer within six weeks. Higher management knew this was an unrealistic schedule and decided to have a key manager take charge of the overall effort. The manager and supervisors of the department responsible for the modification set up a tight schedule and reviewed it with the staff and key manager. While everyone agreed that it was difficult to meet, work was begun. The key manager insisted on reviewing status with the department manager and supervisors everyday. Because of this attention, the department manager took great interest in the progress of his staff and was highly visible. He let his people know that if they had any problems, he was there to help with immediate action.

The project was begun with enthusiasm and was kept moving at a fast pace until its completion. The items were delivered to the customer two weeks ahead of schedule.

8.5 Set Personal Example

Whatever rationale a manager may have for justifying not working hard, it's not valid. Managers set examples for their people and their power to fire, hire, and reward does not exempt them from a day's work. Certainly the kind of work differs and should. However, when the manager spends a lot of time talking to stock brokers, making real estate deals, or reading stock reports, the need for greater productivity will not appear great to the staff.

Case in Point: One manager in a small company spent much of his time away from the facility working on special projects of his own, such as setting up a new restaurant. Although his staff was conscientious, it resented the manager's outside activities and its morale was affected. Sometimes work stopped because he was not available to answer questions or help solve problems.

8.6 Offer Incentives for Superior Performance

It is a well-known fact that you can't get something for nothing. Unfortunately, people sometimes think they can get superior performance without equivalent rewards in return. Very often a new person replaces a manager who has been promoted or left the company, but he/she is not given a raise that is commensurate with his/her skills and contributions. This often creates a negative or cynical response in the person. Too often in industry, the outstanding performer is turned off because he/she is expected to contribute more than others, but his/her pay is not proportionately increased. The end result is that productive people find jobs elsewhere or gradually tune down to their lowest output level.

Case in Point: A particularly productive design-draftsman was at the top of his scale. Yet, he was not qualified for promotion to a higher designer classification. The personnel department would not allow him to be paid above his classification limit nor would they establish a new classification making him a specialist, as was commonly done for other classifications. Shortly after being told of the decision, the designer-draftsman left the company—taking with him know-how and loyalty that were not replaced by a new hire. The manager estimated that the company lost about $12,000 in the first year due to recruiting and training costs. In addition, it lost an average of $6,000 a year due to the lower productivity of his replacement.

Another approach that can affect productivity is the belief that a program for increasing productivity can be successful without an investment of some sort. While a manager may feel that his/her staff are being paid to increase production, that is usually not a key part of most jobs. Productivity increases are usually the responsibility of the manager or an industrial engineer. In this case, special rewards may not be essential, but if a program's success is to depend on grass roots support, some form of a reward for increased productivity should be offered.

> **Case in Point:** Scanlon and LeSieur have developed well-known plans involving giving bonuses to the staff for increased productivity or reduced costs. Profit sharing is another method for rewarding outstanding performance.

8.7 Provide Better Facilities and Tools

Experiments have shown that an improved environment can boost productivity; one report gives 8%. The improvement due to new equipment and tools can be much larger, perhaps 50% and more.

Factors that should be considered to determine whether new facilities or equipment are needed follow:

FACILITIES

- Are people so close together that they get in each other's way or spend too much time talking?
- Is the environment depressing when you enter the area?
- Are the noise level and other distractions too high?
- Are the temperature and humidity uncomfortable?
- Is the lighting adequate or do people suffer fatigue from eye strain?

EQUIPMENT

- Do frequent equipment breakdowns occur?
- Is it difficult and expensive to get replacement parts?
- Do the staff suffer from fatigue because of excessive physical requirements?
- Are too many accidents occurring?
- Are competitors outbidding you?
- Are the more successful competitors in your industry using new equipment?
- Is production on a gradual downswing?

8.8 Set Up Cost Improvement Suggestion System

Cost improvement suggestion systems are common in industry. Even small companies of 30 or fewer people have them. The reason for this is that experience has proved that good ideas can come from just about anyone.

> **Case in Point:** At one medium manufacturing company, a new man noticed that many parts were being rejected because inspectors couldn't really tell if the parts met tolerancing requirements. He proposed a low-cost template that could eliminate most of the guesswork for the inspectors. The template was evaluated and approved for use. Within a year the company found that it saved at least $15,000 a year in scrapped parts. Over a 10-year period the company management projected a $200,000 savings in labor and material.

While most companies don't need encouragement for a cost reduction/suggestion program, they often fail to implement the program properly.

> **Case in Point:** A designer had recommended that an expensive practice of redoing engineering change notices be avoided by having the change notices checked by designers before issuance. Thus, errors could be corrected and the unnecessary expense of issuing new change notices could be drastically reduced.
>
> He anxiously waited a week for a response from the committee in charge of evaluating and approving cost reduction suggestions. He waited three more weeks and no response was received. He confided to a friend that at least a call saying that the idea was being reviewed would have made him feel better. A month later, he told a number of people that he would never submit another idea to the committee. The company not only lost potentially good ideas, but the frustration and anger evoked reduced the suggester's productivity and probably cost the company hundreds of dollars in lost output over this period. His experience also affected the attitudes and morale of those who heard about his experience.

The solution to this potential problem is to assign someone to the evaluating committee who is sensitive to other people's feelings and needs to be recognized for their attempts to help the company. He/she should be given clear instructions that all suggestions received are acknowledged and a tentative decision date given.

Cost-effective ideas should be rewarded in terms of concrete benefits: money, extra vacation time, dinner for the family at a good restaurant, awards, etc.

8.9 Eliminate Company Politicians

Politically oriented managers are often necessary at the highest levels of a company's management. However, they should not engender the same practices at the working levels. Great care should be taken to avoid filling operational jobs with people who are good manipulators and talkers. When it comes to getting work done, managers are needed who are primarily interested in completing the job as efficiently as possible and keeping their staff working as an enthusiastic and cooperative team. The politician is overly concerned with advancement and spends most of the time developing alliances, polishing image, and letting higher management know of readiness to take the next step up. Lack of sufficient care about people becomes known eventually. The result is lower productivity and loss of respect for the company and its higher-level management. The successful advancement of politicians tells the staff that true merit and performance are not really important in the scheme of things.

8.10 Don't Force Good Individual Contributors to Become Unspirited Managers

While good managers are hard to find and deserve good financial rewards and status, exceptional technical experts are also a rare commodity. Therefore, a technical expert should not be made to feel that he/she must become a manager to get top pay and recognition in the company.

> **Case in Point:** At a large company in Northern California, a superb analytical engineer was promoted to a manager's job so that the company could give him the pay and status he deserved. Unfortunately, he had no interest in being a manager and tried to do both jobs. The result was that neither job got done well because his poor performance as a manager affected his analytical work. After six months, he was returned to his original job but with no reduction in pay. While he would be making more than his supervisor, the company managed to keep a very good engineer and showed others that the management path was not the only way to get top pay and recognition.

Competent individual performers are often lost in industry by promotion to supervisory jobs. This can be dangerous to the company's competitive position and can result in lost business and productivity. Thus, two equal but divergent paths to success should be open to management and technical people.

8.11 Keep Turnover Down

Turnover is a normal part of the industrial world. It is often given little attention, but can be a big factor in productivity. Some managers fail to understand that people are not always interchangeable like identical parts of a machine. Individual talents, specialties, experience, and effectiveness vary considerably. Thus, when a skilled person is lost, the cost to find and train a replacement can be high. Certainly no one is indispensable, but many people can only be replaced with lesser beings. The result is lower productivity and creativity, and greater operating costs.

> **Case in Point:** One company estimated that for every loss of an engineer with three years experience with the company, $16,000 in recruitment, training, and associated costs went down the drain.

While $16,000 may be high, even less-skilled people can cost a few thousand dollars to replace. And sometimes the errors or confusion that result during the breaking-in period can exceed many thousands of dollars.

8.12 Watch Out for Deflating Performance Reviews

Performance reviews should be primarily aimed at helping people to improve their work quality and productivity as well as letting them know their good qualities. Unfortunately, experience indicates that performance reviews turn out to be demotivators rather than the opposite. See Chapter 17 for a more extensive discussion of this topic.

8.13 Control Overtime

Experiments have shown certain optimum patterns in achieving the most productive output when overtime (OT) is used. These results[2] follow:

- The most productive use of OT is the 10-hour day split into 5-hour segments for not more than 8 days in a row. Then a 4-day rest before returning to the OT schedule should be allowed. (This involves returning to an 8-hour day on Thursday and Friday with the weekend off.)
- The use of half a day of OT on Saturday was found to be least productive.

---

[2]Don Fuller, "Organizing, Planning, and Scheduling Engineering Operations, IEI," 1962, p. 13–17.

8.14 Eliminate Unneeded Reports and Paper Work

Studies have shown that about 20% of all reports can be eliminated without harming company operations. Therefore, a continuing program of dropping reports or forms should be implemented to save much wasted time and labor. A typical 5-page report should cost about $250 to prepare, depending on the subject and skill of the writer. If this report is prepared monthly, the annual cost would be $3,000. The cost of distribution, reading, and filing could be another $900 a year, assuming no unneeded discussions are created as a result of the report.

Unneeded forms can increase costs significantly.

> **Case in Point:** At one company, two forms were found in use that had similar functions. By combining the two, the company saved $1,000 per year in printing, handling, storage, and filing costs.

8.15 Keep Operating Systems and Procedures Stable

Operating systems and procedures are often subject to change as already discussed in Chapter 1. Most of the time they should be left alone even if they are not perfect. Operating systems and procedures rarely cover every aspect of the operation nor should they. However, they should focus on critical areas. In attempts to achieve perfection, there are always some people who feel that they can do a better job. And maybe they can, but the big question is: "Is the result worth the effort and confusion involved in designing and implementing a new system"? Unless the benefits are significant and obvious to almost everyone, they probably aren't worth implementing.

> **Case in Point:** At one company that was undergoing frequent changes in structure, people, and procedures, a manager submitted a request to the Manager of Systems and Procedures that stated his people were tired of relearning new systems and procedures every year, and that he would stop wasting their time in training sessions if systems didn't stabilize.

New procedures are expensive to design and document; it takes time to become familiar with them; errors are more likely to occur; people become demoralized; and management loses sight of what practices are being followed and thus is less able to manage effectively.

8.16 Don't Take Your People, Facilities, or Customer for Granted

The law of entropy was mentioned in Chapter 2. This law states that disorder tends to increase by itself in a system unless someone does work to reduce it. This is another way of saying that when you take your organization for granted, it will tend to deteriorate. This law also applies to relations with your people. If you take them for granted, they will tend to deteriorate with time also and their productivity and morale will suffer. Therefore, constant attention to your organization and people is needed to maintain optimum productivity.

The same principle or law applies to production equipment and customer relations. Just because you have sold products or services to a company for 10 years doesn't mean that you will continue to do so. Therefore, a conscious effort to keep on good terms and responsive to your customer's needs can reduce the chances for his going elsewhere. Of course, even if you keep your own organization in proper order, problems can arise with customers. They too are subject to internal and external deterioration. While you can't do much about this, being aware of the entropy law can help minimize troubles with your customers or at least to develop strategies in dealing with a customer who is in a progressively higher state of entropy.

8.17 Praise Increases Human Energy

Studies have shown that praise releases productive energy in people. On the opposite end, criticism has been found to decrease human energy available for useful application. Therefore the manager must keep alert to opportunities for praising his/her people. Certainly this praise must be sincere and based on performance. However, unless the manager makes a conscious effort to praise his/her people, they will begin to suffer the ill effects of lack of recognition and attention that most people need, including managers and supervisors themselves.

Praise can be given in private or in front of others. However, public praise is more rewarding to the person than private praise. Many people find praise given in writing, such as a commendation certificate, very rewarding.

8.18 Use Job Rotation

Job rotation involves reassigning people to different positions after they have mastered the work they are doing. While this technique has certain problems, it offers the company significant improvements in staff versatility and improved productivity and morale. Of course, not all people like to be reassigned to a new job periodically. They prefer a stable routine and the security of doing work in which they have a proven ability to do. However, a certain percentage of people do require frequent challenges and changes in the nature of their work to keep their interest and motivation high.

Case in Point: At one company on the West Coast a designer strongly objected to his supervisor about his doing virtually the same kind of work for six years. He was bored and unchallenged by the work and wanted a reassignment to a different technical area so that he could expand his capabilities. He confided to an associate that he was probably working at 50% of his capacity because of the boredom of the job.

In the preceding example, the supervisor's efforts to have the designer transferred from structural work to mechanical work was thwarted by the structural engineering manager because he did not want to lose his experienced designer. (While this can be a serious fault of job rotation, a wider view in terms of its value to the entire organization must be taken into account.)

The benefits of job rotation include:

- A new person may see better ways of doing things because he/she has a fresh view of the operation.
- Morale is improved because the bored expert has a new challenge—that of being a good teacher and having the opportunity of exercising leadership skills.
- Versatility is improved. Under special situations, experienced people will be available from other groups to be temporarily assigned to one function that is behind schedule and needs more people power.
- It can help train people in various aspects of the organization so that they can be promoted into jobs that require an understanding of its overall activities.
- It can motivate people into added effort because of the desire to show that they can learn quickly and do good work in this new area. (Special pay increases tied to multiple skills can help energize people into widening their capabilities.)
- The experienced person training someone from another discipline or group will be motivated to use his/her time more effectively so that normal assignments are completed in addition to performing the training activity.

8.19 Use Brainstorming to Increase Useful Ideas

Every company has a reservoir of new, profit-making ideas that can improve its competitive status. This reservoir is its staff—ranging from the maintenance people to the president of the company. These normally latent ideas can be brought to the open through a technique called Brainstorming.

Brainstorming involves establishing an environment where people are completely unafraid to give out any idea that comes into their heads. This means that the group coordinator makes it clear to everyone before the meeting that no idea will be considered too wild and no one will be laughed at. The idea is to get a completely relaxed, unthreatening, and open atmosphere established. Under these conditions, numerous ideas will be generated and proposed. No attempt to evaluate these ideas should be made during the meeting. They are simply collected for later study by management or a committee.

A 30-minute get-together of 8 to 12 people can result in 50 ideas.[3] Five or six of these will be worth evaluating further.

Other benefits of brainstorming include opportunity for rank and file to participate in improved company operations, improved communication among a wide variety of people, team building and generating of trust between management and staff, and stimulation of people's minds and energies who normally have rather routine work to do.

Some rules for making the brainstorming process work include:

- The objective is to get as many ideas as possible. Quality is not important.
- The more unconventional and unusual the idea, the better.
- The combining and modifying of other ideas is desirable.
- Criticism or negative expressions are not allowed.
- Sessions should be held regularly, preferably in the morning when everyone is alert.
- Sessions should be about 30 minutes and no more than one hour.
- Record all ideas.
- After the meeting, submit the ideas to a review committee. (The names of the people should not be associated with the ideas so the committee will not be influenced by anything but the value of the idea itself.)

8.20 Remove Roadblocks to Productivity

In attempts to keep people informed, increase productivity, and implement participative management techniques, managers sometimes place unintentional roadblocks in their people's paths. A few roadblocks to watch out for include:

- Too many reviewers or approvers needed to release a report, drawing, or study.

[3]"Brainstorming," *Small Business Report*, October 1978, p. 17–19.

- Too many meetings.
- Establishment of a committee to complete a task instead of assigning a competent person to do the work and have it reviewed by the committee.
- No delegation of responsibility, authority, and accountability.
- Too many layers of management involved in decision making. (Decisions should be made at the lowest level possible by people in direct contact with the realities of the situation.)
- Environment of fear to make a mistake results in excessive caution and lower work output.
- Poorly trained people (see next section).
- Absence of management responses to staff pleas for help, special equipment, or other resources.
- Unrealistic and uncoordinated setting of schedules and budgets.
- Manager is not available to answer questions of staff or to help solve problems.

For roadblocks to motivation, see Chapter 17.

8.21 Train People to Improve Productivity

The better trained people are, the more productive they can be. Training involves teaching, informing, or educating people so that they can become well qualified to do their work or to perform in jobs of greater difficulty and responsibility. It differs from education in that it is devoted to developing proficiency in a specific job or organization.

In addition, training focuses on a specific objective that can be attained in a fairly short period.

Effective training increases productivity by accelerating the progress of people on the job by expanding their abilities so that they can contribute more to the company's welfare. To successfully train people with subsequent improvement in productivity, the manager must implement the following practices:

1. Stimulate people into being interested in learning.
2. Adjust the program to the specific needs of the people being trained.
3. Conduct or direct the training activities.
4. The amount of training should be consistent with the person's ability to absorb it.
5. People can learn from being told or shown how to do a job. However, the best method is for them to do the work under someone else's guidance.

6. People respond best to a planned and scheduled program that is implemented and evaluated on a systematic basis.
7. A schedule of re-training should be followed to keep people at their optimum performance.

The cost effectiveness of a training program depends on its cost to implement versus the lost productivity when a formal training program is not used. For example, if a new person is found to produce only 50% of the work over a year that an older, more experienced one does, we can determine that half his/her pay is lost. If he/she is making $12,000, the loss comes to $6,000. However, if the supervisor can spend $1,000 of his/her time training the new person so that he/she is 75% efficient for the year, the net savings will be $2,000 ($3,000–$1,000). Therefore, the training program is worthwhile. However, without an objective cost-benefit study, it cannot be automatically assumed that the cost is worth the results obtained.

Chapter 17 describes coaching and its method of implementation.

8.22 Install an Effective Safety Program

The cost of accidents in industry is staggering. Over 4 million people have accidents at work each year at a cost of over $40 billion. Property loss due to fires comes to roughly $450 million for 50,000 fires per year.[4]

Based on these statistics, an effective safety program can not only save lives and avoid tragedies, but can save the company much money and lost people-power. A few items to include in the program are:

- Have a safety officer assigned, even if only part-time because the company is small.
- Teach the basics about safety in industry. The Government or library can provide material on this subject; also have a safety consultant train a few people or send them to a safety course/seminar sponsored by a college or other institution.
- Examine the company for possible safety hazards such as equipment, facilities, type of work and chemicals.
- Prepare a safety manual that deals with various safety hazards that may apply to the company.
- Instruct people on safety practices and what to do when an accident occurs.
- Post emergency phone numbers in a conspicuous area.

---

[4]Burton E. Lipman, "Successful Cost Reduction and Control," Prentice-Hall, Inc., Englewood Cliffs, NJ, 1978, p. 135.

- Keep complete accident records and investigation reports.
- Establish a system of self-inspections for all work areas.
- Establish a safety committee for small, medium, and large companies.
- Provide staff and management with periodic training in safety.

8.23 Obtain a Return on Your Wastes

Wastes often can be salvaged and sold for a profit. Therefore, a careful analysis should be performed to determine whether the effort of a salvage program will more than pay for itself. Some companies have found that they can earn hundreds of thousands of dollars from their manufacturing wastes. A few possibilities to consider are:

- Rejected parts that may contain valuable metals, such as platinum, gold, silver, or palladium.
- Wire that is plated with silver or gold.
- Excess waste material from machine processes, waste paint, silver from old films, and scrap from silver soldering.
- Old equipment or instruments no longer used from obsolete stock.

Burton E. Lipman in his book "Successful Cost Reduction and Control," Prentice-Hall, Inc., 1978, reported that there are companies that test scrap for valuable metal content. They analyze the scrap and assay it. If it is more valuable than the refining process, you can make money on it.

8.24 Avoid Unnecessary Quality Requirements for Your Products

Unnecessary quality control requirements can add up to high product costs. A harmless appearing tightening of a tolerance can sometimes increase manufacturing and quality control costs exponentially. Therefore, very great care is needed to avoid unneeded requirements. To minimize these costs, follow these practices:[5]

- Be sure that all specifications are needed to satisfy the customer.
- Identify those specifications and requirements that account for the greatest costs. Look at these requirements for reducing labor and material costs.

---

[5]Lipman, *op. cit.* p. 130–131.

- Verify that a change in the specification doesn't create additional manufacturing and inspection problems.
- Find out if changing a tolerance for one operation will make a following or preceding operation easier and cheaper.
- Remember that the requirement to create an excellent product is good, but setting standards for perfection leads to excessive costs, delays, and demoralization.

8.25 Use Standard Parts

Standard parts should be used whenever possible to save costs in materials, labor, waste, and redesign. Every time a new part is specified by an engineer, the company can wind up investing about $3,000 in processing, handling, documentation, and storage costs. Therefore, a firm standards program should be implemented. Some savings that can follow are:

- Fewer purchase orders will be needed (a P.O. may cost $80 on an average).
- Larger price discounts can be obtained because of larger orders.
- Storage and handling costs are reduced because fewer separate orders must be unpacked, checked, and placed in stores.

8.26 Reduce Inventory Costs

Inventories are a cost item that can be controlled to increase efficiency and profits. Several techniques for reducing inventory costs include:

- Work with supplier to reduce lead times and maintain minimum stock for use.
- Buy items on a make-and-hold agreement with supplier.
- Standardize the number of items kept in the stockroom.
- Purge stockroom of obsolete items.
- Don't shut down company during busy periods.
- Minimize the number of outside warehouses—several warehouses will require more items than a single warehouse because each must maintain a minimum stock for adequate customer service.
- Discourage make-and-hold orders from your customers.

8.27 Work Sampling Can Increase Efficiency

The purpose of work sampling is to observe or sample work to find out the percent (ratio) of downtime delays and nonworking periods. It is basically a statistical technique based on the law of probability; e.g., a small number of chance occurrences tend to have the same pattern as the total universe being studied. The work observed must be done on a random basis. This technique has been used for many years to reduce costs or increase production.

> **Case in Point:** A group of new assembly machines had excessive downtime. After two weeks of random sampling, the main problem areas and their related downtime costs were identified. These problems were corrected by redesign effort and the downtime was cut by 85%.[6]

The procedure for doing work sampling follows:

1. Define the study's objective; e.g., to determine machine utilization or set time standards and allowances.
2. Set measures of production for correlation with study results and collect data on production or work rates for each day of the study.
3. Prepare definition of each element that is to be studied.
4. Do initial statistical work; e.g., estimate percent of each element or set up tolerances.
5. Let management and others know what is being done and select and train study team.
6. Create form for recording information on study and collect data.
7. Evaluate results of study (early part of study may have to be discarded because people may have been reacting abnormally while being observed until the novelty wore off.)
8. Prepare a report and present results.

8.28 Cost Reduction Checklist

As was mentioned, there are innumerable ways to reduce operating and production costs or to increase efficiency. These techniques are usually based on one or a combination of the following actions:

1. Elimination of an operation, paper work, part, or condition.
2. Reduction in energy, materials, parts, or space needed.
3. Rearrangement of steps in an operation to increase production or efficiency.

---

[6] Lipman, *op. cit.*, 170–172.

4. Substitution of a new technique, material, part, equipment, or person for another.
5. Acceleration of an activity or operation by using improved systems or procedures.

The checklist in Table XI illustrates the preceding techniques for reducing costs.

TABLE XI
COST REDUCTION IDEA CHECKLIST

1. Can you obtain salvage fees from wastes or obsolete materials, parts, and products?
2. Can you reduce the number of reports produced and distributed? (Over 20% of reports produced are not needed.)
3. Can you reduce document storage costs by microfilming, using a low-cost document center, or renting a remote, inexpensive storage building?
4. Can you buy more efficient drafting machines and equipment to reduce design and drafting labor?
5. Can you reduce accidents and injuries?
6. Can you reduce turnover by some relatively inexpensive technique, such as more recognition of good work performed and attention to people's feelings and needs to be treated humanely?
7. Can you simplify or use lower-priced parts and materials in your products without reducing their marketability?
8. Do you have on-line video screens for frequent and immediate access of design, status, or cost information to the staff?
9. Do you use part-time help to do routine work and reduce overhead expenses?
10. Do you maintain close ties with local schools and colleges for obtaining part-time help and new permanent people with minimum hiring costs?
11. Do you have an active campaign to obtain cost reduction ideas from the staff?
12. Do you have a file of standard descriptions for use in new proposals so that they don't have to be rewritten?
13. Do you use short-interval scheduling to increase productivity?
14. Do you set up mutually agreed-to objectives with your staff?
15. Do you have a standardization program to reduce variety and inventory costs.
16. Do you have branch warehouses that can be consolidated into one warehouse?

TABLE XI (Continued)

17. Can you use thinner metal or lighter gauge plastic in your products without reducing safety or reliability?
18. Do you make optimum-size orders to take account of maximum discounts, but still avoid excessive storage costs?
19. Do you submit bids for materials, parts, etc. to at least three suppliers for competitive prices?
20. Do you make a concerted effort to negotiate lower prices on raw material, parts, packing materials, etc.? Include transportation, terms for future purchases, rebates, price protection, and payment terms.
21. Do you buy replacement parts from manufacturers other than the original equipment manufacturer (OEM)?
22. Can you tint windows to reduce air-conditioning costs? (10% to 25% of air-conditioning costs may be saved.)
23. Do you use flexible work schedules to reduce turnover, absenteeism, and tardiness? (Most surveys show more advantages than disadvantages to flexible work schedules.)
24. Do you use certified mail instead of registered mail? It's cheaper and just as efficient.
25. Do you attach letters to parcels and mark them "First Class Mail Enclosed," and then add a letter fee to parcel post charge?
26. Do you buy materials or liquids in bulk to reduce purchasing, handling, and use costs?
27. Do you evaluate new manufacturing equipment to determine whether it is faster and more economical than existing equipment?
28. Do you check the weight or quantity of materials, liquids, or parts received from vendors?
29. Do you specify a stock item that can eliminate one or more manufacturing steps?
30. Can you rearrange production equipment to allow one operator to run two or more machines?
31. Can you redesign the shipping package to reduce costs?
32. Can you use less expensive cushions or packing material?
33. Can you eliminate fasteners so that parts can be fabricated together to eliminate cost of assembly?
34. Can you reduce window area on outside walls to reduce heating and cooling costs?
35. Can you reduce energy costs through sealing air leaks and routinely cleaning filters, chimneys, and flues?

36. Can you lower thermostat settings to reduce energy costs?
37. Can you turn off every other light to conserve electrical energy?
38. Can you order long-lasting light bulbs to reduce maintenance costs due to more frequent replacement?
39. Can you use special outdoor or indoor paint that has superior durability which will require less frequent painting costs?

9

Configuration Management—Product Management for Today's Needs

Configuration management is an esoteric term that identifies a discipline which is 100% practical when properly applied. This discipline was created about 25 years ago to provide a viable system for the technical and administrative management of complex hardware as it proceeded through its life cycle from conception to installation and operation.

The aim of configuration management (CM) is to assure that a product meets customer requirements under a dynamic environment that involves numerous changes and interfaces with different groups within the company and external to it.

This discipline achieves its aim through several key functions, which are described next.

Configuration Identification: This function of CM involves identifying the product configuration by specifications, drawings, parts lists, test procedures, and system descriptions. The identification function also includes assignment, use, and control of document numbers, equipment numbers, part numbers, and serial numbers.

Configuration Control: This function of CM applies to the process of evaluating, processing, approving, and implementing changes to the approved configuration identified by various engineering documents. These documents include drawings and specifications. Table XII gives the kinds of questions asked by people responsible for controlling the product's con-

TABLE XII

CONFIGURATION CONTROL BOARD CHECKLIST

1. How does this change affect total CI performance?
2. Are other projects or CI's in the system affected by the change?
3. How does the change affect the reliability of the CI?
4. Can the change be implemented by manufacturing as proposed?
5. Is special tooling required and how much will it cost? How long will it take to make this tooling?
6. Will previously delivered CI's have to be returned for rework or will they be field (in-service) retrofitted?
7. How will the CI change affect the delivery schedule?
8. What effect will the change have on the total project cost?
9. What drawings, specifications, manuals, and procedures will have to be changed?
10. How are the CI weight, size, balance, stability, and power consumption affected by the change?
11. Is the CI or operator safety affected?
12. Does the change affect spare parts and assemblies?
13. Is the service life of the CI affected?
14. Are repair and maintenance made more difficult by the change?
15. Will the magnetic and radio interference characteristics of the CI be changed?
16. Will the mechanical and electrical installation of the CI be affected?
17. Will the qualification CI have to be modified?
18. Will parts procurement present any problems?
19. Will completed assemblies without the changes have to be scrapped?
20. What is the effectivity[a] of change incorporation? Which serial numbered assemblies must have the changes made to them?
21. Will additional tests be required? What is their schedule and cost impact?

[a]The approved use of a change in specific CI serial numbers.

Note: A configuration control board usually consists of the project manager and representatives from key functional groups, such as engineering, manufacturing, purchasing, contracts, and quality assurance.

(Used with permission of Wiley-Interscience, New York, "Fundamentals of Configuration Management, Samaras and Czerwinski, 1971, p. 38.)

figuration before they approve a change. Change requests and engineering change notices are key documents for implementing effective change control. Note that the term CI is used to refer to an item designated by the company management or customer for formal configuration management practices.

Configuration Accounting: Configuration accounting involves keeping accurate records of the product's configuration as defined by drawings, specifications, and other documents. It also involves keeping records of proposed changes, approved changes, and changes incorporated into hardware.

> **Case in Point:** A medium-size electronic equipment manufacturer found that configuration accounting records had to be maintained for about 4,000 active drawings and 500 change notices per month.

Typical accounting records include a drawing release file, indented (indentured) drawing lists, where used reports, change-notice-status lists, and as-built and as-modified lists.

Configuration Verification: This function involves checking the product configuration against the documents that were used to build it. For complex products, it has been found to be necessary in spite of the fact that they were inspected by Quality Control.

> **Case in Point:** At one company a configuration audit team found a 10% discrepancy between a newly developed digital voltmeter and its drawings. Another company found an average of three discrepancies between simple mechanical parts and their drawings.

9.1 Why Is Configuration Management Needed?

Although many of the practices for this discipline have been around for many years, they were not formalized into an integrated system until about 1960. The Air Force took the lead in CM development because it found so many problems with the new equipment it was buying. It conducted an in-depth study of these problems and decided that a new discipline was required which would ensure that the product's configuration would be identified, controlled, and accounted for in accordance with a much tighter and formalized set of requirements. Other military services soon found that a more formal system was required for their products and they began requiring similar systems to be followed by their contractors.

To appreciate the importance of effective configuration management, a few examples of the problems that commonly occur when a formal system is not used follow.

Case in Point: One company built a complex product that required numerous changes during installation at the customer's site. No formal system of change control, identification, accounting, and verification was used. A few years later the customer found that its drawings did not reflect the true product configuration and the company was forced to update them. A meticulous process of comparing the product against the drawings and revising them to reflect the as-built configuration was required. It cost the company over $1 million.

Case in Point: Another company found that changes in the product in the field were not reported back to the main engineering division. As a result, the as-designed records did not match the as-built configuration. When a new order for the product was received, the same errors were repeated and the company lost thousands of dollars in retrofit costs that could have been avoided by proper documentation and communication between field and design engineers.

Case in Point: A proposed design improvement was not submitted for evaluation to other groups that may have been affected by the change. After spending $2,500 revising the design and drawings, the engineer accidentally discovered that the new design would require revision of another major component that interfaced with it. Since this change would have required an investment of an additional $13,000, management canceled the original change and the drawings had to be returned to their original configuration.

These are only a tiny sampling of the specific problems, costs, and delays that result from poor configuration management. However, the areas that need configuration management attention are fairly broad and are described next.

9.2 Scope of CM Discipline

Configuration management is a cross-discipline that involves virtually everyone in the company from contracts to inspection. For example, if the product is not controlled with formal contract change notices, then somewhere along the project, people will forget what changes were actually authorized and the final product will fail to be accepted by the customer or if he accepts the product as is, he may refuse to pay the extra costs involved.

Figure 9-1 is a sample chart identifying the various areas that need to be addressed to avoid loss of configuration identification, control, and accounting. (Verification is often considered a part of the control function.)

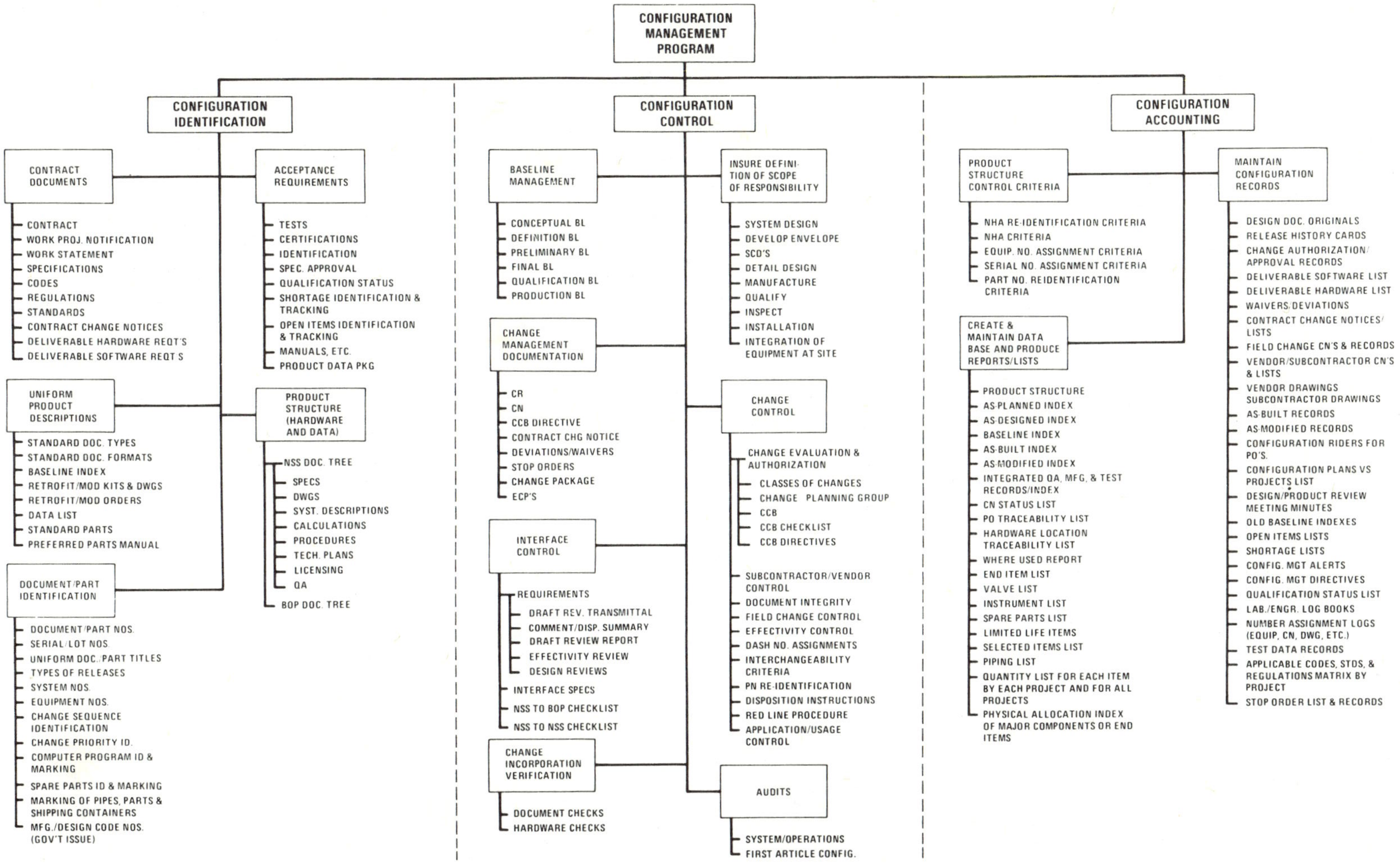

Figure 9-1. Scope of Configuration Management Discipline

Extensive systems and procedures are not necessarily needed for all the areas covered, but there should be a formal review of each area by management to determine the criticality and possible project impact of ignoring the area. In many cases only a flow diagram (see Figure 6–1, page 122) may be adequate. The final choices for in-depth treatment by the company depends on the nature of the company, its product, customer, staff, and past experience or problems.

> *Caution:* Because a company has not had problems in the past does not mean they will never occur. For example, the company may expand its operations, add new product lines and become involved in a new environment that introduces special requirements. Or it may acquire an advanced technology company that appears to need better general management, but actually has CM problems. And as a result of expansion, new people will be hired who may not have the training of the older staff.
>
> Failure to recognize the pitfalls that may result could be disastrous or at least very expensive to the company. Thus, management awareness of the problems that have given birth to this discipline is necessary to help it take corrective action when conditions require it.

9.3 Who Is Responsible for Its Design and Implementation?

For larger companies, a configuration and data management group may be created to spearhead the design and implementation of a configuration management system. However, responsibility for the system design rests with higher management and division-level managers or directors. (Any new system presents numerous difficulties and conflicts that require high-level review and decisions to be resolved.)

Higher management is responsible for verifying that the system selected is being followed. The Quality Assurance group can perform the necessary audits needed by management. However, middle management is responsible for assuring the cooperation of its staff in implementing CM on a day-to-day basis.

In small or medium-size companies, the general manager or a key administrator may be assigned responsibility for designing and implementing a configuration management system. In some cases, he/she may obtain the help of a consultant when needed.

9.4 How Should It Be Implemented?

As mentioned, configuration management is a company-wide function and can't be delegated to a department called Configuration Management (although one may be set up as a resource organization to help other functions and to take the initiative in designing and implementing needed CM systems). Therefore, it is important that the system designed be capable of being implemented by the working staff. The following guidelines can help in its implementation:

- Design a system with inputs and comments from all key groups.
- Design a system that makes sense for your company.
- Prepare a system description and submit it to staff.
- Resolve and respond to criticisms or questions related to the system.
- Obtain high-level approval of the system.
- Prepare detailed procedures when necessary.
- Explain the aims, needs and scope of the system to the staff.
- Let people know that as with anything new, problems will be evident during initial implementation and that their help is needed to correct them.
- Periodically review system implementation and take corrective action when needed.

9.5 Baseline Management

Baseline management is a key element of configuration management. It assures progressive definition of the product by establishing strategic control points called baselines and detailed configuration descriptions. Baseline management covers three phases (usually called conceptual, definition, and acquisition) and six baseline points, three of which are usually contractual* and three internal project baselines. The initial contractual baseline (functional or project requirements) is established by performance and objectives criteria documents that consist of specifications which define project requirements. Once these documents have been approved, any changes to them must be reviewed and approved by management.

When the functional requirements baseline has been further allocated to various elements [called configuration items (CI's)] of the product and their design requirements have been defined by next lower tier specifications, the allocated baseline is established and approved by the customer (or management if the project is internally funded by the company). When this step has been taken, the customer must then approve all changes affecting specifications defining both project and design-to-requirements for the product or its configuration items.

---

*For product development funded by the company, a contractual baseline would be the same as a top management baseline.

Next the project follows a series of baselines (e.g., design, development, and production) into the operational design and prototype or qualification model fabrication and test portion of the acquisition phase (the period between the end of the definition phase and delivery of the last product to the customer.)

As shown in Figure 9-2 the design baseline is represented by a full set of engineering model drawings, preliminary engineering drawings, and support information for the qualification, prototype, and operational product items. The released qualification and prototype drawings, updated performance specification, initial design specifications, test plans, and test procedures form the development baseline. A third baseline, the production baseline makes up the operational product drawing package (prototype update), final specifications (parts, process, and materials documents), final test procedures, etc. (See page 180.)

The next level of configuration baseline authority now consists of design documentation that includes build-to-specifications, engineering drawings, manufacturing and quality data, test procedures, and other detailed technical documents. It is these data that establish the product baseline. The most formal phase of control is begun at this time and the customer insists that he approve all changes affecting the configuration to the extent specified in the contract. A few areas that would require customer or higher management change approval include:

- Performance
- Weight
- Interfaces with other CI's
- Contract price
- Delivery schedule
- Operator safety
- Reliability

Baseline management makes good sense; however, the discipline required to implement comes hard and many companies do not use it. Also for small, simple, routine products, this CM requirement may not be necessary although it could be helpful in managing a small project if tailored to its needs. For more difficult projects, involving a schedule that exceeds a year and the design, development, and fabrication of a high-technology product, the absence of a formal baseline management system can result in major schedule slippages and costs.

> **Case in Point:** One company, staffed with some of the best scientists and engineers, found that the absence of a baseline management system resulted in numerous backslidings from the conceptual, development, and design phases of the project. By failing to

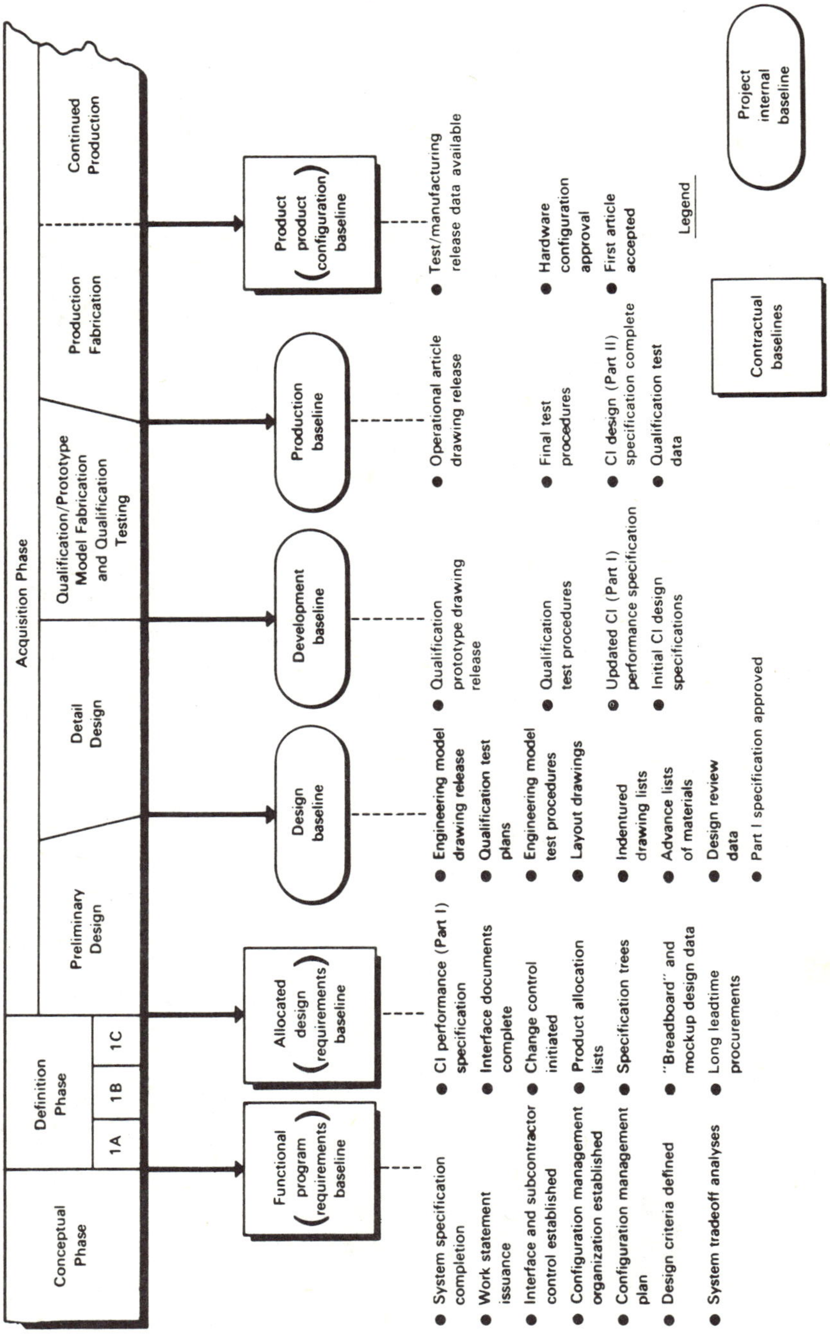

Figure 9-2. Typical Baselines

Used with permission of Wiley-Interscience, New York;
"Fundamentals of Configuration Management," Samaras and Czerwinski, 1971, p. 8

establish firm baselines as the product evolved from conception to final design, the project was kept in a highly fluid and dynamic state. Since baselines were never established by mutual agreement of engineering and management, changes were relatively easy to make. Engineers, being perfectionists by nature, never tired of making improvements to the design.

The result was that cost of development exceeded the contract value by four times and the customer lost confidence in the company's ability-to get the job done.

It should be emphasized that baselines can do five things for higher management when it really wants to manage internal product development:

1. Provide management with an opportunity to formally assess project progress in discrete steps.
2. Help ensure the product is on the right course before it has gone too far awry.
3. Establish a mutually and explicitly agreed-to design status, which cannot be easily tracked back on without management knowledge and agreement.
4. Allow management to cut off a project that is floundering with little chance of success. Thus, funds can be conserved or transferred to a more promising product.
5. Allow management to temporarily stop work on a project because of funding problems or a higher priority task. The baseline provides a hard reference point from which to reinstate the project in the future without returning to ground zero.

9.6 Typical Documents Used for CM

A variety of documents are used to achieve effective configuration management. These include industry-wide specifications, drawings, procedures, operators manuals, and parts lists. It is beyond the scope of this chapter to describe them in detail. However, sample documents are given in "Industrial Documentation Handbook," published by Prentice-Hall, Inc., in 1978. Engineering drawing documents are described in "Engineering Graphics Desk Book," published by Prentice-Hall in 1975.

A few control accounting documents are included in Figures 9-3 through 9-8 to illustrate the types of documents that are needed to implement a configuration management system. These are:

Engineering release form: makes sure there is a record of the engineer's authorization to release a configuration document for use by manufacturing, purchasing, etc. Also provides inputs for the as-designed data base.

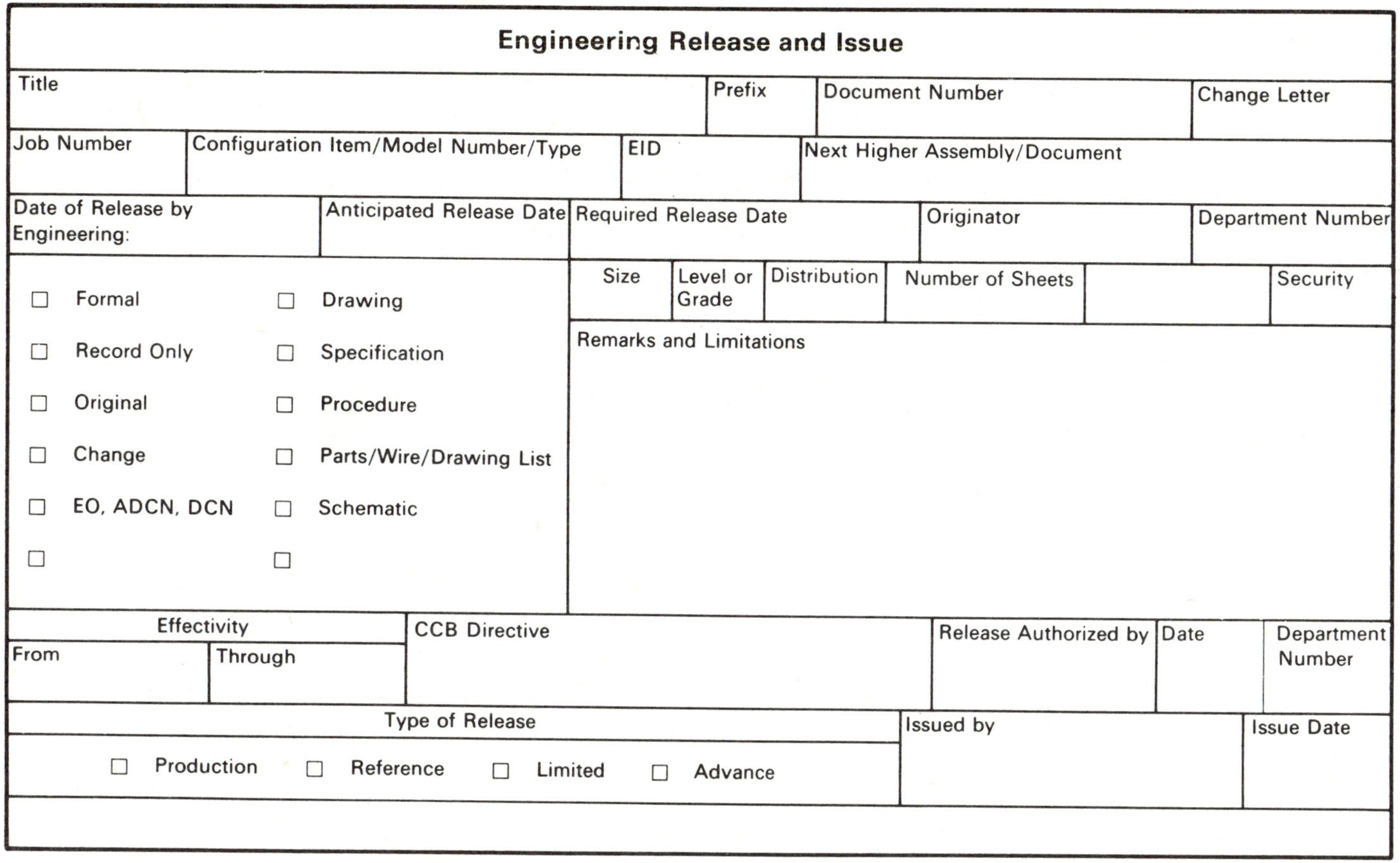

Engineering Release and Issue

Title | Prefix | Document Number | Change Letter

Job Number | Configuration Item/Model Number/Type | EID | Next Higher Assembly/Document

Date of Release by Engineering: | Anticipated Release Date | Required Release Date | Originator | Department Number

☐ Formal ☐ Drawing
☐ Record Only ☐ Specification
☐ Original ☐ Procedure
☐ Change ☐ Parts/Wire/Drawing List
☐ EO, ADCN, DCN ☐ Schematic
☐ ☐

Size | Level or Grade | Distribution | Number of Sheets | | Security

Remarks and Limitations

Effectivity: From | Through | CCB Directive | Release Authorized by | Date | Department Number

Type of Release: ☐ Production ☐ Reference ☐ Limited ☐ Advance | Issued by | Issue Date

Figure 9-3. Engineering Release Form

Used with permission of Wiley-Interscience, New York; "Fundamentals of Configuration Management," Samaras and Czerwinski, 1971, p. 98

Out Out Out

Document Number 123456

Title Preamplifier

Project Number 4001 | CI Seismometer M201

NHA-Document 123000 | Classification U[a]

Originator's Name T. T. Brandoux | Department 34

Location 11174 Foothill, Claremont, Calif. | Size A B | Sheets 2 1

Date Released	Change Notice Number	Grade / Level	Distribution[a] Code	Remarks	Change Letter
8/20/70		2	D	Prototype	N/C[a]
10/11/70		2	D	Re-release-original lost	N/C
1/2/71		1	D	Flight	A
2/10/71	EO 0003	2	D		A-1
2/19/71	EO 007	2	D		A-2
3/2/71	EO 008	2	D		A-3
3/21/71	EO 031	2	D		A-4
4/14/71	EO 0101	2	D		A-5
4/24/71	EO 0112	2	D		A-6
4/24/71	DCN 0022	1	D	Revised drawing	B
6/3/71	EO 0236	2	D	Drawing is obsolete	N/A

Status Card

[a] Dist = Distribution
U = Unclassified
N/C = No Change
DCN = Design Change Notice

Figure 9-4. Document Status Record

Used with permission of Wiley-Interscience, New York; "Fundamentals of Configuration Management," Samaras and Czerwinski, 1971, p. 180

Change Request

Date ____

Revision ____

CR ____________

Contract Number ____________ CI P/N ________ CI Name ____________

Item Affected (P/N) ________________ Name ________________

Next Higher Assembly P/N ____________

Description of Change

Effectivity: S/N ___ Through S/N ____ Priority: ☐ Emergency ☐ Urgent ☐ Routine

☐ Production ☐ Rework ☐ Retrofit Model Affected: Engineering ☐

Remarks:

Prototype ☐

Qualification ☐

Operational ☐

Spares ☐

Class I ☐ Class II ☐

Accepted ☐ Rejected ☐

Originator:	Configuration Manager:	Engineering:
____________ ____ Date	____________ ____ Date	____________ ____ Date

Figure 9-5. Sample Change Request Form

Used with permission of Wiley-Interscience; "Fundamentals of Configuration Management,; Samaras and Czerwinski, 1971, p. 79

Change Cost and Scheduling Estimate	Date	Number ______
	Revision	Project ______

Contract Number ______ CI P/N ______ CI Name ______

Change Request Number ______ Assembly Affected P/N ______

Models Affected ______ Name ______

Cost Estimate

Direct Labor	Burden Rate	Hours	Rate/Hour	Total Cost	Job Number

Materials

Item: ______

Travel: ______

Total Cost (includes G and A) ______

Schedule (Workdays from Go-Ahead)

Go-Ahead Date ______ Completion Date ______

Drawings and EO's ______ Specification Revs. ______

Test Procedures ______ Parts Received ______

Tooling ______ Manufacturing Planning ______

Planning and Control Manager	Date	Project Manager	Date
Configuration Manager	Date		

Figure 9-6. Sample Change Cost and Schedule Estimate

Used with permission of Wiley-Interscience; "Fundamentals of Configuration Management," Samaras and Czerwinski, 1971, p. 80

DISCREPANCY REPORT - DESIGN VS. AS BUILT FOR CI S/N—151

CI NAME: ELEC INSTL, ENGINE C PKG   CONFIGURED ITEM PART NO. 09778 -001   CI NO. E318   REV

PROGRAM LEMDEN   CONTRACT NAS9-11   DATE 13 OCT 19XX

SEQ NO.	PART NUMBER	IND	BASIC NOUN	ENGR ASSEMBLY	NHA QTY	DS EO	P-R-S E	P-R-S M	TAC E M	RELB E	RELB M	MFG SER	MFG LOT NO.	PURCHASE ORDER NUMBER	MSO/KIS WORK ORDER
C24430	SP0213-1	3	INDENT STRAP	228791-001	1				S L					J3322 -1 -1	
C24440	MS21980-156	3	FERRULE,	228791-001	AR				L	1	2			H3010 -1	
C24450	MS21980-175	3	FERRULE,	228791-001	AR				L	1	2			H3011 -1	
C24460	MS21980-187	3	FERRULE,	228791-001	AR				L	1	2			J33051	
C24470	MS21980-205	3	FERRULE,	228791-001	AR				L					J3259	
C24490	MS21981-096	3	FERRULE,	228791-001	AR				L					H3009 -1	
C25500	MS21981-101	3	FERRULE,	228791-001	AR				L					H3009 -1	
C25510	MS21981-115	3	FERRULE,	228791-001	AR				L					H3009 -1	
C29300	C224538-002	3	BOOT,JCT	228789-001	1	C	C1	B	L					K7255 -5 -1	
C29400	C224539-001	3	BOOT,	228789-001	2	C	C1	B	L				351-E-	K3330R	
C29500	C224539-002	3	BOOT,	228789-001	1	C	C1	B	L				351-B-	K7255 -2 -1	
C29600	C224540-003	3	BOOT,	228789-001	1	C	C1	C1	L					K7255 -2 -1	
C29700	C224540-004	3	BOOT,	228789-001	1	C	C1	B	L				351-B-		L0754 -669-1
C29800	C225184-001	3	BOOT,JCT-	228789-001	1	C	C2	B	L				351-A-	K7255 -3 -1	
C29900	C225185-001	3	BOOT,JCT-	228789-001	1	C	C1	B	L				351-D-	P0903 -3	

Figure 9-7. Configuration Discrepancy Report

Used with permission of Prentice-Hall, Inc., "Industrial Documentation Handbook," Thomas T. Samaras, 1978, p. 334

AS DESIGNED/AS BUILT PART TRACEABILITY BY P. O. DATE OCT 19, 19XX

PART NUMBER	MFG	CI NO.	CI SER	SEQ NO.	IND	ENGR ASSEMBLY	NHA QTY	DR EO	O K	P-R-S E M	TAC E M	RELB E M	MFG SER	MFG LOT NO.	PURCHASE ORDER NUMBER	MSO/KIS WORK ORDER
MS21980-261		E318	151	C60000	4	228796-001	AR				L				H3009 -1	
MS21981-096		E318	151	C20155	3	227949-001	AR				L				H3009 -1	
MS21981-096		E318	151	C33100	3	228789-001	AR				L				H3009 -1	
MS21981-096		E318	151	C24490	3	228791-001	AR				L				H3009 -1	
MS21981-096		E318	151	C59500	4	228796-001	AR				L				H3009 -1	
MS21981-101		E318	151	C33200	3	228789-001	AR				L				H3009 -1	
MS21981-101		E318	151	C25500	3	228791-001	AR				L				H3009 -1	
MS21981-101		E318	151	C59550	4	228796-001	AR				L				H3009 -1	
MS21981-115		E218	151	C25510	3	228791-001	AR				L				H3009 -1	
MS21981-219		E318	151	C33300	3	228789-001	AR									
MS21981-219		E318	151	C59650	4	228796-001	AR									

Figure 9-8. Part Traceability to Purchase Order List

Used with permission of Prentice-Hall, Inc., "Industrial Documentation Handbook," Thomas T. Samaras, 1978, p. 317

Document status card: an historical record for each document. Indicates the latest authorized release or change status of document.

Change request: a formal technique for describing, reviewing, and authorizing a proposed change to an approved product configuration.

Change cost and scheduling estimate: a supplementary document that provides a cost and schedule analysis of a proposed change.

Engineering order: a document that formally revises an approved engineering document. It is usually attached to the document until five EO's are issued and the document must be revised for clarity and reissued.

Depending on the company, an EO may be called a design change notice or engineering change notice. See Figure 5-5 (page 108).

Stop Order: a document for stopping work on a product because of an upcoming change that will require new parts or different fabrication requirements. Helps reduce rework and receipt of unneeded parts. See Figure 5-2 (page 100).

Deviation request and authorization: a document that allows a change from official configuration documents for a limited application to specific serial numbered products. A deviation request usually refers to a change before it has occurred while a waiver allows an already accomplished change to be accepted by quality control. See Figure 5-7 (page 116).

Configuration discrepancy report: a configuration accounting document that shows product discrepancies between the hardware and the approved engineering configuration documents.

Part traceability to purchase order list: an accounting document that allows tracing a part or material to its purchase order. This is necessary when a part is defective and needs to be traced to its supplier for corrective action.

9.7 Checklist for Minimum CM Requirements

Regardless of whether a formal system for configuration management exists, certain minimum requirements apply to any company that plans to stay in business for a long time. Table XIII gives a checklist for determining whether your organization meets these minimum requirements. If your company does not have all of these CM elements, careful consideration should be given to adding them soon because virtually all successful manufacturing and construction companies have found them necessary for efficient operations.

TABLE XIII

CHECKLIST FOR MINIMUM CM REQUIREMENTS

- Do you have a company-wide engineering document and part numbering system?
- Do you have an independent release and record control center for the entire company?
- Do you have a catalog of approved engineering documents required by your company, including their formats and content requirements?
- Do you have a change control system that is followed by the staff and which requires management involvement?
- Do you have a purchase order rider that establishes minimum requirements for document identification, change control, and part number control or interchangeability requirements?
- Do you have a document tree or computer index that identifies all the documents required for the product and what other documents they are subordinate to or superior to in the product structure and their release status?
- Do you have an index that gives the number of times a part or item is used in a product?
- Do you have an as-built list for each product that tells you exactly which documents were used to build it and the serial numbers of the parts installed in it?
- Do you have a formal system for controlling changes to interfaces within the company and between project and other companies or contractors?
- Do you require lists of deliverable hardware and software (word documents) to be prepared at the beginning of a project so that everyone knows what is required?

9.8 Where to Get More Information

The Government has printed a number of manuals describing configuration management requirements and systems. The Department of Defense, NASA, Navy, and Army may be contacted for how to get copies of these documents or they may be obtained from the Superintendent of Documents in Washington, D.C. A book by Samaras and Czerwinski, "Fundamentals of Configuration Management," is available from Wiley-Interscience, N.Y.

Seminars are conducted by consultants like Rudy H. Kempter, KRI, 900 National Press Building, Washington, D.C., and universities.

9.9 Pitfalls to Watch Out for

A low-cost and successful CM system is difficult to obtain. It requires high-level attention and top-notch professional people to implement properly. To minimize the dangers involved in implementing CM, keep these pitfalls in mind:

- Beware of using CM technicians or cultists to design and implement your system. People with only a little knowledge or without professional-level system management experience will foist a complex and unworkable system on the company if management abdicates its responsibility. The management and staff must insist on understanding what each component in the system will do for the company and why it is needed.
- Controls and requirements must be based on real need and justifiable in terms of cost vs. benefits. If the controls will not result in improved schedule compliance and considerable cost savings, they should be rejected (except when they are needed for safety).
- Don't try to implement a CM system to supplant responsible performance on the staff's part; e.g., if an engineer is insensitive to configuration identification and control requirements, the system won't fix things up by itself.
- Inadequate funds for proper planning and training.
- Overreaction to CM requirements and needs.
- Failure to enforce system requirements—if a requirement is set up, then it must be followed. Otherwise, get rid of it.
- Failure to periodically review system for missing elements or no longer needed requirements or documents.
- Manager assigned is ambitious and builds an empire that progressively increases the energy and funds required to maintain the CM system.
- Frequent CM system design improvements and changes create confusion and waste the staff's time and energy.

10

Benefits and Risks in Using Small Computers

Computer systems are no longer the province of large companies. The cost of complete computer systems has fallen so low that most companies can afford to pay $4,000 to buy or rent a small computer along with an output printer, TV display, and data storage units. Many of these small systems are surprisingly effective; for example, many can provide the computing power of a $400,000 system of 15 years ago.[1] With the rapid pace of computer development, the installation of a computer in a company of 10 or 20 people has become profitable when it can be used for sound applications.

> **Case in Point:** A $1.5 million firm had a little computer installed in the company. The computer, keyboard, CRT display, and printer fit on a desk top.
>
> The head of the firm reported that the computer cut paper work time by more than half and provided better organized, and more, information than the old manual methods.

While computers—small or large—are not always practical, managers should be aware of their capabilities, cost, and application problems. This chapter provides some of this background. However, an in-depth treatment of computerized management techniques is available from the book: "Computerized Project Management Techniques in the Manufacturing and Construction Industries," Prentice-Hall, Inc., 1979.

[1] "Going After the Small-business Market," *Business Week*, May 16, 1977, p. 51.

10.1 What Is a Low-Cost Computer? How Does It Differ from a Full-Scale Computer?

A low-cost computer is a scaled-down version of the computers often seen in large companies. Years ago, when computers used vacuum tubes and transistors, the quantity of these devices needed to provide the required processing capabilities resulted in very large machines. Over the years, however, miniaturization technology has advanced greatly, especially during our space program, when small computers were a necessary ingredient for success. The extensive use of integrated circuits, microprocessors, and chips allowed the size of computers to decline sharply along with costs in labor, materials, maintenance, and operation.

The major components of small and large computers are the same. They include:

- A data processor unit.
- An input device for allowing people to tell the processor what to do.
- A memory for storing instructions and data resulting from input and processing operations.
- An output device for allowing the processor or memory to provide data to the user.
- A user who defines the problem, tells the computer what to do, and interprets and uses the data provided by the computer.

The differences between large and small computers are primarily in capability, size, and number of peripheral devices available. Small computers have limited capability because they have less expensive and fewer parts and components. Thus, their speed of processing, precision, and the amount of information that can be handled are much less than those of big computers. Also, they can't perform as many operations or functions as large computers.

Depending on the application, these differences may not be significant. Determination of what size computer is the most practical for a company requires some expert advice. This could include the technical representative of the computer supplier, an experienced computer systems expert on your staff, or an independent consultant. Whichever route is followed, the manager cannot give up his responsibility for the final decision. Therefore, he/she must take an active role in the evaluation of company needs and selection of the right computer.

10.2 What Are Its Benefits and Applications?

The benefits of computers lie in the areas of saving time and labor when numerous computations or data manipulations are needed. (Data manipulations include comparing data against each other or a standard and sorting them into different locations in the computer memory.) Computers can also reduce the amount of paper reports and records by keeping large amounts of information on magnetic tape or discs. Accuracy, speed, and repeatability are other good qualities associated with computers. In some cases, a computer can perform calculations in hours that would take a person years to perform.

The business applications of small computers are already great and continuing to increase. They can be used in performance measurement and general management, material management, accounting and finance, drawing preparation, and configuration management. An abbreviated list of small computer applications follows:

Non-Technical	Technical[2]
Payroll	Printed-circuit artwork
General ledger	Schematics
Accounts receivable/payable	Mechanical assemblies and details
Advance payroll	Wiring diagrams
Inventory control	Maps
Statistical analysis	Parts lists
Purchase order processing	PERT charts
Sales analysis	Flow charts
Writes invoices, generates checks	Plots of numerical data
Prepares government reports	Perspectives, isometrics, three-dimensional views
Financial statements	
Job status reports	Paper tapes for driving N/C equipment

According to one small computer leasing company, the preceding list can be expanded to hundreds of off-the-shelf application programs that can be plugged into the computer. (A computer program is a series of instructions prepared in a form that the computer can understand and follow.)

10.3 Who Can Use a Small Computer?

The use of a small computer depends on two key factors. The first is whether the work done at the company can be performed more efficiently

[2]This requires a special plotter, software or digitizing devices.

and accurately than the present methods. The second is whether the company can afford the initial investment and temporary decline in productivity during the installation and early operating stages. Any new equipment inevitably involves delays, mistakes, and problems with people and hardware. Therefore, in spite of optimistic claims of how well a computer system worked at a neighboring company, each company has unique situations that can affect the degree of problems associated with any computer installation or application.

Before deciding to purchase or lease a computer, these questions should be asked:

1. What size computer, associated software, peripherals (e.g., printers, disc memories, and tape drives), and manpower can the company afford to invest during the 6 to 24 months required for the installation?
2. Do I have the people and time to properly analyze my needs, problems, and applications for a computer?
3. Do I have the time to do an accurate cost-benefit analysis to find out whether a computer will pay for itself over the next few years?
4. Do I have a good feel for near-term business expectations? (A sharp downturn in business could abort the project when it's only halfway implemented.)
5. Is this the best time to introduce a new system? (Perturbations and problems created may have unacceptable repercussions during a peak work load period.)

The answers should be "yes" for questions 2 through 5 before you decide to obtain a small computer.

10.4 Can You Install and Operate It Yourself?

Some microcomputers are designed to be installed and operated by people with little or no computer expertise. However, this is not recommended for most applications. Professional help, at least for the initial stage, should be obtained to assure that the best installation and implementation of the equipment are made, and to train your staff properly in its use. A computer professional can save you money by doing the following:

- More quickly and efficiently design and install the computer system.
- Resolve operational problems more efficiently.
- Deal with the supplier more effectively if problems with the equipment occur.

- Identify the kinds of applications that are not cost-effective. (Novices are likely to develop new uses for fun or without serious analysis of the cost effectivity of the computer. The idea that the computer is a toy can lead to much wasted time and trouble if its applications are not controlled by management.)

In summary, while it is possible to install a small computer without expert help, it is probably less efficient in the long run and can drain much labor from other jobs that your staff can do much more efficiently.

10.5 What Special Controls Are Needed?

Even a microcomputer system is a complex instrument. Therefore, its physical protection is necessary. Controls here might include its operation by properly trained people and location in a locked room. In addition, since the data stored in it may be private or sensitive, controls may be needed on who has access to it and what that person may do with the information printed out. Regulation of who may change data is also needed. Allowing anyone in the company to modify data stored in the computer can create a lot of mischief as well as serious problems. For example, altered business or project data may be used by management for a critical decision that could have been different if the data had not been changed by someone who didn't realize that he/she had introduced incorrect changes.

10.6 What Characteristics Should You Look for?

Once a computer system has been determined to be cost-effective or necessary because of its speed or accuracy, a number of factors need to be considered before a computer is purchased or leased. Before discussing the specific features to consider, an overview of a typical small computer in terms of desirable characteristics follows. It should:

1. Be a desk-top system
2. Work in your existing environment
3. Operate with existing staff
4. Work with off-the-shelf programs
5. Allow programming the computer in plain English
6. Handle all the computing needs of your company or department.
7. Be integrated with the existing, larger computer if necessary. (Small computer systems sometimes are used when the main computer is overloaded or near capacity.)

10.6.1—Simplicity: The system should be easy to install and operate. Normally, a small computer operates off a conventional 110VAC outlet and is turned on without complex procedures. It is programmed with a Program Generator that makes the process of instructing the computer relatively easy. Programming is usually done in some form of BASIC language,[3] which doesn't require a professional programmer's skills and can be readily learned by just about anyone. (Other techniques, such as COBOL and PL-1, are more difficult to learn and use.)

Another characteristic of a small computer that should be considered is whether it can operate in two modes. Some computers have foreground/background modes that allow the computer to work on two jobs at the same time; e.g., someone can be entering customer orders while the printer is creating a report.

10.6.2—Plug-in Programs: The availability of already developed and proven programs is a highly desirable feature. Most companies provide a number of off-the-shelf computer programs (software) packaged for commonly performed business functions. These include sales analysis, inventory control, and accounting procedures.

10.6.3—Basic Hardware Available: A variety of hardware should be available to allow for growth in use and new applications. One manufacturer offers this complement of hardware:

- Standard central processing unit
- 16K main memory unit
- Video display (27 lines × 64 characters)
- Typewriter keyboard for inputting instructions
- Random access, high-speed disc drive with a storage capacity of 1.3 million alpha-numeric characters or 2.6 million numerical characters

10.6.4—Modular Construction: Modular construction allows the computer system to be assembled in a variety of configurations to provide for growth and flexibility in use. This feature is achieved by designing various functional units as separate packages that can be easily connected or disconnected to each other to accommodate your needs.

10.6.5—Growth Potential: The capability of expanding your system to meet new demands or needs is another important feature to consider. It is expensive to start off with a small system and then to find out that you

---

[3]Beginner's all-purpose symbolic instruction code.

have outgrown its capacity and must replace it with an entirely new system. A well-designed system will allow the existing hardware to be modified or expanded to accommodate more processing capabilities, greater data storage, or more operators.

10.6.6—Program Generation: Although numerous computer programs are available from suppliers, each company usually has special needs and desires that require special programs to be developed. Ordinarily, a professional programmer is required for this task. However, the manufacturers of small computers have worked hard to develop methods that eliminate the professional programmer and allow just about anyone to develop programs. This simplification is achieved by designing the computer to interpret a few simple instructions provided by the user into the exact programming syntax required for automatically creating the complete program necessary to achieve the new application.

10.6.7—Report Generation: Again, the suppliers have developed software or programs to produce standard reports. However, as time passes, new reports may be needed. Therefore, it is desirable for the computer to have a software package that will allow the user to create new report formats as simply as possible.

10.6.8—Maintainability: All equipment needs some maintenance and breaks down periodically. The question is how easy is it to perform routine maintenance and can it be done by your staff or must the computer supplier's people do it. Also how often does the equipment break down? What is the mean-time-between-failures? The longer the better. In addition, what response time can you expect when a malfunction occurs? A 2-day or longer delay may be acceptable for your company. In some companies, a 4-hour delay may mean disaster.

10.6.9—Cost: If the computer system is bought, then the selling price is important. One manufacturer offers a fairly complete system for under $4,000. Others lease sophisticated small computer systems for $350 a month plus monthly maintenance costs of $155.

What is the history of increased prices for hardware, software, and maintenance? Some companies may be more expensive in the long run, even though their initial equipment cost is lower, because repair and replacement costs may be higher or be increasing at a faster rate than other suppliers.

Table XIV illustrates the costs of various items for a very low cost computer system.

TABLE XIV

TYPICAL COSTS FOR AN INEXPENSIVE MICRO-COMPUTER

Hardware		Software (Ready made)	
Basic computer:	$800	Payroll:	$20
12″ video display:	200	Mailing list:	40
Recorder:	50	Statistical analysis:	30
Expansion 16K memory:	300	Editor-assembler:	30
Expansion interface:	300	General ledger	100
Line printer:	1300		
TV screen printer:	600	Maintenance (for a	
Mini disk:	500	$500/mo rental	
		system):	155

10.7 Typical Hardware Available for a Computer System

Less than a dozen pieces of equipment are necessary to create a computer system. These include the processor, memory, tape drive, inquiry CRT, printer, chair, and desk or table to hold the equipment. A brief description of each item follows:

Processor: The processor is the brains of the computer. It contains the complex circuitry and microprocessors required to perform computations, comparisons, additions, subtractions, sorts, multiplications, and divisions. It is usually the most expensive item in the system although the printer may cost more.

Tape Drive: A tape drive is an electro-mechanical device that allows information to be recorded on magnetic tape and to be read back into the main memory or processor when required. It is a relatively cheap storage medium.

Inquiry CRT: A video display console for providing instantaneous output data to the user. It is similar to a television set, except that it produces words and graphs instead of pictures. A control keyboard is usually provided so that the user can control the display; e.g., move each line up one notch as he/she reads the data.

Key Board: A keyboard, similar to a typewriter, is frequently used with a computer system. This keyboard can be used to input instructions and data or to print out information on paper.

Printer: Printers are output devices that allow the computer to produce output data that can be read by the user. Printers can be inexpensive or expensive, depending on quality requirements, speed and size. A fairly inexpensive ($1,300) printer will print from 60 to 110 characters per second on paper about 10 inches wide.

Peripheral Disk Memory: Disk memories are popular off-line storage devices that are fairly inexpensive but have considerable storage capacity. For example, a mini-disk can be purchased for about $500 that can hold up to 80,000 (80K) characters. It has a transfer rate of 125K bits per second and an average access time of 1/2 second. Mini-disks can be connected together to extend the storage capacity well beyond that of a single disk.

10.8 Risks and Pitfalls in Using Computers

As was mentioned, computers like all sophisticated equipment have risks and pitfalls to watch out for. The primary risk in the use of a computer is that it will be ignored by management. When this happens, computer usage may continue to expand beyond the limits originally defined and users will find performance slipping. Delays in processing will get longer, material will be lost or misplaced, and work needed for the well-being of the company will not be done on time. In addition, computer costs will continue to increase and pressures will build up for newer, faster, and bigger equipment to handle the increased work load. This in turn will require more space or special equipment and facilities. Manpower requirements will also jump. When the computer facility is out of control, it will suck valuable energy from the company's resources and the company's competitive position in its industry will suffer. Of course, if this growth pattern is pandemic, competitors will have the same problems and their decline in efficiency may keep pace with your own.

What makes the computer growth potential a problem is that higher managers generally don't understand computers and they tend to keep away from its operations fearing that their efforts to manage this function will reveal their ignorance or do more harm than good.

While a small company can better manage its small computer because it is designed to be understood and operated by non-computer specialists, there is danger that success in one area, may lead to over-enthusiasm or confidence that may result in misapplications which create added costs through unneeded expansion or inefficient operations.

The pitfalls to avoid in the use of a computer system include:

1. Computer application ground rules are not defined, published or enforced by management.
2. Periodic management audits are not conducted to evaluate the cost effectiveness and performance of the computer system.
3. Management has given up its responsibility for the proper use and operation of the system.

4. A formal change control system is not set up to review and approve all changes in equipment, applications, and operations.
5. Periodic evaluation of operating systems and applications are not held to eliminate wasteful practices or to improve the system.
6. Operating procedures are not written down and kept current.

10.9 Where You Can Get Help

Managers interested in acquiring a computer system can obtain help from several sources. However, the manager must invest some time to assure a cost-effective and successful introduction of a small computer into the organization. Help is available from books on computers—especially practical books that deal with applications of computers. These books usually provide considerable data for evaluating needs and computer equipment.[4]

Journals and brochures from suppliers can be readily obtained for study. Suppliers will also provide advice, demonstrations, and lists of satisfied customers to contact.

Service bureaus are also available to help develop a system and computer programs that are needed for your specific applications or problems.

When hiring people during growth periods or replacements for people who have left, require some expertise in the use of computers. Thus, some in-house capability will be available. This expertise may involve scientific or business applications.

Consultants are also available to help in defining company's needs, designing the system, contacting suppliers, developing specifications and requests for proposals. They can also negotiate the best deal for the company and coordinate the installation and operation of the computer until the staff has everything under control.

---

[4]See Sippl & Dahl, *Computer Power for the Small Business*, Prentice-Hall, Inc., 1979, and Samaras & Yensuang, *Computerized Project Management Techniques for Manufacturing & Construction Industries*, Prentice-Hall, Inc., 1979.

11

Improving Interfaces and Relations with Other Functional Groups

Industrial complexity and the need for increasing specialization have brought interface problems. The impact of these interface problems can be very large on both the company and individual manager. Therefore, explicit attention to interfaces is necessary for effective management.

11.1 Benefits of Good Interfaces

Good interfaces with other functions in the company result in improved understanding of each other's problems and needs. This improved understanding promotes a cooperative attitude and better communication which in turn reduce conflicts, delays, and wasted effort. When problems do arise, they can be settled more quickly and with fewer political repercussions. For example, when two interfacing functions have a disagreement, the managers of each organization can settle the issue quietly without a barrage of memos and ill feelings which often accompany conflicts between different functions that can't work well together or are competitive with each other.

When managers of two or more groups have smooth interfaces among themselves this generally carries over to their people. The result is an open, trustful, and good-natured association that promotes increased productivity and morale. Of course, problems will inevitably arise, but the emotional poison that surrounds groups in friction with each other is missing. Thus, much more objective evaluations of problems can be made by the staff and management. In addition, little or no time will be spent gloating over who was wrong or right.

> **Case in Point:** An inexperienced manager was assigned responsibility for a department. He immediately instituted certain changes and focused his attention on his own people and organization. He did not develop contacts or communication lines with the managers of other departments and divisions. When these other groups complained about problems or asked for special assistance, he ignored them or argued things were okay as they were.
>
> After a year, the managers of the other groups pressured the division director to have him replaced.
>
> A new manager was brought in to straighten out the interface problem. His interest in other parts of the company as well as his department resulted in much better relations, and the complaints ceased.

The specific benefits of good interfaces with other groups within the company include:

- Better flow or exchange of information.
- A sincere desire for each function to perform well.
- Mutual trust and understanding.
- Less wasted energy in unneeded meetings, memos, and individual conflicts.
- Less paper work; when two groups don't trust each other, they tend to want everything written down to protect themselves.
- Less backbiting, with improved morale.
- Help is given by other groups when another is in trouble; e.g., managers on good relations will lend people to the other manager to help in a crisis. When mutual distrust exists, they will find excuses as to why they can't spare anyone.
- Much more efficient resolution of real problems. When people don't have emotional conflicts or feel on a war footing, they are less defensive, more rational, and think better.
- People at the working level will work better with people in different groups instead of taking adversary positions.

11.2 How Your People Can Destroy Your Image

Managers too often judge a person on their staff by how they relate to them. This is a dangerous practice because there is a natural tendency to treat the boss differently from people outside the group. This tendency to argue or offend people outside the group is made worse when the boss is fairly strong and normally backs up his/her people when conflicts occur with other functions or groups.

The secretary with an ugly style is a typical example of how a manager's staff can alienate people. She is an extension of her boss and is very influential in creating a constructive or destructive image for him. Most companies have a few secretaries who are hard to work with. Yet, these secretaries are retained. Apparently the managers don't realize the transfer of the negative image to them that often occurs. People do talk about bad secretaries and they do lose some respect for their bosses. Oppositely, a friendly and courteous secretary helps transfer good feeling to her boss.

> **Case in Point:** One manager in a West Coast company had a secretary with a smile in her voice who made everyone feel good. She treated everyone the same, regardless of his/her position in the company. One manager remarked that he couldn't help liking her boss a little more for having such a pleasant and helpful person working for him.

Of course, secretaries are not the only people who can give their boss a bad image. People in support groups are in very sensitive positions and can really do a lot of harm to their managers. This harm can take the form of using outside consultants instead of the service group, reduced budgets, and pressure to replace the manager as was described earlier in this chapter.

Support groups exist to help the people who produce the basic products of the company. Yet, the people who work in these groups take on an air of superiority with respect to the real producers. This not only causes personal conflicts, but can cripple the effectiveness of the service group and its manager.

> **Case in Point:** A section leader from engineering was talking about a work breakdown structure problem with a representative of the engineering services group. Another person from the service group came in and began listening to the conversation. Suddenly he burst out, with considerable venom, that engineers never follow instructions and have to be forced to do things right. The engineer made a grimace and left the room. The section leader was, of course, insulted and told other engineers and managers about the incident. Even though the manager of the service group was not directly responsible, the section leader later indicated that he had lost some respect for the manager because he kept the person in his department.

The above example is repeated frequently in the average company and sometimes it is someone from a producing group who insults people of support groups. The repercussions may be more subtle in this case, but the manager of the producing group can still be hurt. For example, the supporting group may tend to be less cooperative, keep information of value from the producing organization, or avoid warning the manager of an approaching problem.

How can the manager avoid the creation of interface problems by his people? This is not easy because the incidents that occur are usually outside the manager's view. Thus, if no one complains to him/her there's no way to know. However, a few steps can be taken to minimize the problem:

1. Periodically talk with people in outside groups to find out if there are any personality or attitude problems. (People will not usually volunteer this information because they don't want to be part of the problem or to cause bad feelings.)
2. Hold meetings on a regular basis to review the style and interface relations you want to characterize your group.
3. Emphasize the service aspect of the group.
4. Train or get rid of people who create interface problems because of hostile, superior, or unfriendly attitudes or working styles.
5. Urge your people to help each other from projecting a bad image to outside groups.

11.3 Analyze the Needs of Other Groups

Any serious attempt to improve relations with other groups or functions requires an understanding of their needs, problems, and objectives. The manager needs to first identify all the functions that he or his people interface with during the year. This includes engineering, manufacturing, planning, contracts, marketing, purchasing, publications, and finance. Then he/she needs to list these functions in order of criticality to his/her function. This gives him/her a priority list so that he/she can concentrate on the most important functions first. Next he/she needs to define the responsibilities and needs/objectives of each function. The manager should do this first based on his own perceptions and experience. Then he/she should meet with the manager of each function to determine if this information is consistent with the needs of the functions being supplied support services. By following this procedure any serious misconceptions about each function will stand out when the manager compares his/her list and the list prepared after talking with the group's manager.

After the list is revised, the manager should have the functional group review it to be sure it is right. Then he/she can discuss it with the staff so they will better understand each function's activities and needs.

The end result could be an interface chart as shown in Figure 11-1.

Table of interface responsibilities and needs*

Interface Personnel	Responsibilities	Needs
Manager/Boss	Gives over-all view of product concept and use. Sets key goals. Provides resources. Approves expenditures and major actions. Solves major problems. Notifies staff of changes in plans/goals/requirements. Approves major changes in design.	Notification of problems. Status reports. New or urgent needs. Early notification of expected schedule slippage, failure to meet technical requirements or to stay within budget. Notice of exceptional achievements/progress.
Designer/Draftsman	Prepares schematics, layouts, assembly drawings, parts lists, etc. Identifies documents and assigns part numbers. Follows change control system and procedures. Informs of design simplification and improvement possibilities, weak design areas and potential problems. Meets schedule and budget and reports on status. Meets standards for drawing quality and format. Gets proper approval of design documents before release to manufacturing.	Product requirements. Design goals and potential problems. Special features and potential problems. Schedule and budget. Notification of changes in requirements/design. Special processes or specifications that must be used and test procedure numbers. Parts selection criteria. Manufacturing restraints/considerations. Names of specialists who can help on critical design areas. Test and checkout considerations. Maintenance and repair considerations.

Figure 11-1 Interface Chart

*"Man-man Interface," Thomas T. Samaras. Reprinted with permission of *Electronic Design*, No. 11, 1971, p. 54; copyright Hayden Publishing Co., Inc., 1971.

Interface Personnel	Responsibilities	Needs
Test Engineer	Designs test setups and gets test equipment and facilities ready. Obtains test fixtures. Schedules testing. Writes test procedures. Detects potential problems. Informs of design changes for simpler testing and checkout. Reports status. Determines environmental test conditions.	Configuration and description of product and usage. Test requirements. Special design features. Mounting orientation, limitations and method. Potential danger areas. Schedule and budget. Notification of changes in requirements/plans.
Quality-Assurance and Reliability Engineers	Ensure that product meets minimum quality and reliability standards/requirements. Notify of design/manufacturing/testing weaknesses and problems. Provide adequate inspection and documentation of incoming parts, material control and hardware. Monitor special processes. Review and approve all documents.	Technical goals and requirements. Budget and schedule. Description of product. Design data. Special features and quality/reliability standards. Applicable specifications. Notification of changes in requirements or plans.
Sales/Marketing Representative	Analyzes market potential and sales strategy. Produces sales literature. Helps set price for product. Informs of problems or needs.	Description of product, especially new or outstanding features. Product specifications. Scheduled availability of product for distribution. Cost of product.

Figure 11-1 Interface Chart (continued)

Interface Personnel	Responsibilities	Needs
Procurement Representative	Purchases parts and materials at minimum cost. Notifies vendors of changes in requirements. Notifies of delays/problems. Ensures timely delivery.	General and special parts requirements. Identification of long-lead-time parts. Names of desired suppliers. Specification control documents. Quality and reliability requirements. Priority of cost, quality and delivery time. Clear-cut notification when substitute parts cannot be used.
Technician	Builds and tests prototype. Evaluates operation and troubleshoots. Recommends design improvements. Keeps laboratory notebook up to date.	Performance requirements and criteria. Schedule and budget. Special features/problems. Notification of changes in requirements or plans.
Manufacturing Engineer	Provides tooling and fixtures. Acquires special skills. Meets schedule and budget and quality requirements. Informs of methods for improving productibility of hardware. (Productibility refers to accessibility of parts and realistic tolerances and tooling needs).	Clear-cut goals. Accurate, complete and clear production documents. Special product features and needs. Production document release schedule. All materials needed. Identification of special processes or materials to be used—may require special training program. Changes in plans/design. Schedule and budget.

Figure 11-1 Interface Chart (continued)

Interface Personnel	Responsibilities	Needs
Facilities Engineer	Provides work areas and equipment when needed. Modifies work areas for special needs.	Exact facility and equipment needs. Special environmental conditions. Scheduled need of facilities and equipment. Changes in plans.
Accountant	Issues job numbers. Provides weekly expenditure reports. Processes time cards. Provides cumulative expenditure reports. Notifies management of dangerous budget trends.	Description of work. Budget control and reporting needs. Subtask budgets. Changes in budgets. Expenditure alert levels requiring notifications.
Publications Engineer	Provides documents on time and in budget. Meets document specs. Distributes documents to staff. Informs of problems or needs.	Document requirements, schedule and budget. Description of product and project activities. Special features of product. Changes in design, schedule or other requirements. Specifications to be followed.
Configuration Manager	Sets up system for ensuring that product meets all requirements and for controlling changes to its configuration. Keeps records of changes and approvals. Reports status of changes.	Product description and requirements. Schedule and budget. Special requirements related to form, fit and function. Notification of all proposed changes.

Figure 11-1 Interface Chart (continued)

The benefits of this process are improved understanding of each other's functions and hopefully better communication and working relations. A secondary benefit is that the manager being asked about his/her operation will be pleased that you are interested in improving working relations with him/her. Even if the manager has an accurate understanding of outside functions, the preceding process also gives him/her an opportunity to describe his/her own function's needs and problems to the other managers.

11.4 Talk with Other Managers and People

Too often a manager tends to get overwhelmed with too much paper work or other duties. As a result interfacing with people or managers of other functions is neglected. The old saying "out of sight out of mind" still has considerable bearing today. This in turn can reduce effectiveness, for people will often turn to other managers who are visible and involved with day-to-day activities of the company.

Besides being visible, much information can be acquired through increased communication with other managers and people in other groups. Information can be gleaned about morale, problems between other functions, problems with your people, and new developments. Even within the manager's own group, internal interfaces exist and these too can be a source of trouble when ignored. By talking with supervisors and their staff, you can identify and resolve internal difficulties.

> *Caution:* When a manager does get out and talk with people, it is important that any corrective action be taken in a constructive way without undermining or embarrassing other managers or supervisors.

11.5 Explain Your Needs and Problems to Others

As was mentioned in a previous section, other managers need to understand your responsibilities, needs, objectives, and problems so that they can take steps within their groups to help you. No matter how cooperative and friendly, another manager can't help you unless this individual is aware of your needs. *Important:* You cannot assume that because you had a very constructive talk six months ago that the other manager is still conscious of your needs. With time, awareness fades and periodic refreshment is required to assure some degree of positive action.

Methods for refreshing memory include:

- Send a copy of a new memo or other document that deals with the problem or need previously discussed. Add a hand-written note on first sheet referring to discussion of several weeks or months ago related to this subject.
- Go to lunch together and discuss problems and other areas of mutual interest.

- Set up a small meeting to review a specific area that needs better handling.

11.6 Try to Adjust Your Operations to Others' Needs

Serious consideration should be given to changing your methods of operation when they create problems or don't suit the needs of other functions. This is rarely done before things get too far out of control. Often entropy works its way and interfaces gradually deteriorate until a major explosion occurs and a new manager is obtained or a reorganization is effected.

In considering changing your organization to help other groups, it is important to evaluate the impact of the change on the total company. If the change will decrease your function's efficiency with a cost impact of $15,000 a year, but will improve another groups's performance so that its annual operating costs are reduced by $35,000, then the total company will benefit. Net gain: $20,000 a year.

Too often managers refuse to change for another group because of a provincial attitude and self-defense. Elimination of these attitudes and obstacles rests with higher management. For example, when a manager is found who puts the company's welfare above his own department's, higher management should make sure that he/she is recognized and rewarded. Only by immediate and positive actions, can people be encouraged to take this wider view of their functions.

An example of a questionnaire sheet issued by a manager of a design and drafting service group is shown in Figure 11-2. This questionnaire is a technique for finding out what others want so that changes to the group can be made. The questions help provide the group with comments from users on the services and interfaces given. Note that this questionnaire gives habitual complainers an opportunity to bring up a lot of trivial problems, but some responses will be of great value and may lead to changes that will improve the performance of the organization.

Name ______________________________ Date ____________

Department _________________________ Title ____________

Actual Board Experience
Yes ______ No ______

Yrs. of Experience ________

Figure 11-2 Sample Questionnaire for Improving Interfaces

Adapted from George Rowbotham, "Yardstick for Performance Expectations," *Engineering Graphics*, Nov. 1972, p. 17–19.

1 COSTS

How do you rate drafting costs? High________ Acceptable________ Low________
Comments ____
____

2 SCHEDULE

How good is delivery? Ahead ________ On Schedule ________________
Very Late ________
Comments ____
____

3 COMPLETENESS

How do you rate drawing completeness? Excessive ________________
Normal________________ Short ________________________________
(a) What information, if any, could be omitted? ________________________
____
____
(b) What information is generally missing? ____________________________
____

4 QUALITY

How do you rate drawing quality (involving accuracy, errors, and appearance)?
Excellent ________________________________ Poor________ Varies ______
Comments ____

5 UNIFORMITY OF PRACTICE

Is uniformity of drafting practice generally applied? Yes________ No________
Comments ____
____

6 DRAWING SIZES

Is the use of oversized (Roll Size) drawings used excessively?
Yes________ No________
(a) Should reduced scales be used? Yes________ No________
(b) Should multiple sheets be used? Yes________ No________
(c) Could views, sections, notes, etc. be arranged more efficiently?
Yes________ No________
(d) Should drawing sizes be limited? Yes________ No________
What size? ____
Comment ____

7 AUTOMATION

Do you think some, or all, of the drawings could be produced at lower cost with improved quality, by automated drafting or computer graphics? Yes________
No________
Comments ____

Figure 11-2 Sample Questionnaire (continued)

8 LEGIBILITY

How do you rate drawings from the standpoint of legibility? Good ____________
Acceptable __________ Poor __________
Comments ____

9 PRODUCEABILITY

How do you rate the design of parts from the standpoint of produceability (ease of manufacture)?
Good________ Acceptable________ Poor________
Comments ____
____

10 INSTRUCTION (For design & drafting supervisors & engineers only)

What was the extent of instruction to the designer/draftsman required from you?
Excessive________ Normal________ Very Little________
Comments ____

11 COMPLAINTS

What are primary complaints about drawings? ____________________________
____

12 What percentage of the drafting effort involves drawing revisions?
____

13 What can be done to reduce the amount of drawing revisions?
____

14 DESIGN REVIEWS

Are adequate design reviews held? Yes________ No________
Comments ____

15 REPRODUCTION QUALITY

Is the quality of reproduction (drawing prints) satisfactory?
Yes________ No________
Comments ____
____

(a) Does the reduced size printed copy, if used, create any problems?
Yes________ No________
Comments ____
____

Figure 11-2 Sample Questionnaire (continued)

16 DESIGN LAYOUTS

Do you believe adequate design layouts are prepared prior to detailing?
Yes________ No________ Comments ______________________________________

____

(a) Do you believe that design layout work is excessive? Yes________ No________
Comments ____

____

17 SUPERVISION

Do you believe that design & drafting personnel receive adequate supervision?
Yes________ No________ Comments ______________________________________

____

18 MICROFILMING

Are microfilming problems involved? Yes________ No________ Comments ____

19 UNINCORPORATED CHANGES

Are you opposed to unincorporated changes? Yes________ No________ Comments ____

____

(a) If you approve of unincorporated changes, do you believe the quantity of outstanding unincorporated changes should be limited?
If yes, by what quantity? ______________________________________ Max.
(b) Is there an alternate to unincorporated changes?
Comments ____

____

20 TRAINING

Do you think designers, draftsmen & checkers should receive special training on company time?
If yes, on what subjects? ______________________________________

____

21 INKING

Do you believe drawings should be inked? Yes________ No________ Comments

22 COST REDUCTION TECHNIQUES

Do you believe greater advantages (profit dollar savings) could be achieved by advanced cost reduction tools and techniques?

Figure 11-2 Sample Questionnaire (continued)

Yes________ No________

If yes, which practices or tools should be applied?

(a) Cut and paste-ups.________

(b) Typed notes.________

(c) Photo drafting.________

(d) Conventional representation.________

(e) Undimensioned drawings.________

(f) Improved design layouts.________

(g) Improved "on-the-board" supervision.________

(h) The use of improved (from the standpoint of cost reduction and accuracy) engineering tools, such as:

  (1) Mobile drafting tables.________

  (2) Track type drafting machines.________

(i) Improved drafting room manual.________

(j) Expanded drawing (more thorough) checking.________

(k) Improved filing systems (horizontal files for example).

(l) Templates.________

(m) Erasing machines.________

(n) Washable films to permit use of existing drawing detail.________

(o) Replacement of several pieces of equipment which have been obsoleted, by development of a single unit capable of doing the work for all of them.________

Comments ________________________________

(p) Replacement of tools to reduce maintenance costs.________________

Comments ________________________________

(q) The use of drafting film.________

(r) The equipment should be replaced because accurate performance in its use requires more and more effort on the part of employees to get the required results.________ Comments ________________________

____

(s) Replace the equipment by other tools which have come onto the market which can do the job in less time and with greater efficiency at less operating costs.________

Comments ________________________________

(t) Implement new equipment that has been developed so that its use requires less strain upon employees.________

Effective use of tools (corrective measures should be taken when employees begin to devise ways and means of avoiding the use of a particular tool whenever it is possible for them to do so).________

To avoid profit dollar loss, other innovations that should be considered include: ________________________________

____

____

(u) Improved lighting in the drafting room.________

Comments ________________________________

____

Figure 11-2 Sample Questionnaire (continued)

23 Are departures from drawings necessary to achieve proper assembly?
Comments ____
____

(a) How frequent are such departures? ______________________
Comments ____
____
____

(b) Are such departures reported to engineering? Yes________ No________
Comments ____
____
____

24 SUMMARY OF COMMENTS

____
____

Figure 11-2 Sample Questionnaire (continued)

Caution to Managers Receiving Questionnaire: Most people tend to respond with criticism and negative comments. This is as it should be. However, the manager who sends the survey sheet out is opening himself and the staff to comments that are normally unsaid. Therefore, the person filling out the questionnaire should be careful in the use of language; e.g., emotion-packed words, such as lazy, incompetent, and dumb should be avoided. In addition, just as much thought to the good things being done by the group should be given, even if they are not specifically asked for. The manager asking for inputs, can still be turned off by the way in which responses to questions are made. Thus, a well-meaning technique can backfire if other managers are overly critical and insensitive.

Another example of a simpler questionnaire from a Division Manager is shown in Table XV.

TABLE XV

QUESTIONS FOR DEPARTMENT MANAGERS

1. What specific actions do you recommend to improve the morale of ABC Company personnel?
2. Is the division of responsibility among the Engineering Branches of the Engineering Division and between Engineering and other Divisions workable and adequately defined? If not, what improvements are recommended?
3. Are the specific engineering tasks defined in sufficient detail to permit

TABLE XV (Continued)

preparation of accurate budgets and schedules? If not, what improvements are recommended?

4. Do the existing schedule and cost reporting systems give you the information you need to monitor engineering progress and cost vs. time? If not, what improvements do you recommend?
5. What changes, if any, do you recommend in the number and level of required approvals and the functions of the various approval boards?
6. What changes, if any, do you recommend to provide better feedback to the engineers on the capital cost of the components and systems they design?
7. To what extent is it desirable to simplify ABC's administrative procedures? How do you recommend accomplishing any desired simplification?
8. What additional administrative matters require immediate attention?
9. What technical matters require immediate attention?
10. What new areas of product and business development should we pursue?

11.7 Watch Out for Power Plays

The non-political systems-oriented manager needs to recognize that other managers are not like himself and that they may try to maneuver him into a position that hurts his function and the company.

> **Case in Point:** The manager of a large department convinced another manager that it would be more efficient to combine their groups under his leadership. He argued that since his department consisted of only 12 people, it really would be more easy to achieve integrated operations under one overall manager. The other manager agreed and the change was made. However, the less experienced ex-department manager soon found out that the real aim of the other manager was to get control of his operation.

While these kinds of actions are constantly going on—especially in larger companies—they should not deter good managers from being objective about new proposals for consolidation or improved organization and operations. Through a good communication system, however, the manager can hear things from others that may reveal the true intentions of the people recommending the changes.

11.8 Be a Straight Shooter

Devious people may occasionally succeed in industry. However, they pay a high price in lost respect—their own and others—and they are always threatened by the possibility of the truth coming out.

> **Case in Point:** One manager at a large company was constantly manipulating people and reporting their statements incorrectly to others to further his advancement. After a few years his obvious disruptive influence resulted in his termination. He went to another company to start fresh. However, some people who had also worked in the other company related his activities to the new company's managers and he was watched closely. He was soon laid off when he began similar tactics in his new job.

Managers who try to succeed through good interfaces and superior performance are more likely to reach their objectives over the long haul. But even if they don't quite reach the level of management desired, they will still do a good job where they are as managers and this should still be the primary goal of every manager.

11.9 What to Do If Company Politics Get in the Way

Company politics exist everywhere. However, some companies have more than others. What can the junior or middle manager do about it? If well-liked and respected, he/she may be an influence in eliminating some gross aspects of the political structure. However, it is unlikely that he/she can really effect a major change. Therefore, if company politics are really unacceptable, the well-intentioned manager should leave the company if he/she can find one that is less politically oriented. Otherwise, he/she will be frustrated in developing effective interfaces.

Another alternative exists. If the company is truly overrun with political intrigues, its performance will eventually be degraded as a result of poor interfaces. When things get bad enough, a new top management team may be brought in. This new management could improve things considerably and provide the manager with an acceptable operating environment.

11.10 Avoiding Common Interface Pitfalls

The most common interface pitfall is to ignore the needs, problems, etc. of other groups that interface with your organization. The next most common cause of interface problems is higher management's neglect in establishing the authority and responsibilities of various groups within the company and recording them on paper to avoid jurisdictional disputes and bad feelings later on. The third most common cause of problems is assigning people jobs involving frequent interface contacts with others who are politically oriented and insensitive to other people's needs. Also power-oriented people should not be assigned to jobs requiring proper maintenance of interfaces with other groups.

12

Managing Industrial Documentation

Traditional organizations generally include a functional department called Publications. This department is responsible for establishing standard company report formats, style guides, editing, artwork, typing, reproduction, document identification, and storage of various publications, such as reports, studies, brochures, catalogs, and specification sheets. While this is certainly an important function, it is quite limited in terms of today's role of paper work in many parts of industry. For example, even a small company of 20 people can have stringent documentation requirements to meet when it works on sophisticated or complex products. These requirements may include the need for preparing hardware and computer manuals, drawings, specifications, system descriptions, customer status reports, performance reports, operational and test procedures, management plans, proposals, press releases, work statements, corrective action reports, manufacturing data packages, and test reports.

The amount of time, labor and cost involved with these documents can be a major part of the total project cost. For small-scale production projects, the cost of documentation can exceed hardware costs. Yet, most companies handle the documentation aspects of a project or product in a loose or random way. Detailed planning, budgeting, and control of documentation are not given much attention or are assigned to inexperienced people.

Failure to take an organized systems approach to the preparation of industrial documentation can reduce profit margins, cause delays in product development and manufacture, and result in the loss of valuable information. A systematic program of documentation management can provide a company with many benefits. It can:

1. Reduce operating costs by producing documents for less funds than allocated to this work.
2. Improve people's performance by providing documents that meet specifications on schedule. This in turn can reduce wasted effort, errors, and confusion.
3. Ensure the availability of documents and the information they contain for future projects, thereby minimizing repetition of work already done.

Case in Point: A company established a centralized index of design documents prepared for parts and products over the past 10 years. Designers were encouraged to use the system so that they could find drawings, specifications, etc. of previously built items that were similar to those needed for new projects. The engineers and designers found that 50% of their searches were productive. About 25% of old designs were directly usable and another 25% required minor changes.[1]

4. Improve hardware schedules by producing documents when needed by the staff.
5. Minimize project overruns by having specialized competency in estimating documentation costs.

12.1 Checklist for an Effective Documentation Management System

A number of characteristics are needed by an effective documentation or data management system. The following checklist (Table XVI) should provide an overall picture of how your company stands in the various facets of this specialized and essential discipline.

TABLE XVI
DOCUMENTATION SYSTEM CHECKLIST

1. Do you have one person or group responsible for the overall implementation of a documentation program?
2. Do you have an experienced documentation specialist on the job? (Very often a company recognizes a need for the discipline, but assigns someone who is not doing a good job elsewhere or who is not interested in this area.)
3. Do you have a documentation manual that defines the types of documents needed, their content, and formats?

[1]Samaras, "Engineering Graphics Desk Book," Prentice-Hall, Inc., 1975, p. 69

Case in Point: One company found that a chaotic state resulted when everyone was allowed to create their own documents. The documents had no similarity in content, format, or style. As a result, much time was wasted as each reviewer and approver argued that a particular document didn't fit the specifications normally applicable in industry. Also, without a guide to follow, the authors spent much more time trying to figure out what material should go into the document and in what order.

4. Do you identify what documents are needed for the project and which of them must be delivered to the customer?
5. Do you develop task descriptions, budgets, and schedules for project documents?
6. Do you have a centralized location for storing released documents safely and for preventing unauthorized changes?
7. Do you have a duplicate storage of key documents in case of fire or flood? Thousands of fires occur each year and the loss of vital records and documents can put the companies involved out of business. (A microfilm system is often used to provide a compact medium for remote, long-term storage.)
8. Do you have a system for allowing easy retrieval of records and documents that have been produced on past projects?
9. Do you have a document numbering system that is simple and stable?
10. Do you have a formal change control system for ensuring that changes in documents are reviewed for impact on the schedule, product, budget, and other functions or documents? Without management review, many seemingly simple changes can create bad ramifications.
11. Do you have complete records of the as-built configuration of each serial-numbered product shipped or in stores.
12. Does your system provide for traceability of parts to their documents? Can manufacturing, engineering, testing, quality, operational, and vendor data be tied together when a problem part needs to be traced to its source? Do your product records identify next higher and lower assemblies or parts for a specific item?
13. Do you have a system for identifying and controlling company private and proprietary data? (Private data deals with information about sensitive internal or external company operations. Proprietary data relates to information that could undermine the company's competitive edge, such as new designs, materials, or product ideas.)

12.2 Types of Documents Required for Industrial Operations

Industrial documents come in exceptionally varied formats, contents, page counts, and physical dimensions. They may include 10-square-foot drawings, 8½ × 11-inch, 50-page specifications, 2-page manufacturing orders, single-sheet corrective action requests, test plans, memos, inventory logs, financial reports, proposals, and computerized project status reports.

A survey at one 2,000-person company found that 145 types of documents were in existence. They consisted of 102 technical, 19 control, and 24 administrative types. While the types of documents used are similar for many companies, the format, style, and content vary considerably from company to company.

Typical documents prepared in industry include:

Drawings
Specifications
Management plans
Procedures
Reports
Policy and procedure manuals
Financial statements
Operation/product manuals
Statements of work
Manpower charts
Brochures
Product specifications
Newsletters
Computer programs
Product as-built lists
Purchasing status records
Employment application forms
Employee status records
Accident reports
Feasibility studies
Employee Benefits Manual
Purchase orders
Stop orders
Design document indexes
Correspondence
Parts lists
Manufacturing plans
System descriptions
Design verification plans
Manufacturing rework instructions
Schedules
Work plans
Product catalogs
Press releases
Inventory lists
Inspection reports
Discrepancy reports
Material review board reports
Change notices
Work order lists
Cost and schedule variance reports
Test data sheets
Budget plans
PERT charts
Flow diagrams

Each of the preceding documents has its own distinctive format, scope, and content requirements. However, descriptions of these documents are beyond the scope of this chapter. For samples of most of these documents, see "Industrial Documentation Handbook," Prentice-Hall, Inc., 1978.

12.3 Organizing for Effective Preparation of Documents

The preparation of documents includes a number of key steps. However, each step may not be explicitly defined or followed in a formal manner, depending on the mode of operation of the responsible manager, his/her experience, and the formal requirements of the company, project, or customer. Regardless of whether the operations are performed to written or unwritten procedures, the steps described next are essential for producing effective documents.

1. Analyze job (types of documents, purpose, need and user requirements).
2. Identify documents needed.
3. Determine scope, content, review, approval, and distribution requirements.
4. Estimate document preparation costs for research, writing, typing, art, reproduction, and revision.
5. Develop and approve budget.
6. Establish schedule.
7. Assign staff to document tasks.
8. Prepare documents to a system developed to meet company/project needs.
9. Check completed documents, for contract or work order conformance.
10. Submit documents for management review and approval before release.
11. Submit for final editing, printing, and delivery to customer or management.
12. Revise documents to meet customer requirements or to correct errors.
13. Perform final printing and distribution to users.
14. File and store documents.
15. Maintain (revise) documents to reflect changing requirements or needs.
16. Provide rapid retrieval of documents when requested by staff.
17. Destroy documents when no longer needed by company or required by law.

Table XVII gives a checklist of document characteristics that require definition before the preparation process is begun.

TABLE XVII
DOCUMENT CHARACTERISTICS CHECKLIST

Format and method of section numbering
Number of text pages
Number of illustrations
Number of photographs
Number of equation pages
Number of copies
Number of submittals expected before final acceptance
Number of revisions expected
Frequency of submittal (once, monthly, quarterly, etc.)

TABLE XVII (Continued)

Names of persons to approve the document	Quality level
Name of person to prepare document	Method of printing and binding
Names of customer representatives to approve document	Documents needed before preparation can begin
Start and stop dates	Person or persons responsible for supplying source information
Delivery date	Department responsible for preparation (engineering, data control, publications, etc.)
Persons authorized to release document for distribution (may be the same as persons responsible for approval)	Level of editing (15 minutes per page for light, 30 for medium, and 60 for heavy)
Names of reviewers	Requirement for certification by a registered professional engineer
Period allotted for review	

12.4 Who Should Be Responsible for Documentation Management?

An officer of the company should be assigned specific responsibility for assuring that an overall systematic approach is developed for managing company/project documentation. This individual should be sure that a centralized and integrated approach is taken and that diverse areas are brought together as much as practical. Certain areas, such as legal and financial data, may be difficult to assemble under one function or person, but the entire documentation picture should be evaluated, and explicit decisions made to exempt certain areas from a centralized control system. The following areas within the company generally retain significant autonomy but should be examined for complying with overall company requirements:

- Financial documents
- Data processing documents
- Contractual and legal documents
- Purchasing documents
- Project, engineering, manufacturing, and construction documents

For a large company, one group reporting to a V.P. should be in charge of managing documentation for the entire company. He/she should be given authority to design and implement a system that ensures the greatest amount of conformity in the preparation, approval, reproduction, distribution, control, storage, retrieval, and destruction of documents. This function could be combined with configuration management operations described in Chapter 9.

For small companies, one person can be assigned the overall documentation management responsibility. He or she should report to the President, V.P., or General Manager to provide the authority needed to make the system work.

Failure to provide this centralized control of the documentation function can lead to great expenses and trouble as the company grows.

> **Case in Point:** One company that lacked a centralized documentation function had each division develop its own documentation systems. As a result, documents were not stored in a central area. For instance, a survey found that test data could be found in any one of five different locations. Thus, considerable difficulty in tracing down test records existed and the possibility of lost data was high since control was not in the hands of people experienced with records management and control. The problem was compounded by having three independent records storage groups in different parts of the company.

12.5 Design and Drafting Document Administration

Engineering drawings are a major cost element in most companies involved in the development and production of hardware. The cost of the average drawing may be as little as $100 or may exceed $1,000. If a company produces 1,000 drawings a year, this adds up to an expenditure of $100,000 to $1 million a year. The function responsible for a sum such as this cannot be ignored without an impact on overall company performance.

Design and drafting operations are often given little attention in organizations because management either doesn't understand their activities and considers them subordinate to engineering and manufacturing activities, or doesn't realize that performance improvement in this area can affect other activities very favorably.

> **Case in Point:** A Design and Drafting (D&D) group at one company was allowed to exist without too much attention. As a result, entropy took its toll and things deteriorated; e.g., when manufacturing asked for change notices to be expedited so that equipment could be finished, inspected, and shipped, the manager merely put the job request in the hopper to be dealt with on a first-in, first-out basis. The resulting delays in equipment shipments created a steady stream of late penalty payments that added up to many thousands of dollars a year.
>
> When the D&D manager left for another job, his replacement had a different viewpoint about holding up production. He set a maximum

time of 8 hours for a change notice holding up production. He took a personal interest in expediting any change notices that were holding up shipments. Penalty payments due to late shipment dropped by about $17,000 in the first year.

This is only one small area of cost savings that can be attained by a well-run D&D operation. Other savings that a competent specialist in D&D management can bring about include the following areas:

- Simplified drafting (10%to 30% savings)
- Improved productivity through better equipment and environment (8%to 10% savings)
- Use of existing drawings for new projects (up to 50% savings)
- Use of cut-and-paste techniques (up to 35% savings)
- More accurate bids (up to 400% savings)
- Increased productivity through performance measurement (up to 30% savings)
- Use of automatic drafting (up to 35% savings)
- Use of short interval scheduling (up to 50% savings)
- Design improvements (up to a few hundred percent savings for individual designs)

For further information on D&D administration and cost saving techniques, see "Engineering Graphics Desk Book," Prentice-Hall, Inc., 1975.

12.6 Forms Control for Economical Paper Work Processing

Forms are commonly used in industry to save labor when information requirements are the same each time a specific action is required. Thus, purchase requests and orders are almost always standard documents that are used by the staff. Requests for internal service support, vacation, transfer, promotion, and capital equipment are also submitted on standard forms.

While in principle forms are efficient tools, they tend to get abused. Every time someone thinks he/she has a repetitive operation or requirement, a new form may be generated. These forms, when multiplied by $300 to cover all the internal and external labor involved, can add up to a sizable investment. To avoid this, a central forms center is often set up to evaluate all forms requested and to design them as efficiently as possible. In this way, forms proliferation is kept under control, less confusion occurs, and of course, costs are kept down. The problem with a forms center is that a fixed cost center is now established even if the need for new forms is minimal. Thus, the initial purpose of cost reduction may be lost and the staff, in order to keep busy, may increase entropy by acting in a bureaucratic way and delaying the requests of the staff for new or revised forms. Therefore periodic appraisal of the contributions of the forms center is needed to make sure it's worth the investment.

Table XVIII is a forms need evaluation checklist. This list should be followed even if no formal forms control center exists. Table XIX is a checklist to be used when the need for a new form has been established and a new form is to be designed.

TABLE XVIII

CHECKLIST FOR EVALUATING WHETHER A FORM IS REALLY NEEDED

1. Does a long-term and repetitive need for the form exist?
2. Are similar forms already available that could do the job?
3. Will this form reduce errors, lost information, clerical handling, and repetitive entries?
4. Can the form be used to combine two or more other forms and thereby create one form instead of two or more?
5. Will this form increase productivity or efficiency?
6. Will the cost of the form be less than the savings expected; e.g., is the cost of its design, approval, paper, printing, filing, and storage significantly (e.g., 20%) less than the savings to be achieved?

TABLE XIX

FACTORS IN FORMS DESIGN—A CHECKLIST[2]

- Data elements—are they all identified?
- How will the form be laid out or arranged for best efficiency?
- Are instructions legible?
- Is the language simple, grammatical, precise?
- Is the paper quality identified and suitable for the form's use?
- Is a multipart form needed? How many parts?
- Is it designed to facilitate input to the computer?
- Have the users been consulted?

---

[2]Julius B. Kaiser, "Forms Design and Control," American Management Association, 1968, p. 44.

TABLE XIX (Continued)

- What about form numbers? Are they to be preprinted or added manually?
- How are subsequent revisions to the form going to be identified; e.g., will revision letters be added after the form number or the date of the latest revision?
- Are instructions needed to fill out form?
- What kind of printing process will be used?
- Are the following production specifications given: quantity, paper stock, and proofing requirements before printing.

12.7 Records Management

Records management is a discipline that is devoted to the systematic creation, organization, control, evaluation, classification, storage, protection, retrieval, and destruction of records.

The major objective of records management is to support company management by controlling the burgeoning records jungle that is engulfing modern industry. A key responsibility of the functional manager is to work with the records manager in achieving this objective. This person can assist the records group by learning about the records system in use and current plans to change it. Also, if a records management manual is available, the responsible functional or project manager should familiarize himself with its contents. For further information, a number of books[3] are available on records management in the library or can be bought from their publishers.

Table XX lists some handy facts about records.

TABLE XX

HANDY FACTS FOR RECORDS MANAGEMENT[4]

1. The largest common overhead expense in a company is its business records.
2. A typical company creates about 2 cubic feet of records per employee per year.
3. A company keeps 13 to 37 cubic feet of records in files and storage per employee.

---

[3]Maedke, Wilmer *et al.* "Information and Records Management," Glencoe, 1974.

[4]"The Records Survey: Practical Guidelines for Getting One Going," *Administrative Management*, May 1973, p. 20–28.

4. The monthly rent paid for keeping a 6-square-foot filing cabinet in a typical office is about $80.*†
5. A typical 4-drawer file cabinet can contain up to 18,000 sheets of records or documents.
6. The common filing cost is 6¢† per unit filed.
7. Each misfile costs about 1.09.†
8. 1% of the documents filed are misfiled.
9. It costs $30 to $45 to microfilm 1 cubic foot of records.
10. The typical cost for storing 1 cubic foot of records in a records center is $2.70† a year.
11. It usually takes 3 to 5 minutes to retrieve a record from an inactive file in a records center.
12. Records should be kept for about 5 years to justify the cost of microfilming.
13. Most records should be kept for less than 6 years.
14. About 5 percent of the records should be stored for more than 10 years.
15. Permanent retentions should seldom occur.
16. 85% of the files are never referred to again.
17. 87% of all inquiries to inactive files are for records up to 2 years old.
18. 20% to 25% of reports in an organization are either duplicated or serve no useful purpose or do not justify the costs of their creation.

*May be as low as $9.
†Adjusted for inflation.

13

Critiquing and Improving Existing Systems, Operations, or Products

Most systems that have been in use for a few years are subject to review and improvement. The reasons for this condition are that few companies remain static for longer than a year or two and new techniques or developments occur with such rapidity that they may offer significant productivity or efficiency benefits. However, as mentioned in Chapter 1, care must be taken to avoid uncontrolled innovation that creates a climate of constant change and instability.

The following material gives an overall picture of a systematic method for critiquing and improving existing systems or operations. It has been successfully used by companies with resultant considerable savings.

> **Case in Point:** One company reported a 5% to 95% reduction in costs for each operation subjected to value analysis, the technique described in this chapter.

13.1 Value Analysis Technique Provides Effective Critiques

The aim of value analysis is to identify and remove areas of high and unnecessary costs from existing systems or products. It can be applied to paper work, operating systems, hardware, procedures, packaging, shipping, spare parts, sales activities, and field services. Because of its critical nature, there is a danger that the system or hardware creators will be threatened and problems could arise from this. Therefore, the basic philosophy of value analysis needs to be communicated to everyone involved with the critique. To ensure good human relations, it is essential that everyone understand that virtually any system or hardware can be made simpler and less costly and this does not reflect poorly on the original designers. The three key ideas in value analysis are:

1. We can always do a better job.
2. We are not in competition with each other because internal competition increases entropy or disorder.
3. If we improve value, we increase company profit and success and these ultimately help everyone.

In the context of value analysis, value is characterized by the lowest cost that allows the desired function to be reliably achieved. The principal concern of value analysis is economic. In achieving economic value, the following steps are needed.

- Crystallize and describe the functions of an operation, part, product, system, procedure, or organization.
- Establish cost vs. function relationships.
- Stimulate the desire to creatively achieve functions at the lowest cost without compromising performance or delivery requirements.

13.2 Why Is Value Analysis Needed?

If a company has the best people available, then why can't it expect to have them produce the best products, systems, methods? For the manager who is highly selective and pays top wages, it might seem unnecessary to have a value analysis program. However, there are several reasons why there is always room for improvement. One reason is that there are too many things to think about when designing a new system or product and time and budget limits prevent following through on all alternatives possible. In addition, design inputs from the designer's manager may be imposed which the designer accepts because he/she doesn't want to contradict the boss or doesn't have the time to develop a counter proposal to these inputs. Also a system must be integrated with the existing environment and this may require less than an optimum design.

The reasons for unnecessary costs being created in a system or product include:

- Inadequate definition of product specifications or what the customer needs or wants.

- Lack of ideas or consideration of alternate approaches.
- Lack of information on new materials, processes, components, or products.
- Temporary circumstances cause imperfect designs because of urgent delivery schedules, inadequate design budgets, changes in construction codes, or lack of people.
- Honest wrong beliefs or ignorance about a design, material, or process. New developments occur at such a rapid pace in some areas that designers cannot know all of them.
- Habits and attitudes block objective evaluation of alternate solutions, new techniques, or new materials; eg., "We didn't do it that way at Z.K. Bodden Co." or "We tried that method 2 years ago and it didn't work."

The process involved in value analysis is described next. For more detailed information and guidance, refer to "Practical Value Analysis Methods," 1972, Hayden, by John H. Fasal.

13.3 Identify Real Need for System, Operation, or Product

Most systems or products have a single function or need that they fulfill. It is extremely important that this function be identified and specified in clear and unambiguous language. Once the need or function has been identified, it should be reviewed by others to make sure that it is in fact the basic function required by the user or customer. Incorrect identification of the need will, of course, result in an unsatisfactory value analysis effort.

In addition to the primary need or function, secondary needs or functions should also be identified. For example, the primary function of a purchasing system is to buy parts, materials, and services for the company. Its secondary functions are to communicate company requirements to vendors and to negotiate contracts.

13.4 Identify Each Step of Operation

A thorough examination of the system or product is then required. This means identifying each step or element of the operation. Figure 13-1 shows a sample listing of the steps required to initiate a work plan. Each step is listed in its sequence of occurrence under the column "WHAT?" Then the person or function responsible for each step is recorded along the row marked "WHO?" Research is usually needed to obtain this informa-

SOFTWARE SEQUENCE FLOW CHART

PROJECT INITIATE WORK PLAN – 620 PLANS PER YEAR = $76,837 TEAM NO. 236

WHO? / WHAT?	SEC'Y	BR MGR	QA ENGR	COG ENGR	PURCH	MFG						EVENT TIME	EVENT COST	HRLY RATE USED	ELAP TIME	OTHER COSTS
Receive traveler	○											1 min	0.13	8.09		0.15
Log in/out	○											5 min	0.65	8.09	8 hr	0.10
Review		○										30 min	9.29	18.57		
Assign responsibility		○										10 min	3.10	18.57		
Distribute (2 hr each)	○											10 min	1.30	8.09	1 hr	0.56
Prepare work plan			○	○	○	○						8 hr	80.96	10.12	40 hr	2.00
Type plan	○											2 hr	16.18	8.09	8 hr	0.20
Approve		○										15 min	4.56	18.57	1 hr	0.20
Copy	④											10 min	1.30	8.09		
Distribute	④											10 min	1.30	8.09	3 hr	0.56
File (secretary files original)	▽1		▽1	▽1	▽1	▽1						10 min	1.30	8.09		
Total												9.7 hr 581 min	120.16		61 hr	3.77

Figure 13-1. Sample Operation Flow Chart

tion from the people intimately involved with making the system work or creating the product.

13.5 Identify the Cost and Time of Each Step

The cost and time are determined next for each step. This information is obtained by interviewing the people responsible for each step and finding out how much time they spend on the average to perform their work. This time is then converted to dollars by multiplying each person's burdened hourly rate by the labor required. Figure 13-1 is used again to record this information in columns to the right. Note that elapsed time refers to the total time required to accomplish the step—this may not be the same as the labor involved because the work may sit unattended for hours or days due to higher priority items or assignments. "Other costs" refers to materials, computer time, forms, and other non-direct labor costs.

13.6 Develop Flow Chart

A flow chart is usually developed next by recording circles in each step and drawing interconnecting lines between the steps (see Figure 13-1). These steps, functions, costs, and flow paths now represent a complete sequence flow chart for the system used to initiate work plans.

13.7 Determine Need for Each Step

The next step in the value analysis process is to critically examine each element in the system to see if it really contributes to the main and secondary functions or needs of the system/product. Some guidelines for helping perform this process follow:

- If I remove this step can the system still work well?
- If I remove a step that does not prevent the system from working, what benefits or secondary functions will be lost? Will these unneeded benefits become necessary in the next year or two?
- Is the retention of these functions worth the cost? For example, is the customer willing to pay for them now or in the near future?
- Are these secondary or tertiary functions being satisfied by others that are associated with this system?

13.8 Simplify Flow Chart

Eliminate all steps or subelements that do not contribute to the basic needs or functions desired by the user or customer. This elimination should be based on the worth or lack of worth of each step and its cost impact. The before-and-after flow charts should be kept together for easy comparison by management and the user if any questions should arise.

13.9 Recompute Time and Cost for Each Step

After simplifying the flow chart, recompute each time and cost element. Recompute the total time and cost required for the system or product. Also determine the total elapsed time involved.

13.10 Verify That No Bad Ramifications Will Result from the Simplification

Some risk is always present when simplifying a system or product; e.g., it is possible that some unforeseen defect will result that could compromise the system or product performance or reliability. Therefore, the value analysis person or team must carefully check the new system to be sure that a needed activity has not been inadvertently omitted. The user or a third party can be helpful in identifying a system defect of this type.

13.11 Compare Before and After Costs

After computation of the new costs, a chart should be prepared comparing the key features of the two approaches. This comparison chart should include the following before-and-after parameters:

- Actual time required to make system work
- Real cost (break out labor, material, and other costs separately)
- Elapsed time for the system to work
- Annual cost (cost per system, operation or product times the number of times it is repeated per year)
- Annual savings

13.12 Sell New System to Management and User

The analysis and resulting benefits of the new system should be brought together in a simplified form for presentation to management and the user. The form of presentation must be oriented toward convincing everyone that a change will result in significant cost savings with little or no risk in undermining the effectiveness of the system or product. A view graph or flip chart presentation should be made. Also a final report is desirable. A list of possible objections or problems with the changes should be created and answers formulated before the presentation is made.

13.13 Pitfalls of Value Analysis

As with any technique or system, implementation pitfalls exist. The primary pitfall is recommending a change when the benefits to be obtained are marginal or contingent on a number of assumptions that could turn out to be wrong. The worse thing a value analysis program can do is be found guilty of foisting system or product changes onto the company that do not materially reduce costs. In addition to this, beware of these pitfalls:

- Approved revised systems or products that have been analyzed for maximum value are not implemented by staff—a schedule and formal implementation completion report to management may be needed.
- The total cost of the value analysis effort is more than the benefits derived. For example, a formal value analysis program may cost the company $100,000 a year but resulting cost savings may only be $50,000 because most of the improvements do not contribute to significant cost savings. Of course, if $50,000 is saved each year and cumulative with each succeeding year, the $100,000 cost will eventually be less than the savings. For example, assuming a savings of $50,000 for each year over a 5-year period, the net savings will be as follows:

Year	Cumulative Savings
1st	$50K
2nd	$100K ($50K for 1st and 2nd years)
3rd	$150K ($50K for 1st, 2nd, and 3rd years added together)
4th	$200K (same as above plus 4th year savings)
5th	$250K (same as above plus 4th and 5th year savings)
Total for 5 yrs	$750K (savings attained for each are added to previous year's savings if they still apply)
Cumulative costs:	$500K ($100K/yr × 5 years)
Net savings:	$250K ($750K − $500K)

- Creation of an atmosphere of criticism and personal insult that alienates the original designers and users of the system and breeds a defensive attitude.
- Failure to discuss changes with users and to obtain their backing.
- Lack of proper rewards to people simplifying the system and those making the new system or product work.
- Value analysis program is put in the hands of amateurs or people

who really don't understand the problems in implementing a successful value analysis program.

- Lack of top management backing and interest.
- No historical records and follow-up to verify that the cost savings were actually attained.

14

Evaluating Need and Designing New Systems and Operations

The preceding chapter dealt with an approach to improving existing systems and operations. This chapter focuses on design of a new system or operation. While new product development is not covered, the principles are similar, except that much more sophisticated techniques are required for evaluating customer interest or need for a new product.

14.1 Set Clear Definition of System Objective, Need, and Cost Effectiveness

The stimulus for designing a new system, operation or organization may come from two main sources. The first source is the discovery of a deficiency or problem area within the company that needs correction. The second source is a spontaneous or externally induced idea that a new system will be needed in the future or that it can provide immediate benefits in terms of improved performance.

Regardless of where the idea comes from, a clear definition of the key system objective and why it is needed is essential. The objective should also be set down in tangible form; e.g., "The proposed change control system will reduce the number of undesirable product changes by 70% or last year's unrecovered costs for product changes will be reduced from $150,000 to $50,000."

In defining the real need for a new system, the following considerations must be evaluated:

- Will the cost of implementing the new system or technique be offset by the cost savings derived? Over what period?
- Can I simplify the technique or reduce its scope of application to minimize its cost, but still obtain the benefits?
- Can I use the system with minor modifications to do more than meet one specific need and thereby increase the benefits obtained to justify its implementation?
- Is the risk to product safety and customer dissatisfaction dangerous to the company's future if I don't implement the system, regardless of whether I can justify its cost in terms of cost savings?
- If the technique is not practical at this time for my company, does the anticipated long-term growth indicate that the technique will be needed in a year, two, or five? If it will be needed in a year, it may be wise to start now.
- Will the new system free my people from routine work so that they can apply their expertise to more creative work?
- Is the new system acceptable to the staff? If they are against it, it's likely to fail without strong management backing and a greater amount of energy or effort than would normally be required.

In responding to the preceding questions, the need for a cost-benefit analysis will arise. Figure 14-1 illustrates one approach that can be used for this analysis. In usint this chart, different cost figures for labor and facilities will be needed to reflect your own company's rates (page 240).

If the resulting cost-benefit analysis reveals a difference of less than 10%, very great care should be taken in deciding to design and implement the system. Minor errors in assumptions or changes in the future business climate or customer demands could wipe away this savings and the new system may not provide any cost benefits. Some managers recommend a minimum savings of 25% to justify installing a new system because of the number of errors possible in the cost-benefit analysis. This is a fairly large savings, and setting this high a level for acceptance could result in the discarding of a good system; also, once this figure gets around to the staff, the people proposing a new technique will tend to stretch future benefits or present costs to attain a 25% savings. Therefore, it is not recommended that a firm minimum percentage savings be officially set, although a manager may have a figure in his head as a personal guidepost.

When a cost-benefit analysis is submitted to a manager, his/her degree of confidence in it should be based on the following:

Prepared By: ______________
Date: ______________

Description of Technique

Reason for Consideration

Cost To Implement

Task	Hrs.	Task	Hrs.	Other Costs	Dollars
Research	____	Training	____	New Equipment	______
Design	____	New/Altered Procedures	____	Facilities	______
Coordination	____	Consultant	____	Supplies	______
Review/Evalute	____	Clerical	____	Materials	______
Implement	____			Tools	______
				Travel	______
				New/Altered Forms	______

Total Burdened Labor $ ________
Total ODC $ ________
Grand Total $ ________

Probability of Success (Profitable): ____________________%

Potential Benefits

Reduced Turn Around Time: $____*
Reduced Labor (__Hrs.x$15/hr.) $____
Reduced Materials (Qty. per yr) x ________(Unit Cost): $____
Reduced Equipment ($__cost + $__Maintenance): $____
Reduced Facilities (__x$.75/ sq. ft.): $ _____
Reduced Consultant ($__/hr.x _____ hr.): $ _____
Reduced Travel/Other: $ _____

Net Savings Over 1st Year = $____; Next 5 Years = $ ______
Approved By: ______________________ Date _______
Approved By: ______________________ Date _______

Rejected By: ______________________ Date _______
Reason for Rejection:

*(Estimated Savings due to Fewer Delays)

Figure 14-1. Evaluation Summary

Used with permission of Prentice-Hall, Inc., "Engineering Graphics Desk Book, Thomas T. Samaras, 1975, p. 35

- Is the analysis effectively prepared and logically consistent.
- Is the expected savings realistic based on experience with similar systems or techniques?

- Is the person who made the analysis generally conservative and accurate in his/her estimates?
- How closely have past accepted new systems or operations met their expectations?
- Are assumptions and constraints that need formal attention and examination explicit in the analysis?
- How much have other companies that implemented this system saved over the last few years?

14.2 Establish Specification for Controlling Design of System

A system specification is a must for any new system. Yet, in practice it is not often prepared. The reasons for this neglect include the lack of direction and discipline to prepare this vital document, not enough time, or the system is so simple it doesn't appear to need one.

A system specification provides a baseline for the design and development of the new system, and assures that all key areas of the system have been identified and defined. It also provides managers with a document that allows them to review so that the system designer does not go off in the wrong direction.

> **Case in Point:** The manager of a medium-size organization, instructed his systems designer to develop a status reporting and control system for his department. The two men met once and discussed the requirements for about one hour. The designer left and began working on the system. After about two months, he returned with a sophisticated computerized system. He had worked hard and had done a fine job. However, the manager found the system did not meet his requirements. It was too complex and required too much labor to keep the information provided up-to-date. He asked the designer to find another job and hired someone else.
>
> Reliance on verbal inputs for the design of a system that requires a few thousand dollars to create, is more expensive in the long run and creates manager-worker problems. A written and approved system specification would have avoided this wasted effort, lost time and personal distress.

A system specification need not be a long document. If a single page covers all the material needed to define the purpose, scope, and design features, then that's all that is needed. The key elements of a system specification are:

- Purpose

- Objectives
- Needs or functions to be fulfilled
- Assumptions
- Constraints
- Input/output requirements
- Interface requirements
- Key design features
- Preliminary system concept
- Quality assurance requirements

14.3 Prepare System Diagram and Description

A system diagram is needed to visually define the key blocks or functions that must be performed by the system and the sequence and interrelationships that must be met. Figure 14-2 shows a sample flow diagram that illustrates the activities and functional responsibilities for a work authorization system.

This diagram helps the creator visualize the system, to detect things omitted, and to have a baseline for revision. Of course, it is an excellent means of communicating the designer's ideas to others for evaluation and understanding.

Many system designers tend to explain their systems with words. This is difficult to do without diagrams and is more time-consuming and less effective. If a choice exists between a flow chart and text, the flow chart is usually the best way to go.

For complex systems, separate flow charts may be needed in addition to the overall flow chart. Thus, for a performance measurement system as described in Chapter 6, 13 detailed flow charts may be needed.

If textual descriptions are needed, they should concentrate on dealing with system elements not readily discernible from the flow charts. If the system description is to be sent to people outside the company, more textual material may be needed. However, if the system will be implemented within a single organization of people who already have considerable knowledge of company operations, then the flow diagrams with minor textual material should be adequate.

14.4 Design System to Meet Users Needs

Very often the system designer loses sight of the purpose of the system and the people who will have to use it. Great care must be taken to avoid designing a system that will impose unneeded work or activities on the user. Failure to work closely with the user and to find out which tasks

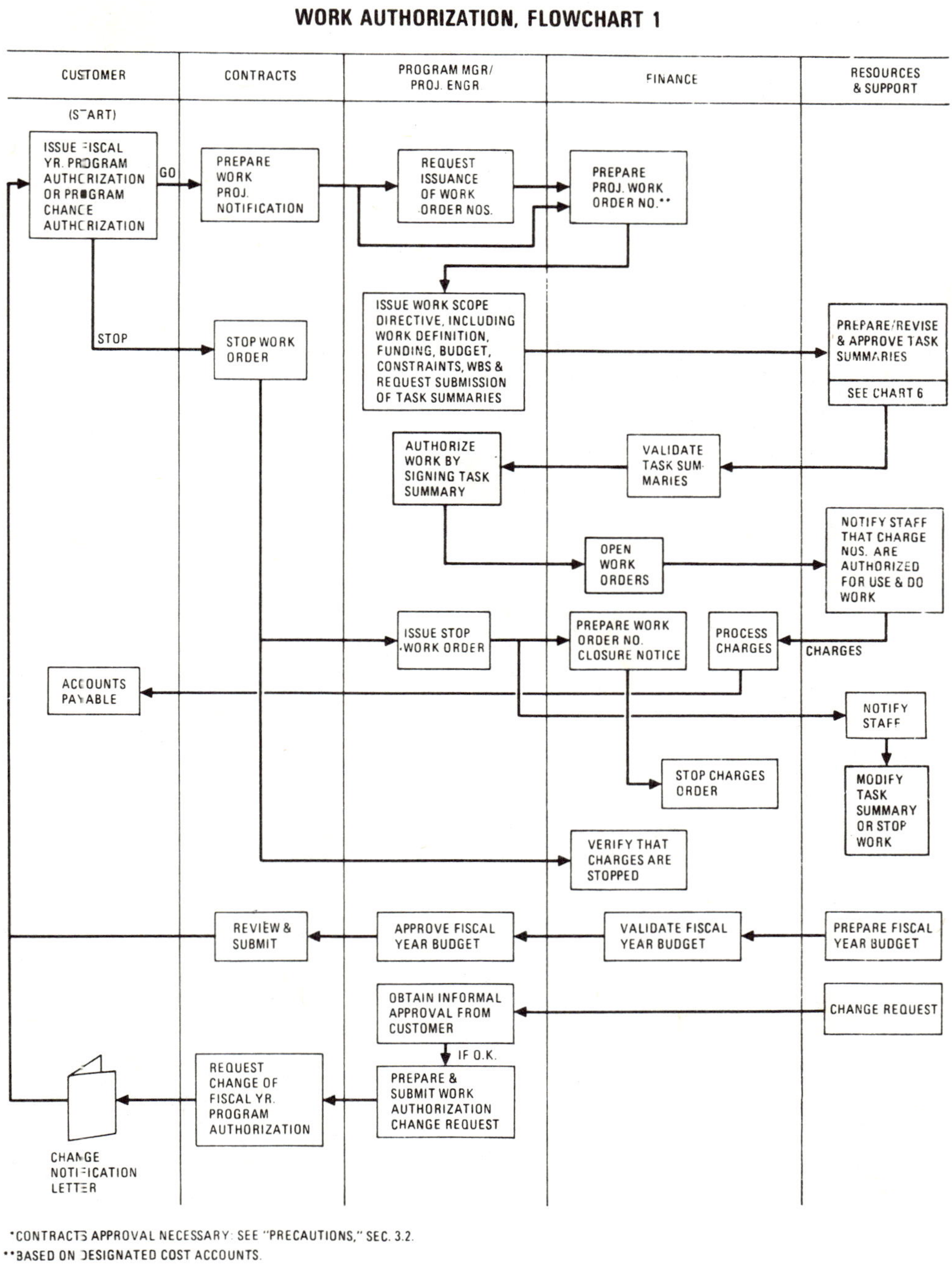

Figure 14-2. Sample Flow Chart

will be resisted creates a negative attitude that can seriously undermine the effectiveness of the system. Some of the questions that the system designer should ask in creating the system are:

- How much time and effort will be required from the user? Does he/she have the time available to meet system requirements?
- How much extra paper work will be required from the user? Is the user already fed-up with present documentation requirements?
- Is the user happy with things the way they are? If so, how are you going to convince him or her that the new system is worth implementing? What benefits will the user derive or are they all beneficial for someone other than the user?
- Can the user readily supply the information needed to make the system work right? For example, if a performance measurement reporting system is being designed, does he/she have the work and milestones accomplished data handy for recording on the input sheet for the report?
- What information does the user need from the system to make him or her happy? In what format should it be?

Of course, careful consideration of the user's needs will not insure his/her support. No matter what is done, a new system is another burden to many users and they are more likely to be hostile or unenthusiastic even when they get a lot of attention. Therefore, don't expect open support from the rank-and-file users even if the person who asked for this new system is their boss or higher management.

14.5 Keep System Design Simple

The system should be made as simple as possible. There always are people, usually not related in any close way to the users, who want to capture everything possible in a system. As a result, the system becomes very complex. Any system is a compromise between what is theoretically desirable and what is achievable in real life. A complex system will tend to fall apart of its own weight after its initial setup. Therefore, the long-term success of the system must be viewed. If the amount of energy needed to keep it together is great, the system will deteriorate in accordance with the entropy law and the final result will be a system that people don't like and won't follow. Therefore, the simplest system that will provide perhaps 80% of what is desired or needed may be the best in the long run. In summary, attainment of the ideal system can cost an infinite amount of money. In addition, the cost is likely to increase exponentially as pressure increases to approach perfection. Very often the cost of reaching for perfection winds up being more than the company can afford. Therefore, the system should be designed to meet the minimum acceptable performance requirements and then the remaining available energy should be spent in making the system really work.

14.6 Keep People Informed of Purpose and Status of System

From the inception to the completion of a new system, it is important to keep people informed of the purpose and status of the system. As was mentioned in Chapter 2, people are usually very interested in knowing what is going on in the company, especially if it affects them directly. Therefore, a program of communication should be established. This requires a list of people and functions (e.g., manufacturing, finance, and engineering) who need to be kept informed of system progress. The following techniques may be used:

- Person-to-person contact
- Group briefings
- Periodic written reports highlighting events and focusing on special impacts on various functional areas
- Special bulletins or notices

14.7 Develop Detailed Procedures

As the system design progresses, detailed procedures may be required to allow the system to work. These procedures may apply to the whole company or may be used by specific functions. The procedures should embody the key design features specified in the system specification and description or flow charts.

Procedures should be drafted, submitted to people or functions affected by them, and revised as required. Major changes should be first incorporated into the system specification before the procedures are revised. This keeps the system requirements documents and working subsystem elements in synchronization and consistent.

Other areas needing attention during the procedures development or detail design phase, are the creation of forms, reports, and other documents needed to make the system work.

As mentioned, procedures and other documents should be kept brief and to a minimum.

14.8 Follow-up Design

There is always some follow-up design needed after the system has been implemented, as will be described in Chapter 15. A system audit, after it has been working for 6 months or a year, is needed to make sure that it is doing what was expected from it and that no unnecessary or impractical steps or features exist. Generally, this should not be a major effort. However, the process itself helps show the users that management is really interested in the system and that it cares about its effectiveness and their needs.

14.9 New System Design Pitfalls to Avoid

Some of the pitfalls of new systems have been already discussed in Chapter 1. A brief listing of potential problems or mistakes in designing a new system or operation follow:

- System requirements not documented and reviewed by management and users before design begins.
- The system is not soundly applied; e.g., application not practical.
- System design is too complex and ambitious (trying to do too much).
- Systems designer assumed responsibility for the design and management abdicated responsibility.
- System is designed to replace people rather than to help them get their work done better and faster.
- Over-optimistic expectations; of course, optimism is needed—otherwise the project would not get off the ground, but optimism must be tempered with realistic expectations and awareness of potential problems.
- Search for a perfect design creates funding problems, delays, and interminable discussions and revisions.

15

Implementing New Systems Effectively

A superb system design is no guarantee that the system will also be effectively implemented. Great thought and care are needed to make the system work as intended. Manufacturing people don't need to be told this when it comes to systems for producing hard goods. However, they often tend to look at soft systems (such as management systems and paper work) as much less demanding and important. As a result, after using fairly high-level people to conceive and design a system, someone with less experience and background is assigned to make the system work. And what's worse, management often turns its attention to new problems and assumes that everything will move smoothly once the system design has been approved; and that the benefits of the new system will be accrued without any more effort on its part. A manufacturing company in a small town in California found that this assumption wasn't valid.

> **Case in Point:** After having an expert team of specialists and administrators evaluate a new operating system for one year, the Director obtained top management approval to invest $300,000 for the new equipment that was intended to improve the efficiency of the design and drafting department by 30% to 70%. The feasibility study leading up to this decision indicated that the system would be operating at its optimum level in 3 to 6 months, based on other companies' experience.
>
> Perhaps the short implementation schedule gave management the impression that the system installation was a simple process and they focused their attention on other areas. Two-and-a-half years later, the specialist in charge of the system's implementation hedgingly admitted that the system bugs and people problems had been

finally worked out and the system was now working at its optimum level.

While the implementation of a new system is subject to a large variety of pitfalls that can prevent achieving the benefits desired, there are several key steps that can help assure success. These are described next.

15.1 Top Management Support Is Essential

Experience with implementing new systems indicates that top management support is absolutely essential for complete success. This means that top management must invest a certain amount of time in understanding the new system and being convinced that the benefits are real and justify the trouble and expense of implementing the system. This support must then be communicated to the staff so that the system implementers will get the cooperation needed from everyone involved to make the system work. This communication may be through memos, management directives, presence at implementation meetings, and periodic appearance at the location of the system implementation efforts.

15.2 Anticipate Problems and Formulate Advance Solutions

Hopefully, problems were anticipated during the proposal or feasibility stages of the system. However, the problems identified should now be re-evaluated and new ones added if previously overlooked. Some possible problems that should be considered along with solution development include:

- What if the forms, equipment, or people needed to implement the system are not ready when needed?
- What if the special facilities needed are not ready?
- What if people resist changing over to the new system?
- What if a key system person leaves the company?
- What if a new manager enters the scene and doesn't like the new system?
- What if the computer is not available to tie into the new system because of other more urgent work (assuming a computer is needed)?
- What if the budget allocated is suddenly reduced because of company fiscal problems?

- What if more funds than approved are needed to complete system implementation?
- What if system bugs and malfunctions and delays exceed expectations?
- What if the supplier of new equipment goes out of business?
- What if business declines and the need for the system is no longer economically justifiable?

15.3 Implement a Pilot Program

Sometimes companies decide to move from the old system to the new in one giant step. They close down the old system and open the new system, expecting a smooth transition because a careful analysis of the system and potential problems has been done and the problems taken care of. Unfortunately, there is no foolproof way of ensuring the immediate success of a new system. Even with highly competent people, things get overlooked or unexpected developments occur. Therefore, many companies set up a pilot system in one area to test the system and to get rid of any bugs before the old system is completely turned off. This way, if problems occur, the old system is there to do the work until the new system is fixed.

While management may find a one-step conversion to the new system desirable from a cost viewpoint, people experienced in implementing new systems generally don't recommend it. Therefore, be cautious before taking this step and make sure that everything has been planned in detail.

15.4 Communicate Closely with Users

Communication with the users was already mentioned in a previous chapter as being important. At this point in the system project, it is vital that the system implementers work closely with the users. This includes giving them an overview of the implementation process and reviewing the aims and benefits of the new system. Hopefully, some benefits will be available to the users. These are not always readily apparent and in fact, no near-term, tangible benefits may exist for the users. This situation, of course, is undesirable and the system implementer will have some trouble in getting full cooperation from the users.

In summary, the users should be told the following:

- Benefits of new system to company and users; why it is needed.
- How the system works.
- How the system will be implemented.

- Some of the potential problems to be expected during the break-in period.
- Availability of the systems people to help solve operational problems that may result after turnover of system operation to users.

15.5 Offer Rewards to Chief Implementers and Users

By the time the system is fully implemented, the company will have spent from a few thousand to hundreds of thousands of dollars—for big companies, millions may be invested. It is natural for management to oppose spending any more money than is absolutely necessary. Therefore, rewards to the staff for its successful implementation are often ignored. The rationalization goes something like this: "Harry and his crew are being paid a good salary, so why should we reward them for the new system?" While this may be true for managers whose job descriptions may include improving company productivity, most people are not officially required to create or implement new systems. This is not a routine job and special talents, efforts, and attitudes are required for success. In addition, the systems people responsible for its success are subject to higher risk of failure compared to working on routine tasks. In a way, a systems implementer is like a combat soldier who receives higher pay for greater exposure to danger.

Even if management feels that the salary structure for systems people takes this into account, it's shortsighted to be cheap after investing so much money and time into the new system. A pre-system implementation reward plan for the key people involved—at all levels—can be a great motivating force and will increase the chances for success. If the system is successful, the company will not lose any money when the rewards are tied to the net savings obtained.

If money rewards are against company policy, then other techniques can be used, such as a special afternoon celebration at a restaurant, a weekend party, free dinners for each participant and his/her spouse or friend, or letters of appreciation from the President.

> **Case in Point:** A new system person at one large company was asked to simplify a system for processing documents. The original designer had created a complex system that had many controls and paper work requirements. The new system was designed and implemented by the new designer. After two years, the staff and management were happy with the new system. A survey revealed that the company had saved about one-half million dollars a year with the new system. Yet, no recognition or rewards were given to the designer. Failure to be rewarded for his efforts goaded him to leave the company, taking with him other cost-saving ideas that had not yet been proposed.

A modest reward would have saved the company much money in the long run. Therefore, management should be constantly alert to sharing some of the benefits of a new system with its creators and implementers.

15.6 Train People Well

Even simple systems take time to learn. Therefore, a formal training program should be set up and implemented so that everyone thoroughly understands what's going on. Training should be more than a one-shot affair It must be repeated periodically or people will inevitably drift into bad modes of operation or may unknowingly be doing something wrong.

One company found that by assigning training responsibility to line managers, the staff learned more efficiently because their instructions came from their boss rather than an outsider. This was found more effective than the previous method and reduced putting systems people on the defensive, which interferred with the training process. (People are more likely to attack a new system when it is presented by someone outside the group rather than by their boss.)

Visual displays are important for effective training. View graphs, flip charts, movies (for complex systems), and handouts describing the system can be effective training aids. The extent of these depends on the particular system, available funds, and staff needs.

15.7 Insist on Periodic Audits of System

Chapter 2 discussed the entropy theory and stated that it is the most natural thing in the world for a system involving an on-going process to decay with time if work is not done to maintain its configuration. This means that elements or steps within the system will tend to be done less carefully than required for optimum system performance or that steps may be short-circuited because of time, laziness, or failure to understand the importance of the step. Also new people may not understand the system completely or correctly and errors will occur and may be repeated indefinitely until they become obvious to the customer or manager. Therefore, periodic surveys or audits of the system implementation are needed to detect any system deterioration or trends that could impact system performance.

A secondary benefit of system audits is that the auditor may detect a system design deficiency that needs correction; or that a deviation from the design might be found to be more effective and the system should be revised to officially require the unapproved practice to become a part of the system and communicated to other users who may be following the old process.

15.8 Hold Managers Responsible for Success of System

Managers of the using organizations must be held responsible for the successful implementation and operation of the system. Failure to hold them responsible will remove a great motivating force for success. If the systems people can be blamed for problems and the system not working, then the system is very likely to fail if the managers are not enthusiastic about the system in the first place and if someone else outside the group thought of the new system.

On the other hand, if top management holds the managers responsible, it can point out that the managers had an opportunity to critique the system before it was implemented and to raise problems that needed solutions. Thus, their failure to identify these problems rests with them just as much as with the systems people. While the managers may have legitimate complaints, holding them responsible will reduce scapegoating and will normally bring forth greater efforts to make the system work.

15.9 Avoid Building Over-Expectations

A problem with implementing a new system is overselling it. To obtain management approval and funding, the creators tend to emphasize the benefits and positive aspects of the new system. They feel that if the problems and uncertainties are presented or given significant attention, they will be used by others to stop the project. Therefore, an aura of success is created and the negative elements are suppressed. (While suppressing problems is not recommended, each manager must be realistic in terms of the environment that he/she must work in.)

Potential problems or negative factors can be deadly to the new system if they are not adequately communicated to the staff during the implementation phase. Management and the user must be informed of the problems and delays that may occur until the system bugs are removed. Of course, they can't be given a pessimistic picture or failure may result from a self-fulfilling prophecy. It takes considerable skill to keep people keyed up and believing that the system will do what the creators promised, but still realistic in expectations of troubles during the initial operating phase.

If the staff is not prepared for some difficulties, then as soon as an unexpected delay occurs, their confidence in the system will be shaken and the system may have a black eye for a year or two.

> **Case in Point:** A manager vehemently complained that a new performance measurement system was a joke because he spent hours completing a variance analysis report (see Chapter 6) for overrunning his budget only to find out that the comptroller had made a mistake in reporting his budget status. While the systems person tried to assuage him by explaining that some rough spots still had to

be smoothed out, the manager was still highly agitated and down on the system when the systems person left his office.

15.10 Modify System to Eliminate Deficiencies or Make Improvements

Some changes to the system will normally be needed to correct errors, new conditions or requirements, or satisfy complaints of the users. In addition, new elements or processes may be found desirable and some follow-up design work may be needed.

While the company should always be open to making the system better, care is needed to avoid a continuous improvement syndrome that consumes much people power, money, and time. If too loose a policy is allowed, the benefits may never be realized since the system will be a constant money/resource sink, which never quite provides the benefits originally wanted. For example, assume a new system cost of $50,000 was estimated and cost benefits of $10,000 a year were projected. Now, if annual improvements are made that cost $5,000 a year, the payback period would be 10 years instead of the original 5 planned for. If management knew the payback period would have been 10 years during the proposal stage, they could very well have chosen another area for investment of company funds. Of course, the costs of improvement or upgrading may be $10,000 so that no benefits are obtained as long as these costs are being incurred.

15.11 Expand System to Entire Operation or Company

Once the pilot program has proved to work, the new system should be expanded to the entire operation or company. The old system should be discontinued. Discontinuation of the old system should not be assumed to occur automatically. A plan should be made and management should follow up to be sure the old system is no longer in use.

15.12 Implementation Pitfalls

A number of pitfalls should be avoided when implementing new systems. These are summarized below:

- Top management support is not obtained.
- Inadequate training.
- Failure to use a dedicated, talented, full-time implementation team—few new systems can be implemented properly on a part-time basis.

- Poor discipline.
- Company is not used to working to a system; e.g., following procedures and operating requirements.
- Hostile or uncooperative staff.
- Lack of preparation for problems, delays, and setbacks.
- Failure to make maximum use of existing systems.
- Failure to conduct an audit before turning over system to user.
- New systems designer or manager gets involved in the middle of the implementation process. (The perturbations of new people can be deadly because the project's momentum can be broken and may never return as a result of conflicts, redesigns, and delays.)

16

Manager's Troubleshooting Charts

Companies get into trouble for a number of reasons. Sometimes their troubles can be traced down and pinpointed to one or two causes. Other times there may be several causes contributing to problems and failures. The ability of the manager to examine and correct a specific or generalized problem is therefore of great importance to successful performance. This chapter provides a rough framework for this problem detection and isolation process. However, it is only a start and the manager must carefully consider a number of factors that only he/she is in a position to know because of personal experience and involvement with the company or department.

The following troubleshooting charts deal with organizational, financial, production, people, marketing, and operational problems. Each chart identifies a common problem, gives its possible causes and identifies solutions that may apply. While these charts only provide general solutions to problems, they can serve to stimulate the manager's creative powers in developing solutions for specific problems within the organization.

16.1 Organizational Troubleshooting Chart

Problem	Possible Causes	Solutions Inventory
Frequent conflicts between projects and functional groups or between functional groups themselves.	1. Poorly defined responsibilities by higher management.	1. Define and document division of responsibilities more precisely —avoid ambiguity.

Problem	Possible Causes	Solutions Inventory
Frequent conflicts between projects and functional groups or between functional groups themselves.	2. Immature managers	2. Increase standards for manager selection; use management development programs. Replace with superior managers.
	3. Power-oriented—not systems-oriented managers.	3. Re-educate managers that company wants managers who get results and are systems-oriented rather than managers who can only evaluate actions or decisions in terms of their own organizations; reward systems-oriented managers whenever possible.
	4. Lack of direction or interest in operations by higher management.	4. Devote more attention to operations; keep in direct contact with staff on a regular basis.
	5. Failure to issue charters for each organization.	5. Issue charter for each major group and maintain current.
Frequent organizational changes.	1. No one knows what type of organization is best.	1. Need professional help or special task force to study problem.
	2. Change is being used as a coverup for past failures or to show board of directors or stockholders something is being done.	2. Real causes of problems need to be pinpointed and specific solutions developed for each.
	3. Frequent changes in managers.	3. Obtain agreement that systems or organization will not be changed by new managers except when specific problems exist.

Problem	Possible Causes	Solutions Inventory
Objectives and goals set by higher management not being met by staff.	1. Lack of discipline.	1. Tighter control and monitoring by higher management. Formal MBO program may help. Short interval scheduling may also be useful. (This involves breaking up a task into more numerous milestones so that progress can be measured by shorter time spans.)
	2. Unrealistic setting of goals/objectives.	2. Re-assess goal setting techniques. See Chapter 7 for MBO.
	3. Fluid environment creates conditions that make meeting objectives impossible.	3. Allow for anticipated changes in environment when setting goals/objectives.
	4. Frequent unpredicted emergencies distract staff from objectives.	4. Introduce better planning system. See Chapter 3.
Too many parallel efforts going on and decisions not being made by middle managers because they can't come to agreements on how things should be done.	1. Lack of central control/authority. 2. Too much autonomy on part of middle managers. 3. Managers are allowed too much discretion on deviating from proven standard operating procedures.	1-3 Operations manager needed to act as a focal point and authority center for minimizing impasses, expediting decisions and avoiding redundant efforts.

16.2 Financial Troubleshooting Chart

Problem	Possible Causes	Solutions Inventory
Negative cash flow	1. Invoices are not being paid on time by customers.	1. New, faster invoice system needed; closer follow-up on overdue

Problem	Possible Causes	Solutions Inventory
Negative cash flow		payments; give refunds for early payments. Also, sell accounts or notes payable to a bank or sell assets; hold off dividend payments, or limit withdrawals by partners; limit pre-paid expenses; e.g., buy 6 months of insurance instead of 1 year.
	2. Billings are being paid too soon.	2. Set a longer time between receipt of bills and payment dates; accounting may be too efficient.
	3. Material and labor estimates too low.	3. Reassess bidding and cost estimating techniques and people. Establish an estimating manual. Use historical costs as references.
	4. Charges are not being controlled by management.	4. Need a formal work or charge authorization system; back off unauthorized charges.
	5. Overhead or support services costs are out of control.	5. Need to examine where money is going; zero base budgeting may be needed. See Chapter 3. Negotiate cost reduction program.
Project costs exceed budgets	1. Mischarging on various jobs.	1. Tighter control by project manager and comptroller; disciplinary action on overruns; formal stop work order system.
	2. Project estimates are poorly done.	2. Obtain more competent help; set up training program; allow more time for estimates during proposal stage.

Problem	Possible Causes	Solutions Inventory
Project costs exceed budgets	3. People are doing work not covered for on project or task.	3. Tighter review of work by supervisors. A performance measurement system is needed as described in Chapter 6. Prohibit staff responses to customer requests for additional work unless approved by Contracts.
Insufficient funds are available to continue operations or expand facilities	1. Insufficient profits.	1. Set up system of performance measurement or increased productivity techniques; stop unnecessary product improvements.
	2. A one-shot large investment has drained capital resources.	1, 2, 3 & 4. Issue stock to gain capital; obtain loan—try other banks or other sources even if denied by one bank; obtain more financial backers; affiliate with a larger company that has extra capital to invest in your company; contact small business administration, or ask staff to become backers of company. Sell patents.
	3. R&D has been using up more funds than planned.	3. See above; re-examine R&D work plans and eliminate or postpone work that is not essential for near term.
	4. Cost of materials has escalated beyond forecasted trends, draining finances.	4. See 2 above. Negotiate longer payment period. Search for ways to reduce material wastes and thereby cut sizes of orders.

16.3 Low Productivity Troubleshooting Chart

Problem	Possible Causes	Solutions Inventory
Production rates not being met or declining	1. Inadequate supervision.	1. Review supervisory procedures with staff, add training course.
	2. Frequent equipment malfunctions.	2. Improve preventive maintenance program; buy new production equipment; renovate equipment.
	3. Low morale.	3. Improve wages or working conditions; offer bonuses or incentives for increased productivity.
	4. Frequent material shortages.	4. Improve materials planning system; tight buyer followup on orders; change vendors.
	5. Special processes or techniques or materials are slowing down progress.	5. Replace with simpler, easier items or give staff more training or special tools to improve efficiency; give work to vendors with special facilities or skills.
	6. Quality defects require rework.	6. Retrain or replace workers who are guilty of numerous mistakes; relax inspection requirements or engineering standards when possible.
	7. Production rates not realistic.	7. Supervisors and managers may need better techniques for estimating production rates or pressure from the top needs to be relaxed because it's forcing supervisors to commit to unrealistic rates.

Problem	Possible Causes	Solutions Inventory
Production rates not being met or declining	8. Production procedures are inadequate or too complicated.	8. Revise procedures or manufacturing instructions; implement work simplification procedures/techniques.

16.4 People Troubleshooting Chart

Problem	Possible Causes	Solutions Inventory
High turnover	1. Poor wages.	1. Raise wages or introduce bonus/profit sharing system.
	2. Poor working conditions.	2. Add color, carpeting, more lighting, air conditioning, partitions, new furniture, etc.
	3. Unsatisfying work.	3. Job rotation; expand job responsibilities; involve staff in planning/decision making; reward suggestions for improvement of productivity; give staff more recognition for good work.
	4. Lack of growth opportunity.	4. Promote from within; indicate that if profitability increases, expansion will occur and new jobs will be opened. Add more responsibility to existing jobs.
	5. Political environment.	5. Caution supervisors and managers from favoritism based on friendship or other non-performance related qualities. Reassign those who persist in this behavior.

Problem	Possible Causes	Solutions Inventory
High turnover	6. Insecurity.	6. Use certain amount of job shoppers to cushion periodic declines in staffing; relocate people in departments that are overstaffed rather than laying them off. Work with other companies to get people being laid off jobs.
No esprit de corps	1. See high turnover above.	1. See 1-6 above.
	2. Company doesn't care about its people.	2. Managers and supervisors need to spend more time with their people and take steps to correct areas of dissatisfaction. Improve communication. Top management should visit with people at working levels.
	3. People feel exploited.	3. Wages should be competitive with other companies; superior performance should receive superior rewards; work output standards are excessive and should be reduced.
	4. Staff doesn't trust company or leader's good intentions.	4. Improve communications with staff; provide tangible evidence of company interest in its people and loyalty to them.
	5. People feel unappreciated.	5. Provide more visible and frequent signs of appreciation of work well done.

Problem	Possible Causes	Solutions Inventory
Numerous personal conflicts	1. High internal competition and rivalry.	1. Avoid rating people against each other or setting contests between them; issue formal company policy emphasizing cooperation vs. competition; hold special training seminars.
	2. Unfair reward system.	2. Make sure people are rewarded on ability and performance and not on personal relations with supervisors; set up objective guidelines for providing rewards.
	3. Certain people are allowed to break rules or get the best assignments consistently.	3. Discuss problem with supervisors and have them take corrective action; audit implementation; conduct management training seminars describing the problems created when discipline is inconsistently applied.

16.5 Marketing/Customer Troubleshooting Chart

Problem	Possible Causes	Solutions Inventory
Losing business	1. Salesmen are turning customers off.	1. Identify behavior that is offensive; e.g., overselling, use of jokes no longer considered in good taste, or making delivery promises that can't be met; retrain salesmen in new techniques; stop salesmen from wasting calls on old customers who don't buy much anymore.

Problem	Possible Causes	Solutions Inventory
Losing business	2. Dissatisfaction with use and serviceability of products.	2. Revise procedures and policies to emphasize customer satisfaction, rather than repair income; improve user manuals.
	3. Products lack certain features desired by customer or provided by other companies.	3. Request that engineering add these features to product; provide survey results to support request; get more creative engineers.
	4. Market demand has had a general decline.	4. Develop marketing strategy to obtain larger share from competitors; increase advertising budget or change style; look for new growing market demands and develop products to meet them; consider exports.
	5. Competitors have lower prices.	5. Implement cost reduction or value analysis programs; lower profit margin; emphasize value of special product benefits to justify customer paying more.
	6. Distributers are pushing other products.	6. Find out reasons; offer greater incentives to them; have salesmen visit them more; provide more application engineer visits.
	7. Customer is getting more attention and service from other companies.	7. Increase personal contacts with customers; improve proposals; increase responsiveness to customers' queries and needs; add special accessories or add-ons to product that make

Problem	Possible Causes	Solutions Inventory
Losing business		your proposed products more attractive; coach staff to avoid rudeness and improve ability to deal with customers; don't try to reach too broad a market and thus concentrate attention on real customers.
Product doesn't meet customer requirements	1. Configuration is not completely and accurately documented so that customer can order identical products.	1. Implement configuration identification and control procedures—see Chapter 9.
	2. Product doesn't meet specifications.	2. Engineers must be given all customer specs and their designs must be reviewed for compliance to these specs. Any deviations must be approved by customer in writing.
	3. Product is too expensive.	3. Design to cost, not to optimum or desired performance and quality; use value analysis; obtain written customer agreement to pay for changes.
	4. Product doesn't include all changes requested by customer.	4. Formal change management procedures needed; use change verification procedures to make sure products include changes before shipment to customer.

16.6 Increasing Operational Costs Troubleshooting Chart

Problem	Possible Causes	Solutions Inventory
Overhead costs are increasing	1. Too much computer time.	1. Better control of computer usage; new guidelines as to when the computer should be used.
	2. Too much paper work.	2. Do value analysis on paper work systems to eliminate redundant or unneeded paper work activities.
	3. Too much absenteeism, illness, or accidents.	3. Correct morale problems; more interesting work; less pressure; improved safety procedures and discipline.
	4. Inefficient use of secretaries and typists.	4. Establish secretarial or typist pools; verify that managers really need full-time secretaries; hire job shoppers for temporary overloads.
	5. Unnecessary reports being prepared.	5. Eliminate reports not needed to get work done or to document projects; also determine if they are bigger than needed. Make sure copies aren't being sent to people who don't need them.
	6. Frequent reorganizations.	6. Avoid musical chairs with managers; concentrate on improving their performance; find out why they are doing poorly and coach them to rectify the problems.
Product costs are rising	1. Only small number or quantity of material is bought on each order.	1. Increase size of orders to get bigger price discounts.

Problem	Possible Causes	Solutions Inventory
Product costs are rising	2. Too many types of items being used on products.	2. Reduce variety of items needed; use preferred parts list during design phase of products.
	3. Bid requirements are changed after order is issued.	3. Make sure all requirements are identified on original bid request.
	4. Too much scrap.	4. Simplify design to reduce errors and waste; improve manufacturing operations.
	5. Overstocking.	5. Set up more accurate estimates of product needs and waste during manufacturing and testing; use computer material planning system.
	6. Work taking too long.	6. Prepare written plans; set deadlines.
Increasing administrative and support costs	1. Operating systems too complex.	1. Conduct value analysis program. See Chapter 13.
	2. Customer requirements introduce more paper work and planning costs.	2. Negotiate simplifications before signing contract; or follow-up with a contract revision, but be prepared for cutback in funds also.*
	3. Too many reports on status of work.	3. Review all reports for simplification and elimination based on survey results.
	4. Too many changes in systems and requirements.	4. Assign control for systems to one manager and make sure he or she controls the number of changes each year. Critically evaluate all proposed changes;

*Customer will expect you to reduce price if he reduces contract requirements.

Problem	Possible Causes	Solutions Inventory
Increasing administrative and support costs		major changes must be reviewed by higher management.
	5. Too much planning and scheduling of labor being expended.	5. Firm up initial objectives and funding limits before detailed planning and scheduling is begun; reduce scope if practical.
	6. Management reports too expensive.	6. Computerized management report system may be more effective; reduce scope of reports; reduce frequency of publication if action won't adversely affect management's visibility of progress.
	7. System changes are plagued with changes in direction, confusion, and much rework.	7. Insist on written system specifications approved by responsible manager and user.

17

Self-Promoting Practices

This chapter features specific practices any manager can use to improve effectiveness as administrator and leader. The practices described in this chapter are based on actual experience and studies conducted to find out how people feel or react when their bosses act in certain ways. While many of the practices described will be familiar to most managers, it is important to keep in mind that successful management does not result from what the manager knows, but from what he does. To help in doing, the following steps should be followed:

- Identify those practices that are desired but not employed consistently.
- Reread the material on those practices several times—preferably five or six times spread out over a week.
- Make notes or underline those statements that are most important to you.
- Outline a brief plan for implementing each practice selected; list the steps that will be followed and how successful implementation of the practice will be determined. Also set a schedule for completion of the plan. Put practices you want to really follow on 3 × 5″ cards and keep them in your shirt pocket. Review them at the start of the day and before lunch until you feel they have become a part of you.

Note: Too often, intelligent people assume that they only need to be told something once and they will never forget it. Thus, mature people may find the 3× 5″ card approach to learning new things childish. However, a casual reading of a good idea or technique will not result in its implementation for most people. The idea must be reviewed many times until it has become a part of them.

17.1 Maintain a "You" Point of View

Les Giblin, a well-known human relations expert, has frequently reported the fact that people are primarily interested in themselves, not you. Therefore, the words "I," "me," and "mine" are much less interesting to them than the words "you" and "yours."[1] Taking a consistent "you" stand is difficult, but can increase your effectiveness and influence considerably. Thus, the effective manager makes his presentations focus on showing how people can get what they want by doing what you want them to do. For example, show how your idea, product, system, or procedure will help them:

- Meet their objectives
- Save money and time
- Increase their sales
- Increase their influence, power, or status
- Get a promotion

This simple "you-view" of life is difficult to live with, but there is no doubt that virtually everyone is much more interested in his own well-being and growth than in yours. If you can successfully learn to focus on how your ideas or actions will help others, then they will be more friendly and cooperative with you and will enhance your ability to get things done in the organization.

17.2 Help People Feel Important/Worthwhile

Most people have a strong desire to be important and recognized for their contributions to the company. Studies in human motivation show that recognition is a key factor in making people work hard. Oppositely, ignoring or talking down to people are powerful methods for demotivating them. The intensity of this need for recognition is illustrated next:

> **Case in Point:** One supervisor at a company in San Diego was talking to an associate about a manager in another organization. The associate was startled to find the supervisor extremely hostile towards this manager. When he probed the supervisor to find the reason for this hostility, he explained that this manager always looked straight through him whenever they passed in the hall and never said hello even though the two men knew each other. The supervisor simply felt that the manager didn't recognize his existence as a person.

[1]Les Giblin, "Human Relations Handbook," New Jersey, 1968, p. 3.

Besides humanistic considerations, the manager who ignores people loses influence over them and may even create enemies who may eventually get into a position to do him harm. A few ways to help make people feel worthwhile follow:

- Listen to them
- Compliment them when they deserve it
- Acknowledge awareness when someone is waiting to see you
- Pay attention to each person in a group
- Use their names when possible
- Show that you are impressed with their achievements

17.3 Criticize Constructively

Criticism should be given in a positive, helpful spirit. When presented in a negative way, it antagonizes the person who may completely ignore his/her errors or may become worse in order to get back at you. Thus, your effectiveness will be increased through a conscious effort to criticize constructively. Les Giblin offers the following rules:[2]

1. Criticize in absolute privacy.
2. Precede criticism with a kind word or compliment.
3. Criticize the act, not the person.
4. Tell the person how to do it right.
5. Ask for the person's cooperation in correcting the problem. (Demanding cooperation is more likely to produce the opposite result.)
6. End the criticism with a positive or friendly remark; e.g., "Let's work out the problem together."

17.4 Listen to People

In various parts of preceding chapters, a number of key areas were discussed for increasing leadership and managerial effectiveness. These included developing a rapport with people, improving communication, and motivating people. To implement these actions successfully, you must acquire information about their needs, interests, problems, and experience. While some of this information may be obtained from resumes and employee records, the art of listening is a prime source of useful information. This means being able to stop talking and really listen to what the other person is saying—not just courtesy silence while you are developing

---

[2]Giblin, *op. cit.* p. 29–30.

an answer to his/her argument or thinking about what you will be doing on the weekend. Since over half your time is probably spent listening to people, it's worth cultivating effective listening habits, such as:

- Listen for ideas and facts.
- Listen to gain something for yourself.
- Avoid rapid closure because someone said something you didn't like.
- Practice listening by seeing how much information you can obtain from what people say.
- Make a conscious effort to remember what the person said.

17.5 Thank People

An expression of appreciation for good or fast work by your staff is important. While this little action may seem of trivial value, many people do get a big lift when their boss says thanks and pats them on the back. Of course, expressions of appreciation must be sincere and based on real accomplishments.

17.6 Don't Tease People

Virtually every company has people who like to tease others about their ideas, habits, ethnic background, or physical characteristics. However, few people enjoy being the center of a joke or funny remarks. Because most people want to be good sports, they will not show their true feelings. But if the teaser has hit a sensitive spot, the person being teased may resent the teaser for a long time. If the teaser is a manager, his ability to develop a rapport with the other person will be diminished and his cooperative attitude may decline also. Therefore, the manager should avoid teasing his staff, associates and boss, even if others seem to be doing it with no ill effect. Great care should be taken to avoid teasing someone about the following:

- Weight
- Age
- Height
- Baldness
- Eyeglasses
- Speech
- Religion
- Dress
- Mannerisms
- Intelligence
- Race or nationality
- Relatives
- Lifestyle

17.7 Use an Open Performance Appraisal System

Performance appraisal systems are supposed to stimulate people into improving their work or skills. Yet, many systems do just the opposite. For example, the fairly popular method of ranking people in comparison to their peers has been found to turn otherwise good people into cynical, dispirited, and unproductive workers. The experiences of two managers illustrate the problems arising from poorly designed or implemented performance appraisal systems:

> **Case in Point:** "The effects of a declining rating [ranking] are disturbing. If you give a man a rating of 35 [40 is average], he can't look himself in the eye. If you give him a 30, he goes numb; it's a terrible jolt to his pride. When a man's rating is lowered two points, his performance goes to pot. A few men will work harder if you lower their ratings, but most will give up. People need a pat on the back."[3]

> **Case in Point:** "Unfortunately, under the new Technical Performance Appraisal (TPA) system, we have to tell one half of our engineers that they are below average. After we tell a man his score is below 40, he won't do anything for a month. He stews over his low rating and he may even take a few day's sick leave, even though he's not physically sick. After a month or two, we may be able to get him working again with the hope that he'll do better next year, but that is really a false hope. He won't get a better score next year because the men above him now will still be above him next year, even if he does improve a little."[4]

To avoid these reactions—and they are not rare examples—an open appraisal system is needed. This means that a large number of people feel that if they perform well, they can expect comparable rewards. This contrasts with the closed system where only a small number of people believe that high effort will bring them suitable rewards.

An open system can be achieved by measuring a person's performance against a set of pre-established goals or his previous performance in the year before. This approach does not introduce a peer comparison, which can often be negative and unrewarding. Instead it says that if a person's performance improves, he/she is doing well, regardless of what others do. This means that virtually everyone can do well if they want to—a much more healthy condition for both the individual and company.

---

[3]Paul H. Thompson & Gene W. Dalton, "Performance Appraisal: Managers Beware," *HBR*, January-February 1970, p. 52.

[4]Thompson, *op. cit.*, p. 52.

Performance appraisal by objectives greatly reduces the manager's subjective evaluation and minimizes accusations of favoritism or bias. This in turn helps the manager or supervisor when he recommends someone for promotion. Bringing forth past records of goals achieved, provides higher management and industrial relations with more impartial evidence than just the supervisor's opinion.

As with any system, pitfalls exist. The manager should watch out for the following if the open appraisal system is to work:

- Extenuating reasons should not be ignored when someone fails to meet his/her objectives.
- Objectives are too easy to meet, indicating a false measurement.
- Raises and promotions are not generally correlated to performance records.

Regardless of the pitfalls, the open appraisal system is much less likely to turn off people than a ranking system which says that only 33% of the company can get a good rating and that 33% must get a bad rating, even when most of the staff are doing average or above average work.

17.8 Don't Expect Perfection

People are inherently imperfect. If you have extremely high standards or expect people to be errorless, you will soon be disappointed, cynical, and irascible. In addition, your people will become overly sensitive to making errors. This condition will create anxiety, slow down work, and may even create more errors. However, if you keep your moderate expectations to yourself, but let your people know that you expect the best from them, you will often be pleasantly surprised at the quality of work produced.

17.9 Keep Abreast of Affirmative Action Requirements

The extent to which the affirmative action program of a company is implemented, depends on the company. If the company does government work, an active program for hiring and promoting minorities, women, the disabled, and Vietnam veterans might be in effect. In some cases, the company may have specific annual hiring and promotion goals. For example, one employee manual says this about its affirmative action program:

> "The task of contributing to the achievement of the Company's annual hiring and promotion goals is a condition of employment for which every supervisor/manager is held accountable and on which each supervisor will be evaluated annually."

It is thus apparent that a manager needs to be knowledgeable about the many facets of discrimination in order to avoid problems for the company and him/herself. The best source of information is the company's employee manual. However, a few representative guidelines are given here to illustrate the scope of the affirmative action program in terms of do's and don'ts:[5]

- Don't ask applicants questions about their race, national origin, religion, age, marital or family status, height or weight, arrest records, or credit ratings.
- Do record in writing reasons for a person being passed up for a promotion and let the prospect know these reasons.
- Don't prohibit Hispanic or other ethnic people from speaking their own language unless it actually affects performance.
- Apply disciplinary actions consistently. That is, don't fire a woman or older person for coming in late if you don't fire young men for the same reason.
- Don't fire people for excessive garnishments or arrests. This action could be considered discriminatory if it results in a higher proportion of minority firings.

While the above guidelines are subject to change and interpretation, they reflect the kinds of actions that should be followed or avoided by the manager to eschew charges of discrimination. Discrimination charges can siphon off much of the manager's time and drain the company's financial resources.

For additional guidance on setting up a successful equal opportunity program, see Dean Peskin's book: "The Building Blocks of EEO," The World Publishing Company, 1971. Also see "Affirmative Action and Equal Employment—A Guide Book for Employers," Vol. 1, 1974; available from Superintendent of Documents, Wash., D.C. 20402.

17.10 Involve Staff in Organizational and Project Plans

While it is difficult to involve everyone in your plans, anyone who can benefit from the process or shows an interest should be asked to attend meetings on plans related to the organization or a new project. If a large number of people are involved, these meetings should only be used to communicate already defined plans and to answer questions or get ideas on hazy or ill-defined areas. In the case of a project kick-off meeting, only people who will be contributing to the project should be invited. How-

[5]Laurence B. Hambright, Personnel Administrator, San Diego, CA.

ever, a bulletin can be issued to others identifying the aims, scope, customer, and nature of the project. This information can be useful to people working on other projects or proposals that may have some overlap or relevant exchange value. For a large company, this communication could avoid redundant work or proposals that sometimes occur when people in different areas come up with similar ideas for new projects.

During the actual planning process, care is needed in the selection of people at meetings. In this case, selectivity is necessary because as the group grows, its tendency to become entropic (see Chapter 2) also grows. Therefore, a completely open meeting may not get much done unless the manager is simply interested in getting ideas before the actual planning process begins. This situation would then be more of a brainstorming session than a planning effort.

Another approach to obtaining the participation of others in organizational or project plans would be to issue a questionnaire to the staff and ask for their ideas and suggestions for designing or implementing the planning process or a management plan.

Besides participation on projects, the staff should be encouraged to help the entire company as was done by one company:

> **Case in Point:** The Lincoln Electric Company set up an advisory board that met twice a month. The company grew and prospered sharing many benefits with its people. Its turnover rate was also exceedingly low. In addition, in spite of large increases in material prices, the company was able to reduce its product costs by 20%.[6]

A large part of the company's success was attributed to the following:

- The staff participated in running the company through their representatives on the Advisory Board and improvement suggestion system.
- The staff profited from both their ideas and increased efficiency. The profits were received in the form of bonuses, life insurance, pensions, paid health benefits, and dividends from stock purchases.
- No one feared being laid off; job security was strictly related to each person's performance, not factors which were beyond his/her control.
- Promotion depended on the person's performance.

---

[6]William R. Van Dersal, "The Successful Supervisor," 3rd Edition, Harper & Row, N.Y., 1974, p. 51–54.

While the performance of Lincoln Electric Company was not totally related to staff participation, it was a major factor.

17.11 Answer Your Calls

People, regardless of their position in the company, get angry or resentful when their calls are not returned. This in turn may lead to stewing over the situation and lost time. In some cases, the person may have to stop work until he/she can get an answer from you on what to do. And if the person doesn't call back, you may not hear about a situation or event that would have been useful to you in making a decision or avoiding a mistake.

> **Case in Point:** An administrative assistant at one company called a manager to let him know that his annual budget sheet had omitted a $9,600 item needed by his department. The manager was out, but his secretary put the message on his desk. When he returned he put the note on the side to do some other work. Two days later, he came across the note and figured that since the administrative assistant had not called back the message wasn't important. Months later, the manager found that his budget did not include $9,600 for the needed item, but it was too late to change the budget.

Of course, the effects of unreturned calls on customers and clients are even worse. Therefore, great care should be taken to answer calls as quickly as possible. To avoid delays in returning calls to customers/clients, a different-colored note should be used.

17.12 Remove Roadblocks to Motivation

In earlier chapters, it was stated that it is difficult to motivate people because the desire to do good work must come from within the person. Experience indicates that while it is possible for the manager to motivate people, it takes a lot of his/her time and energy to do this effectively and to maintain a person in a motivated state for a long period. Certainly, attempts to find out what a person wants out of life and work can be helpful. For example, information on a person's need for achievement and recognition, security, money, acceptance, status, or professional growth can guide the manager toward taking actions that will spur the person to improved performance. However, some management experts feel that a better approach is to recognize that most people want to do a good job without any prompting from management and to take actions to avoid demotivating them. For example, George Odiorne identified five roadblocks to motivation given in Table XXI.

TABLE XXI

ROADBLOCKS TO MOTIVATION[7]

1. Don't let the person know what you expect; if questions persist, don't respond with a clear answer and be contradictory.
2. Demand high work output; when the work is done be exacting, judgmental, punitive, and hostile because undefined objectives were not achieved.
3. Prevent the person from knowing personal progress when doing well; put accomplishments down and deny any progress; approve wrong and misdirected activities for long periods, then hit hard for being a consistently poor performer.
4. Divorce your rewards from achievement. Be sure there is no correlation among pay, recognition, bonuses, praise, and promotions and achievement of objectives or completion of work on time and within budget.
5. Don't give the person the resources needed to get the job done; take away resources in the middle of the job.

Practical Management Associates, Woodland Hills, California, identified two types of obstacles to motivated people. One type is a performance obstacle. This obstacle makes it impossible or very difficult to get work done well and efficiently. The second type is a work gratification obstacle. This obstacle prevents or deprives a person of feeling rewarded from doing work or having performed it in a superior way. Both types of obstacles can affect human performance and the manager should work to keep these obstacles out of his/her organization. Examples of performance and work gratification obstacles are listed below:

Obstacles to Performance	Obstacles to Work Gratification
Red tape	Absence of credit or recognition
Bottlenecks	Contribution not readily observed
Unrealistic demands on schedule, quality, etc.	No sense of tangible accomplishments (work never comes to an end)
Inadequate facilities	Over or under supervision
Lack of skill, ability or training	Aim or purpose of work not understood
Uncooperative fellow workers	Inconsistent rewards
Conflicting orders (too many bosses)	Unchallenging work
Rapidly changing ground rules or goals	Lack of peer acceptance

[7]George S. Odiorne, "Management and the Activity Trap," Harper & Row, N.Y., 1974, p. 167.

Too much work
Excessive demands on non-contributory aspects of work, such as reports and excessive or unnecessary planning
Rewards for non-contributing aspects of work

17.13 Don't Shoot from the Hip

Some managers have found that they can be fairly accurate decision makers by making snap decisions without time-consuming research, meetings, and thought. However, this approach can be dangerous when overconfidence leads the manager into a quick decision that has many ramifications to his organization and company. Thus, the habit of shooting from the hip without careful aim can miss a major target and really hurt the manager.

Experience has shown that the manager in a complex and dynamic industry can get into trouble even in apparently minor appearing hip-shot decisions. Therefore, while an extensive investigation into each problem is not needed, the ramifications of each decision should be systematically considered before making most decisions. Although the decision-making process may take 10 to 60 minutes of private thought or investigation, it is well worth the investment because an error on even a minor area can result in dozens of wasted hours by others.

> **Case in Point:** A manager was going to a meeting with the director of his division when the director spied a new clerk talking to someone. He turned to the manager and said: "I saw her talking to that engineer two days in a row. Fire her."
>
> When the manager talked to the clerk's supervisor, the supervisor got upset and said he would be back. Some time later, he returned with a grin and noted that the clerk was on her coffee break on both days.
>
> The next day, the director asked the manager if the clerk had been fired. The manager explained that she and the engineer were talking during their coffee breaks. The director shrugged and walked away.
>
> As a result of this snap decision, about two hours were wasted and people were upset. Had the clerk been fired, she could have caused much more wasted time by bringing forth a complaint of discrimination since the engineer was not fired.

Even the manager highly confident in quick decision making should try to keep a record of successes and failures to verify a good record. In spite of a good record, conditions may change—for example, a move to a new company—and the old mode of operation may not work well there.

17.14 Don't Propagate Low-Profile Syndromes

It is natural to feel a certain amount of resentment or irritation with people who frequently disagree with your actions or are independent acting. However, if these people are good performers and have valuable experience and talent, these qualities can override the negative aspects of disagreements and non-conformity.

Since these people perform well, and their insubordination is not at a gross level, managers wait until a cutback is needed to get rid of them. Of course, when this occurs the rest of the staff puts two and two together and infers that Bob Zip was laid off because he was too independent. They thus either look for another boss who isn't so sensitive or consciously establish a low profile so as not to antagonize the manager. This, of course, does not promote a creative and productive environment and everybody loses.

To avoid this, the manager needs to consciously think through attitudes toward people who are independent and outspoken. If there is a tendency to let attitudes affect performance ratings and layoff listings, develop a plan to counteract this quality. If the manager is unable to deal with high-profile people, then he/she must accept the fact that the staff will eventually become a bunch of yes-men as newcomers are told that the boss doesn't like anyone to disagree or argue about his/her policies, aims, decisions, and methods.

17.15 Avoid a Not-Invented Here Attitude

Industry is rife with people who want to change existing systems, procedures, organizations, and product designs. They feel, based on their experience, that they have better ways to do things. As a result, much work done by competent people is subjected to unnecessary scrapping or revision. Certainly, simplification or correction of an error is a bona fide change. But great discipline is needed to keep unnecessary changes in existing systems/products under control. To do this, the manager should give explicit instructions concerning opposition to changing other people's work and should repeat them periodically.

Several reasons exist to explain why people who are asked to take over an organization, operation, system, or design of someone else's want to change it. It is important for the manager to keep these reasons in mind before allowing redesign to proceed. The following questions can help him/her avoid approving unneeded changes recommended by a staff member:

- Is the person relatively inexperienced and really after an opportunity to design a new system on his/her own?
- Is the person suggesting the redesign more qualified than the original designer(s)? What makes him/her more qualified?

- Does the person asking to make the change have a personal reason for the change; e.g., would he/she like to make a good impression by showing the manager all the bad things he/she found in the design?
- Is the person a cultist who believes that every design should contain certain features that he/she strongly believes in?
- Does the person really understand the design—is he/she aware of the specifications, history, and user requirements?
- Does the person have a distaste for being the caretaker for someone else's work, rather than the creator?

The manager is often hard pressed to stop a change recommended by a competent specialist because the arguments raised often have merit; and he lacks in-depth knowledge himself. For example, all designs have deficiencies, could be based on a different concept, or can be done in a radically different way. However, if the manager is not hard when requests to redesign previous systems come in, the system will be reworked as if the original designers didn't know what they were doing.

> **Case in Point:** One company had undergone 10 operating system redesigns over a 12-year period. Each time someone was assigned the task, a new system would evolve and a new operating manual would be created. A temporary hiatus occurred when one new systems person was openly committed to not redesigning the system or manual except for new requirements or clearly ineffectual procedures. This stability lasted for a few years. When he left the organization, the new systems person was already making plans for revising the entire manual for the eleventh time.

The only way from stopping this process is for managers to take strong positions against changes and to require thorough analysis and research that will objectively indicate that the change is necessary.

> *Caution:* A balanced approach must exist. If no pressure exists for some changes, then a company may get into the rigor-mortis stage. In this case, the manager will have to cultivate staff interest in searching for better ways of doing things.

17.16 Don't Throw Out the System with the Bath Water

Related to the preceding topic, is the practice of throwing out a system because one problem has been discovered, or because the system isn t working well. In most cases, a system doesn't work well because people aren't making it work well. A perfect system will fail if people don't like it or are not disciplined in following its requirements. Therefore, before a system is thrown out and a new design initiated, consider the following:

- Is the defect of minor impact and therefore acceptable?

Case in Point: At one company, a part was found defective because a drawing was released with an error. The director held a meeting and requested that a new drawing control system be designed to prevent this error from recurring. The manager assigned to correct the problem found that the cost of the defect was about $5,000 (and had only occurred once that year). However, the annual cost of a new control system would be over $20,000. Also, it would not be infallible and an occasional mistake such as had occurred could still be found. It was decided that replacement of the old control system would not be worth the cost.

- Are people really following the system as specified. If they are not, then will they follow the requirements of a new system?
- Can a minor change to the system fix the problem?
- Will the new system create a host of different problems, such as additional delays and lower morale?

As was mentioned in Chapter 2, frequent organizational changes give the impression of improving things, but in effect can demoralize and confuse people. The same is true if a company frequently changes its operating systems, procedures, and manuals.

17.17 Avoid Constant Nit-Picking

Nit-picking is the criticism of minor details that do not materially contribute to the effectiveness, quality, or use of the system, product, or operation. Nit-picking has a number of harmful physical and psychological effects, such as demotivation of the person being nit-picked, wasting of the people's time, and diverting energy from the purpose of the work being examined. The nit-picker can also gain a bad reputation from this practice. For example, at one company a manager known for his nit-picking was dubbed the "old lady." Therefore, the manager must be constantly on guard against falling into a nit-picking pattern merely to exhibit the care with which the material or system was studied.

17.18 Don't Over-Rely on Specialists

The manager's ignorance of specialized systems, such as computers, can create an unsafe reliance on system experts or specialists. This reliance can get the manager in trouble by developing computer and other systems that are not cost-effective or practical or will be in a constant-improvement syndrome of existing systems. For example, computer people have a natural tendency to get engrossed in their sophisticated and admittedly powerful tools and often see all problem solutions via the computer. Therefore, the manager must be careful not to accept recommendations on computer solutions to problems without careful scrutiny and consideration of alternate techniques.

When a specialist speaks to you about your operating systems, consider that the specialist:

- Often doesn't understand the environment as well as you do.
- May not know everything about the field or discipline.
- May have certain conditioned responses that prevent taking an impartial view of the problem.
- May have some personal reasons for specific recommendations.

17.19 Avoid Top Management Over-Delegation to Middle Management

Because of the pressure and duties incumbent on higher management, middle managers are often officially or unofficially delegated responsibility for policies and decisions that really should be made by higher management. For example, decisions on the operational and organizational philosophy of the company may be assigned to directors or managers who have differing objectives, needs, and viewpoints with each other and probably higher management. Therefore, their approaches to operations and organization may not be best for the company or customer. The normal self-centeredness of middle managers will result in conflicts that will be settled through negotiation and compromise. These compromise decisions will rarely be in the best interests of the company as a whole. In addition, these decisions will be in constant flux or subject to change when new middle managers are assigned. Also, when impasses occur, they will be resolved by inefficient methods, such as establishing redundant functions or uncentralized support functions.

While top management need not spend a lot of time in making these decisions, clear-cut and decisive directions on how the company will be organized and run will eliminate much wasted time, conflicts, and political machinations.

17.20 Avoid Hiring Friends and Relatives

Many managers tend to hire their friends[8] and relatives because of loyalty, knowledge of their capabilities, and the comfortable relations that already exist. However, a number of dangers exist in following this practice in filling openings within the organization:

- Staff feel more vulnerable because their errors, remarks or shortcomings may be reported to the manager when he/she is visiting with his/her friend or relative. While the report may not be done maliciously, the information about people in the group can be damaging to them.
- Staff feel (even if not true) that friends or relatives can get away with things that others can't; such as leaving early for lunch or coming to work late.
- Staff feel that when a good job opens up, the friend or relative will get it even if not as qualified as others.

Case in Point: At one company, there was an opening in a department for a new manager. Two people already in the department were qualified for the job. However, the department manager selected a friend of his who had no background in this area. In the two years that he held the job, he did not perform well and was eventually replaced by someone else. Their friendship also waned. In addition, the manager lost the respect of his staff who observed that he put other friends in key jobs.

- Staff feel that raises and performance ratings will be affected by the special relationship that exists.
- Staff feel that if a layoff is required, friends and relatives will be the last to go, regardless of their performance.

Another problem with putting a friend or relative in a job under you, is that discipline problems become much stickier. As a result, your entropy will increase due to greater frustration and time spent trying to develop effective strategies for getting the person in line.

The effects of the preceding observations can lead to demotivation, transfers, hostility, and resignations.

While relatives and friends can work out well, the probability is that the organization's efficiency and morale will be adversely affected unless they have special talents or abilities that are readily apparent to the staff and helpful to them and their success.

---

[8]A friend is closer than an acquaintance. A friend is someone you spend time with outside the company.

Many companies are aware of the potential problems with relatives and require that they be assigned to separate organizations within the company to minimize problems. However, rules about friends are seldom defined in company policies.

17.21 Don't Lock People in at Their Levels of Incompetence

The Peter Principle states that people tend to rise in an organization until they reach the level of their incompetence. At this level, they are no longer promoted and remain fixed in this position until they leave or die. Of course, not all people who have reached a certain level within an organization are incompetent. A manager could be competent, but have certain undesirable personal qualities that limit his/her promotion to a higher job. Also, he/she may be performing at a marginal level that indicates to management that a step up would not be wise, or that he/she may not be interested in a more responsible position. In these cases, acceptable performance exists and no changes may be needed. But what if the person is out of his league? Many companies tend to live with this situation unless it becomes completely unworkable or the person antagonizes higher management on a personal level. The idea is that the person will be destroyed or will lose face if reassigned to a job that appears to be lower in the organization. For example, if a manager of engineering is transferred back into a staff position, this is generally viewed as a demotion. But if he/she is more useful to the company as a creator or designer than as a manager, what's wrong with this? There isn't really anything wrong unless he/she gets a big pay cut and is really unhappy as an engineer. In fact, people doing poor jobs as managers, would welcome reassignment to something they could do well if no loss in face occurred.

If a company can develop an atmosphere where management and staff work are considered different kinds of jobs, rather than one being higher than the other, reassignment of managers to staff jobs won't have the stigma attached to the action, and the company will eventually establish a top-notch managerial group. In addition, talented individual contributors will stay.

There is no doubt that a manager's job is desirable for the person seeking status, power, and money. However, many people accept promotions to managers' jobs only because of financial rewards. If the company allows individual contributors to make as much as most executives, then people who really don't want to be managers will refuse managers' jobs and the company and individual will both profit. Similar status symbols, such as windowed offices, carpeting, and secretaries (if really needed) can also help minimize the differences.

17.22 Maintain Contact with Firing-Line People

Too often the busy manager or executive stays in his/her office, goes on trips, or attends meetings and has no time to visit the production area or engineering offices. As a result, he/she loses vital contact points for first-hand information on how things are going and what's bothering people. In addition, he/she loses a powerful motivating force. When a higher-level manager or the president of the company visits people at the working level, they feel more important because they think he/she considers what they are doing important. They thus take more pride in their work.

17.23 Conduct Operation Audits

Chapter 15 mentioned the importance of audits for new systems. Audits are also important for checking on conformance with old system and procedures. The manager should insist on these audits on a semiannual or annual basis. For problem areas, more frequent audits should be made.

17.24 Prepare a Policy and Procedure Manual

A policy and procedure manual is important even for small companies. On the surface it may appear expensive to prepare and maintain. But it is really a cost-and time-saver. It saves money because it forces you to define how you will operate your company at one blow and thus ensures that the various policies and procedures will be consistent and known to everyone who works for you. Without the manual, solutions to problems will be re-invented each time because of poor memories or new people.

A manual can save time by allowing people to obtain answers from the document without having to ask you or others. It also saves time by reducing errors that inevitably occur as time causes memories to fade.

Another cost benefit is that the organization will evolve by design and under top management control because all key areas are documented. Without the manual, people will tend to invent things on an ad hoc basis, which you may not know about until much damage has been done. This damage may include lost time in correcting the misdirected actions, confusion, arguments, and poor morale.

17.25 Avoid Over-Reliance on Memos and Reports for Communication

Formal memos and reports should be used when they are more efficient than verbal communications, when a record of the information is needed, or when customer or company requirements make them mandatory. However, informal memos, often referred to as AVO's (avoid verbal orders), are effective when the chances for misunderstanding are high or when the complexity of the message requires it to be written for the user's benefit.

An example of a formal memo that should have been communicated orally is shown in Figure 17-1. The memo was written to a staff member by his manager. It serves no real value and promotes disorder by raising questions as to the motives for writing it and the mental state of the author. In the example shown, a mere tongue lashing would have kept the entropy down. (Note: Of the people mentioned in the memo, Fred Club was the boss of the manager who wrote the memo and Ken Gardino, a peer manager.)

While memos are necessary parts of the corporate communication system, they should not be used to replace face-to-face communication or to resolve problems.

To: Albert Horn Date: Jan. 17, 19XX
From: Frank Posit
Subject: Work Plan and Procedure

I can only assume that you, Fred, and Ken have good reasons for persistently ignoring my repeated recommendations (pleadings?) to retain a one-page work plan which includes only those things the Project Managers need to sign off and to include the other information needed by the Comptroller, Planning and Engineering in a related planning work package. Whatever the factors are, I am unaware of them, but it is too late to try to change now. Let's give your approach a try. After all I agreed to live with your product because my work on Project LTT did not give me time to argue my preference.

Please proceed to get the forms and procedure completed. I vote for using Publications to draw up the example pages.

cc
Fred Club
Ken Gardino

Figure 17-1 Sample of an Unnecessary Memo

17.26 Hold an Undistorted or Realistic View of Manager's Position

A preceding section dealt with the distinction between a manager or administrator and the person doing the work. When a manager looks upon himself as inherently superior to his people he is headed for trouble. Many people today do not feel inferior to their bosses, except in terms of power or specific experience or capabilities. But on a people-to-people basis, they feel equally important. Thus, the manager who loses sight of his main purpose, which is to organize and motivate people into getting the job done with minimum lost time and money, is going to decrease his effectiveness. People are fairly quick to pick out a hypocrite or person who has an overblown view of himself. Therefore, the astute manager views himself as performing a specific job—although a vital one—and that his performance is dependent on how his people do—not on how he wields power.

17.27 Control Waste

Studies have shown that people are turned off by obvious wasteful practices. Therefore, the manager should be careful to avoid an image of not caring how money or material is abused. If he/she practices methods to reduce waste, the staff will tend to follow his/her example.

17.28 Don't Assume That Turnover Washes Out Tired Blood

Experience has shown that loss of old timers with the company does not necessarily result in their replacement with a group of eager, superior performers.

> **Case in Point:** One company found that when it lost three of its top draftsmen due to poor wages, their replacements were about half as efficient and didn't have the conscientious attitudes of the people they replaced.

Certainly, if a person is doing poorly, the replacement may very likely be better. But the blind assumption that attrition is good for the company is completely wrong. The reason for this is that the people who leave are usually the more progressive, dynamic and courageous people. The people who are complacent and don't want to take risks are more likely to stay. This is not to say that they are not competent, because often they are. However, they lack the qualities of the people who left. While the people who are hired to replace those that left may also have these qualities, they still have to learn about the company and require some training even if highly experienced. In addition, the company loses money in recruiting expenses and payment of higher salaries to attract people with good skills and experience.

Thus, while some new blood is desirable, the manager should concentrate on motivating and developing people who show promise rather than wasting much time interviewing and retraining new people.

17.29 Don't Reward Unneeded Growth

As mentioned in Chapter 2, most companies inadvertently promote unneeded growth by rewarding managers on the basis of the size of their organizations. When the manager realizes that his/her salary is a function of the number of people he/she has in the organization, he/she consciously or unconsciously tends to increase the size of the staff. He/she may do this by taking on new functions, other manager's functions, or increasing his/her work load. In slim times, he/she takes whatever action is possible to keep from losing too many people.

The solution to this problem is to measure a manager's worth on how well the job gets done rather on the size of his/her organization. This means that if because of insufficient work, he/she has to transfer people to another group or lay them off, he/she shouldn't be penalized. Also if in losing 50% of the staff, he/she still produces 60% of the work, he/she has shown considerable ability in increasing the organization's efficiency by a considerable amount and therefore deserves a raise, not a pay cut or no raise at all.

17.30 Don't Program People for Failure

The danger of programming your production people for failure is somewhat less than for your support people but it still exists. Setting unrealistic objectives and work rates can make normally productive and good workers turn out shoddy products or become demoralized because they can't meet standards set for them. It is much better to set standards that most people can meet, with bonuses for those who exceed these standards.

In the case of support people, the amount of work that they can do is more difficult to establish and a manager may have no standards at all. More and more work is assigned without an appreciation of the limits of the person. While it can be assumed that the person will complain when the work load gets too heavy, this may not occur until a heavy backlog occurs. If the person is conscientious, the situation can really get out of control; an overworked and demoralized employee may well leave the company.

17.31 Coach Your People[9]

Coaching involves the setting up of an open atmosphere and partnership in planning and reviewing results. It also involves making the more

[9]Hawdon Hague, "Executive Self Development," Macmillan, London, 1974, p. 85–87.

junior person aware of how he/she is managing and using situations when they arise as teaching opportunities. Some coaching practices include:

- Setting up slightly different situations to help the staff to see them from new angles.
- Helping the junior manager or staff analyze his/her operating methods.
- Discussing alternatives.
- Reviewing the "how" as opposed to the "what" when a major decision has been taken.
- Allowing junior manager or staff to make mistakes without interfering unless a serious error will occur.
- Asking questions to stimulate thought and consideration of alternatives and their implications.
- Controlling the rate at which a staff member takes on responsibilities; e.g., delegating them one by one instead of all at once.
- Asking him/her to represent you at the meeting with the power to act; then discussing what he/she did.

A key aim of coaching is to make the manager learn how to think and determine solutions for him/herself. Discussions before and after major events will help achieve this, as well as awareness that he/she is being observed.

17.32 Turn on Middle-Aged People

Middle-aged and older people are frequently accused of lacking the drive and enthusiasm of younger people. Actually, with their experience and maturity, they represent a great resource of potential energy for a company, especially where their work involves considerable knowledge and skill. The reasons middle-aged and older people are turned off or become non-productive include:

- They become cynical because they have seen the effects of politics, stupidity, ignorance, and waste and don't see efforts to improve these conditions.
- If successful, the organization dissipates their creative energies in relatively non-productive meetings, seminars, and public/customer relations. They are frustrated by this situation, but like the financial rewards and feel that they must follow orders.
- Physical deterioration may cause loss of energy and motivation.
- Over-security may incite complacency, which in turn leads to low drive to achieve anything.

- The impetus for continued growth stops due to social attitudes, lack of motivation, and loss of confidence in the potential for success.

Most of the preceding problems can be rectified through effective management and an effort to identify the specific problems of low productivity and creativity. Even the physical problems can be corrected through better nutrition, exercise, and medical care. Thus, a more positive attitude on the part of the manager is required to keep middle-aged and older people more dynamic and productive. He/she must also realize that a full-time commitment is not only important to himself or herself, but to the staff, company, and customer.

17.33 Recognize That Management Is a Full-Time Job

Managers who are specialists or technical people often have difficulty in letting the technical aspects of their work be handled by their staff so that they can focus their energies on managing the organization. Consequently, they don't have enough time to be competent managers and sometimes do more harm than good in the technical area because they don't have all the information needed to make a decision. To avoid doing a poor job in both areas, the manager must make a commitment to manage or request that he/she be replaced. Anything less than this is unfair to the staff, the company and the manager himself because:

- The overall performance of the organization will deteriorate.
- Administrative aspects of the operation will create problems with the staff, other company functions, and higher management. This, in turn, will reduce their efficiency. For example, if planning and scheduling work is not done by the manager, then other people who are less knowledgeable of his/her operations will have to do so.
- The staff will obtain less satisfaction from working in the group and morale will decline.

To avoid the preceding problems, and to obtain real satisfaction from managing an organization, the manager must accept the fact that a great portion of his/her time must be devoted to planning, coordinating, budgeting, decision making, and dealing with people.

17.34 Avoid Rapid Closure on New Ideas

Managers often make decisions based on past experience and do not adequately consider recent changes or new requirements that nullify the validity of a past successful action or solution. Thus, the manager must keep an open mind when a competent staff member broaches a new idea that the manager has already evaluated and discarded in the past. Before he/she rejects or accepts the idea or system, the following questions should be answered:

1. Have performance requirements related to the idea changed since the idea, etc. was first considered?
2. Was the company operating under different conditions when the idea or system was previously submitted?
3. Was the technique rather new and undeveloped when it was considered earlier?
4. Did the kinds of people involved in the past differ from the current staff? How will this affect success of the idea or project?
5. Is a different higher management in charge now? How will the differences affect the implementation of the idea, system, or project?

17.35 Don't Automatically Reject Over-Qualified Candidates

The experienced and higher paid candidate for a job is often rejected because he/she is considered over-qualified. The term "over-qualified" can have several meanings, including too expensive, too difficult to direct or supervise, or too threatening to someone in the organization. Of course, it can also mean that the job can be done as well or better by a less experienced person.

When the person applying for the job is really over-qualified, then the manager's decision to reject him/her is valid. However, too often, a manager has a certain image of what level person he/she wants and automatically rejects a candidate without an objective evaluation. The following example illustrates the benefits of being more flexible in one's filling of jobs:

> **Case in Point:** A manager at one manufacturing company rejected a candidate for a design checker's job because the person had the qualifications to be doing his (the manager's) job. However, a supervisor under this manager saw the candidate's resume and asked him in for an interview. The man was hired as a checker and it was soon apparent that he was more knowledgeable and productive than any of the other checkers. In addition, he had ideas on how to improve operations and was very well liked by everyone. Even if he had been paid his former salary, the manager felt that this man would have been worth it. In his first year, the checker conducted training seminars for inspectors and implemented a new technique that saved the company many thousands of dollars a year.

The preceding illustration indicates that senior people may command a higher salary, but can more than repay it with new ideas, broader experience, and greater productivity and dependability than less experienced people.

17.36 Really Absorb New Ideas and Attitudes

In the rush to cover a wide range of material and information each day, many important ideas or facts are lost. The reason for this is that very few people have the ability to permanently retain information without some repetition and concerted memorization.

> **Case in Point:** William J. Tobin, author and sales consultant, reports what happens to a new idea given to 100 people:
>
> - After 24 hours, 25 have forgotten it.
> - After 48 hours, 50 have forgotten it.
> - After 4 days 85 have forgotten it.
> - After 16 days, 98 have forgotten it.

Dr. Maltz in his book "Psycho-Cybernetics" reported that at least 21 days of practice are needed before an old mental image can be replaced by a new one. In view of these observations, it is obvious that most people need to review and repeat new ideas, facts and behavior many times before they can become an integral part of their mind and body.

This repetition process is especially important when a habit or attitude change is desired. Therefore, a formal technique for improving retention of important data or practices should be used. A few techniques for doing this follow:

- Record the idea, fact or practice on a 3 × 5-inch card and carry it in your shirt pocket. Review the card two or three times each day for a week or more, depending on how long this process must go on for you to really absorb the idea. (Although this practice was mentioned at the beginning of this chapter, it is repeated here because so few people follow this or a similar process in acquiring new information or habits.)
- Record the idea or practice in a special notebook that you take home with you for review. Keep all new ideas, attitude changes needed, etc., in this book and review it frequently—visualizing or repeating the idea until it is mastered.
- Take your notes with you to the doctor's office, lunch, when you take your wife shopping (stay in the car and study), or anywhere you may have some dead time. You can easily pick up more than 3 hours of study time each week this way.
- Tape the ideas and play them back while you're driving to and from work, or in the morning before work is started (only when this doesn't make driving more dangerous).

- Explore the use of hypnotism; some people have reported this an effective means for changing attitudes or habits quickly.
- Use your imagination. Visualize yourself acting the way you would like to.

Case in Point: Golf teacher Alex Morrison taught Lew Lehr to break 90 for the first time with no actual practice. Morrison had Lehr relax in an easy chair while he demonstrated the correct swings for Lehr. Lehr was then told to spend five minutes a day relaxing in his easy chair visualizing himself practicing golf swings.

Several days later with no physical preparation, Lehr shot nine holes in an even par, 36.[10]

While the recommended practices are extremely difficult to do, they can be very effective in improving your performance. Without these techniques, it will take many years to achieve the same results. Therefore, if you feel the need to change an attitude or habit, a disciplined approach is needed.

[10]Maxwell Maltz, "Psycho-Cybernetics, Prentice-Hall, Inc., 1960, p. 36 & 37.

INDEX

D

I

J

K

L

P

Q

R

S

T